Texas Money
All the Law Allows

Mona D. Sizer

Republic of Texas Press
Plano, Texas

Library of Congress Cataloging-in-Publication Data

Sizer, Mona D.
    Texas money : all the law allows / Mona D. Sizer.
        p.   cm.
    Includes bibliographical references and index.
    ISBN 1-55622-926-7 (alk. paper)
    1. Texas--Biography.   2. Businessmen--Texas--Biography.
    3. Millionaires--Texas--Biography.   I. Title.
    CT262 .S59 2002
    305.5'234'0922764--dc21   2002006363
                                                                      CIP

© 2003, Mona D. Sizer

All Rights Reserved

Printed in the United States of America

ISBN 1-55622-926-7
10 9 8 7 6 5 4 3 2 1
0207

All inquiries for volume purchases of this book should be addressed to
Wordware Publishing, Inc., at 2320 Los Rios Boulevard, Plano, Texas
75074. Telephone inquiries may be made by calling:

(972) 423-0090

Other Titles by Mona D. Sizer

The King Ranch Story: Truth and Myth

"...a vivid updated account of the larger-than-life
Captain Richard King and his descendants..."
Elmer Kelton, *The Way of the Coyote* and
The Smiling Country

Texas Politicians: Good 'n' Bad

"...Mona Sizer, a Lone Star writer, like a female
Texas Ranger, is keeping her eyes on them."
Jim McKone, *The Monitor*

"...an anecdotal lark through state shenanigans."
Jan Epton Seale, *Texas Books in Review*

Texas Justice: Bought and Paid For

"Lady Justice, who is usually portrayed blindfolded...
gets a poke in the eye here."
Eileen Mattei, *Valley Morning Star*

Texas Heroes: A Dynasty of Courage

"...a rare volume...that treats both Quanah Parker,
the 19th century Comanche leader, and
Audie Murphy, the most decorated American of
World War II."
Andrew Graybill, *Southwestern Historical Quarterly*

"Sizer is on her way to becoming the
Queen of Texas Pop History."
Eileen Mattei, *Valley Morning Star*

Contents

Acknowledgments

The list of people who aided me in writing *Texas Money* is rich and varied. The people themselves are rich in nature though not in wealth on the level of the men and women in this book. If you are rich in wealth, dear friends, shame on you for holding out on me.

I'd like to acknowledge the rich friendship that I enjoy with Lela Unruh, my woman in Dallas, who gallantly collected newspaper clippings as well as other materials on so many of the people in the book. Likewise, Jon Ann Rucker brought me a wealth of materials on Mary Kay. Orfa Reyes took me to a Mary Kay meeting where I learned so much. Diana Gold and Jennie Moore provided pictures. Thank you all so much.

B. J. and Kristin Joseph provided firsthand information and introductions, as did Laura Castoro. Great friends all. Jan Gracia gave me ideas and went with me to meet people here in the Valley. I really owe you, Jan. Danny Buttery brought me last minute information from an unexpected professional source. Thank you, kind sir.

All these willing people are testimony to the fact that no author really writes alone. Certainly, no author needs to because no author could have better support than my Republic of Texas Press editors Ginnie Bivona and Dianne Stultz, who keep tormenting about meeting my deadlines. Just kidding, ladies. And, of course, Cathy Tindle and Paula Price, to whom no request is impossible, no whining too unbearable to listen to.

To my readers, "The rich are different from you and me." How different and yet how alike is the subject of this book. If you are simply astonished by their stories, then you'll enjoy this book.

Mona D. Sizer
Harlingen, Texas

The Origin of Money

In Scotland, the scene of a violent rebellion ruthlessly put down by England in 1745, Adam Smith completed his book *Inquiry into the Nature and Causes of the Wealth of Nations*. Therein he set forth his most important precept: all social improvement in the business of civilization gets done by a "division of labor." Smith further observed that each such division earns rewards for its laborers who in turn use those rewards to improve their lives.

He explained how this division came about as a natural progression beginning first with primitive man who was the sole provider for his family. He fished, he hunted, and he gathered food. He did not concentrate his energy and his intelligence on performing and perfecting one task. He did it all himself.

Eventually, he found too many people were grouped around him. They couldn't all hunt. The game would be exhausted. Nor could they all fish. Their numbers forced them to divide the tasks among themselves. Those who had natural talents for hunting hunted. He concentrated on a new way of feeding his family—farming. He found he was proficient at it.

So proficient did he become that he began to grow more than enough to feed himself and his family. He had food to trade or sell to others. He traded wheat for meat, but sometimes he felt he was cheated. Rather than barter, he began to sell it outright, keeping track of who owed him what with tokens such as shells or stones or pieces of metal.

Before too long someone in the society discovered that he had no talent for either hunting or farming. He had a talent for buying and selling. With that man civil society progressed to the stage that Adam Smith recognized as commercial. The fruits of man's labor were no longer the things he consumed himself. They became "commodities," literally the things he bought and sold in exchange for other goods. With the invention of paper, the shells, stones, and pieces of metal were discarded or used to a limited degree. The method of exchange became pieces of paper that promised other men would pay him. So men quite literally began to collect paper promises. With the appearance of paper promises, the world suddenly turned into a civilized place.

Smith saw capitalism being born, the system of economic production behind commercial society. It was a system whose productivity and inventiveness put all the rest in the shade. People could earn the means to live together in larger groups. Their conditions steadily improved as more labor saving tools were invented by enterprising souls. Stacks of paper promises could purchase not just necessities, but luxuries as well. Paper promises (and the things they could buy) became every man's goal. Because of paper promises, the capitalistic society, despite all efforts of its other institutions—family, education, religion, and politics—embraced the fifth institution—economics.

Almost immediately, rare members of the society showed unusual adeptness in making and selling very desirable things that more and more people wanted. These men began to acquire stacks and stacks of paper promises until they had more than almost anybody else. It was equally obvious but often ignored that these people consumed relatively little more than those with fewer stacks of promises. A man can only drive one Rolls Royce or one Chevy pickup at a time. A woman can only wear so many necklaces, be they diamonds or seashells.

Yet such a man or woman was admired and envied. Those less adept at individual accumulation of promises were eager to work for those who were, because promises were distributed to them. They in turn distributed these promises to others.

Society became almost unbelievably complicated, so much so that today incredibly intelligent machines take care of and in some cases take the place of the almost uncountable paper promises that our brains can no longer remember.

Those with incredible numbers of paper promises stand on pinnacles alone. We name them The Rich. The rest stand on various levels below and look up longingly.

What constitutes a rich man? He may not be different in thought or deed from other men. He may not be free of responsibility or happy or creative. He may be driven by greed and self-interest to the exclusion of all other feelings. Only one thing about him is different.

One social observer, George G. Kirstein, has concluded that a man is truly rich when he enjoys "total economic freedom." He need never think about whether he can afford anything.

In Texas—thanks to a bounty rivaled by few other places in the world—an unusually large number of men and women enjoy total economic freedom. How some of them came by it and what they have done with it are the stories that are told hereafter.

Society has coined a term for the paper promises.
We call it MONEY.

"It is not from the benevolence of the butcher, the brewer, or the baker, that we expect our dinner, but from their regard to their own self-interest."

—*Inquiry into the Nature and Causes of the Wealth of Nations*
—Adam Smith

Howard Robard Hughes Jr.
"Texas's First Billionaire"

The whole world threw a party for Howard Robard Hughes Jr. It began in New York City on the day he arrived to fly his silver Lockheed 14, a twin-engine passenger plane, to Paris. Though his intention had not been announced publicly, strategically placed rumors circulated that he intended to fly around the world. He hoped to beat fellow Texan Wiley Post's record of seven and a half days.

Not solo as Lindbergh's *Spirit of St. Louis* had been, Hughes had a crew of four including a co-pilot and a radioman, Richard Stoddart, who just happened to work for the National Broadcasting Company. By the time Hughes and his crew of four arrived at the field, five thousand people, led by Grover Whalen, the director of the upcoming World's Fair, had gathered to cheer and see him off. Like Lindbergh's *Spirit of St. Louis,* he had allowed the plane to be named *New York World's Fair 1939* to publicize the upcoming event.

The date was July 10, 1938. At 6 P.M. he arrived at the hangar and received the weather reports. Over the Atlantic everything looked good to go. There were no reasons to delay if one did not count caution or fear of what could happen.

The plane was dangerously overloaded for the takeoff of the 3,641-mile flight to Paris. It carried 1,500 gallons of aviation fuel, 150 gallons of oil, and a laboratory full of equipment. In 1927 Lindbergh's *Spirit* had ten instruments including an ignition switch. Eleven years later Hughes's *World's Fair* had thirty different gauges, many of them duplicated for each engine. It weighed nearly thirteen tons, an amount so prodigious that Goodyear Tire and Rubber Company had made special tires to support it.

As the thirty-three-year-old Hughes gazed at the runway, he felt a thrill of anxiety. Would the heavily loaded plane be able to take off in such a short space?

While Whalen praised him, Hughes became increasingly more doubtful and more morose. At last the entrepreneur finished his speechmaking and turned to the celebrity pilot, who pulled a piece of paper from his pocket. As sweat ran down his back, he bent forward to the microphone in his characteristically deprecating pose. "We hope that our flight may prove a contribution to the cause of friendship between nations and that through their outstanding fliers, for whom the common bond of aviation transcends national boundaries, this cause may be furthered."

He then apologized to the newsmen for being rude earlier. He explained that he had a lot on his mind. Magically, his tension vanished when he climbed in and sat behind the Lockheed's controls. Howard Hughes was always free when he sat in a cockpit. He taxied the plane away from the administration building to the northwest end of the strip. To the southeast, the runway of Floyd Bennett Field in Brooklyn ended in more or less flat ground.

At 7:19 P.M. he pulled both throttles wide open. The Lockheed roared down the runway. A cloud of dust billowed up behind the plane, silhouetting it in the setting sun. At the field's halfway point, no one in the crowd could take his eyes off the spectacle. No one knew whether the rapidly accelerating Lockheed would lift off the tarmac or crash and burn. The noise increased as it screamed by them.

Hughes kept his eyes on the pavement. Even as he gained speed, he was running out of runway. Almost at the last minute, he felt the tail rise. There was a slight bump as the wheels left the pavement and grazed the bare earth. Another great cloud of dust swirled up. For an instant the Lockheed's engines altered as if they had throttled back.

The crowd gasped.

Then the engines' full thunder came roaring out of the distance as the plane began to climb. Hughes dipped his wings over Hollywood actress Katharine Hepburn's Long Island home and pointed the nose toward Boston and the first leg of the great circle route—Paris.

The 3,641-mile flight was accomplished in sixteen hours, thirty-eight minutes. Lindbergh's record, still the best at the time, was thirty-three and a half hours. Though the time was astonishing, the trip had not been without adversities. Hughes had flown the Atlantic through a dense cloud cover even at 7,500 feet. They had lost radio contact for an hour and a half in the middle of the ocean. Most important, strong winds had depleted the fuel supply at a terrifying rate after it was much too late to turn back.

Running on fumes, they approached the French coast. Hughes sent the Lockheed into a power dive at 220 miles per hour toward La Bourget Airfield outside Paris. The NBC radioman sent the word ahead, his voice breathless with excitement.

The French were amazed at the news. They had not expected the intrepid flier for many hours. Thousands of Frenchmen and Americans hurried out to the field. And here it came—a roaring silver streak to make a perfect landing. And there he was—the first one out of the plane. Everyone cheered hysterically. The American ambassador was waiting to shake his hand. Though Hughes was invited to stay, he made his dramatic announcement.

He was bound for Moscow.

For the first time, everyone recognized what had only been suspected. He was not only out to break Lindbergh's record. He was out to fly around the world.

Unfortunately, the plane had damaged a rear landing strut on the New York takeoff. The French had no idea how to repair it. A new one was unavailable. Hughes's engineer spent nearly eight hours fixing it while Hughes paced and fretted.

No one else did. During that time a celebration began in New York and in Paris. Congratulatory telegrams were delivered. At midnight Hughes stuffed them in his pocket and took off with his crew. The crosswinds were so strong that as the plane cleared the runway and began to rise, it actually slewed sideways and the wings dipped. The crowd gasped then cheered as the Lockheed steadied then flew off into the darkness, its roar gradually carried away by the wind.

When he landed in Moscow 1,550 miles and eleven hours later, he had trouble setting the Lockheed down. The Russians were all over the field. They cheered and congratulated him. They had found a box of his favorite food—cornflakes. They wanted to touch him, to shake his hand, to touch the Lockheed itself. The sense of history or tragedy was pervasive.

The Russians replenished his food and water as well as his fuel. Hughes turned down a gift of caviar because "every pound counts" and took off again.

Back home he was becoming a national hero. Americans across the nation followed the flight on the NBC radio. The newspapers carried front-page headlines and maps. Baby boys were being named Howard. Americans had fallen in love with Lindbergh, their "Lone Eagle." Now they fell in love with Hughes but in a different way. He was mysterious and romantic. More than that, he was covered with Hollywood glitz and Texas legend.

On the Lockheed came, flying across the wastes of Siberia, its speed dazzling everyone, records dropping with each passing hour.

Some 1,400 miles later Hughes landed in Omsk in the middle of the night in what the flight engineer said looked like a cabbage patch. As swiftly as they could refuel, they took off to fly 2,158 miles over some of the most desolate country in the world. Very little was known about any of this area. American maps were only estimates as Hughes learned.

When he landed at Jakutsk deep in Siberia, he had covered a little over half the distance of his flight. His next destination was Fairbanks, Alaska, a distance of 2,456 miles. As he took off, the Verchojanskij Chrebet, one of the great mountain ranges of the world, rose in front of him. The U.S. Hydrographic Survey put the maximum height at 6,500 feet high. Hughes's altimeter read 7,000 feet, and he was headed straight for the face of the mountain. Desperately he climbed. Ice began to form on the wings. At 10,000 feet with the ice growing heavier by the second, Hughes managed to slip through a gap at the crest of the range. His only comment to his frightened crew was, "It's a damn good thing I didn't try to fly out of Jakutsk at night."

They landed in Fairbanks on July 13 at three P.M., four hours short of three full days in the air. Wiley Post's widow greeted him with tears on her cheeks. The next morning they fueled in Minneapolis, making the shortest pit stop in flight history, thirty-four minutes.

At two P.M. the next day, Hughes passed over Pennsylvania and began his descent into New York. As he passed over Floyd Bennett field, he shuddered. Was the flight to end tragically after all? Fully 25,000 people lined the field on every side. They stood on their cars and screamed. They waved and jumped up and down. He had no choice. He had to land there.

Setting his jaw, he brought the Lockheed in for a perfect three-point landing between the hordes pressing toward him. Police were unable to keep order. Hughes was in danger of running people down as they raced out onto the tarmac to touch his plane. He had brought the Lockheed in nearly four days faster than Wiley Post's flight. Hughes had set a record flying round the world in three days, nineteen hours, and seventeen minutes.

Grover Whalen's welcoming script had to be abandoned. Mass hysteria among Americans quite mad for the sight of aviation heroes made any prepared ceremony impossible to follow. Even the presence of New York's popular mayor Fiorello LaGuardia imposed no dignity in the situation. Hughes could not land the plane at the designated spot. He had to taxi where he could. When Whalen and LaGuardia arrived puffing, they had to squeeze their way through the throngs.

This time Hughes emerged from the plane last. He was unshaven, smeared with grease, wearing a look somewhere between a frown and blush. He looked around helplessly then clambered down from the plane's wing to be enveloped by people who wanted to hug and kiss him, snap his picture, and even tear a piece off his clothing. They lifted him onto their shoulders and carried him to the reviewing stand hastily moved to the Lockheed's wingtip.

At last LaGuardia got to shake his hand. "Seven million New Yorkers offer congratulations for the greatest record established in the history of aviation. Welcome home."

Hughes mumbled something.

"Louder, Howard!" someone shouted.

"I am ever so much honored," he finally said. "Thank you very much."

That night he slipped away from Whalen's home where he was to stay the night. He tried to go to Katharine Hepburn's town house, but the crowds were waiting there. Nearly dead for sleep, he spent the night alone in the Drake Hotel on Park Avenue.

July 15, 1938, he spoke before a crowd of several hundred in the City Council chamber. In a speech "written ... for me by myself," he deprecated his act as in anyway heroic. He told the crowd that it was merely carrying out a careful plan that succeeded because it was carefully planned. He felt that his flight was important because it had reestablished America as the driving force in the world's aviation. If the sale of American planes would increase by only a little bit, then Hughes said, "the flight was worthwhile." After his speech he had the full treatment of tickertape parade in a huge shiny convertible down Broadway.

At first nervous and a little frightened, he got into the spirit of the thing and ended by waving and smiling constantly—enjoying his celebrity as only a few men in the world are allowed to do.

Hughes's flight did exactly what he hoped it would do. The sale of American planes, especially the Lockheed 14, rose sharply with orders pouring in from the Netherlands, Britain, and France.

The next few days he had tickertape parades in Chicago and Washington and finally July 30 in his own hometown Houston, Texas, where ten thousand people overran the modest field hastily renamed Howard Hughes Airport. A quarter of a million people lined the downtown streets and tossed confetti. That night at the Rice Hotel a banquet was held in his honor attended by his loving aunts, his childhood friends, and Governor James V. Allred of Texas, who said, "All of Texas is proud of your achievement."

It was perhaps the high water mark of his life. When he flew out of Houston a few days later, none knew including himself that he would never return.

> "The embarrassment of riches."
> —Voltaire

Howard was the only child of rich parents, Howard Robard Hughes Sr. and Allene Gano Hughes. His handsome father was characterized as flamboyant, "worth fifty thousand one day, owing fifty thousand the next." His gorgeous mother was from an old, cultured family. She` "looked and acted like a queen."

Their only son was born on Christmas Eve in 1905. His mother maintained that the doctor advised her to have no more children even though she was young and healthy. Moreover, he did not fill out a birth certificate and file it with the authorities. There is no trace of Hughes's birth anywhere in Texas. Only by affidavit from friends and relatives of his mother was his birth authenticated.

At that time Hughes Sr. and his partner Walter Sharp, a brilliant oilman, were going from oil field to oil field buying leases. But the big strikes were mostly bought up at that particular time. They quickly became more interested in supplying tools. Hughes Sr. invented a bit that was different from the conventional fishtail. When attached to the pipe stem of a rotary drilling rig, it bored through solid rock at the rate of fourteen feet in eleven hours. The "Rock Eater" became the foundation of the Sharp-Hughes Tool Company that within five years had turned into a virtual worldwide monopoly to supply drill bits to the oil industry.

While Hughes Sr. was building the business, Allene and her son were growing very close. She had an abnormal fear of disease, which she communicated to the boy. If anyone with whom he played became ill, she would take Howard out of town. She turned him into a lonely child whose only friend was Dudley Sharp, the son of his father's partner now deceased. When Hughes was fourteen, he was paralyzed for a short time by an unexplained illness. Though he seemed to recover completely, the experience left him with a lifetime phobic regard for his health.

After Howard recovered, Hughes Sr. sent him to a private school in Boston, no doubt fearful that his son's mother would "turn him into a sissy." There he had trouble fitting in. He did not make friends though he did quite well in class work and learned to play golf. Unfortunately, he was not allowed to finish there because his father, who traveled around the country selling tools, traveled to the West Coast. Hughes was attending the Thacher School in California when his mother died. He was a young sixteen.

Grief stricken, Hughes Sr. paid for his son to sit in on classes at Cal Tech. There he was under the care of Rupert Hughes, his uncle, a successful novelist turned screenwriter for Samuel Goldwyn studios. Howard saw the movie business from behind the cameras. It fascinated him. He also became infatuated with a young actress, Eleanor Boardman, though she was six years older and not interested in the shy young man.

He was disappointed when at seventeen, still with no high school diploma and a surprisingly small amount of formal education, his father brought him back to Houston. Howard despised school and was lukewarm about the idea of becoming an engineer, but he was a good son who also wanted to please his father. The stubborn, almost obsessive personality that characterized his later years was absent in him at this time. He did what his father told him.

He might have wandered through the next twenty years, content to be guided by his father through education, marriage, and career had his life not changed abruptly. He had barely completed his first semester at Rice Institute, the most prestigious and most highly rated university in the Southwest, when his father dropped dead of a massive heart attack. On January 14, 1924, Howard Hughes was junior no more. He was on his own.

Rupert Hughes tried to supervise Howard's part of the estate and the interest of Hughes Tool Company. Annette Gano, his mother's sister, tried to be a mother to him, but Howard almost immediately quarreled with these family members, probably because they were little more than strangers to him. He had been close only to his parents. Now they were gone. He owed loyalty or affection to no one of his parents' generation. Besides, at eighteen he was a millionaire.

On December 24, 1924, his nineteenth birthday, he filed suit in a Houston courtroom to be declared twenty-one. To insure the success of his suit, he had already set about wooing Judge Walter Montieth, a friend of his father. He had been playing golf with the judge all through the fall at the Houston Country Club. He had studied the workings and the books of Hughes Tool Company and spoke knowledgeably when Montieth questioned him. Although he had no intention of ever setting foot inside an educational institution again, he talked often about going to Princeton with his friend Dudley Sharp. Two days after Howard's nineteenth birthday, he was declared an adult of "full age."

He was master of his own future.

What Montieth thought when Hughes did not immediately take off for Princeton is unknown. Undoubtedly, he knew he'd been fooled, but he was helpless. The damage was permanent. For several months Howard was seen everywhere in Houston squiring Ella Rice, a girl from old money, the granddaughter of the founder of Rice Institute. They were married June 1, 1925.

At the same time, Howard made no effort to interfere in the workings of Hughes Tool. He was content to let others do that work so long as he could spend what he wanted when he wanted.

In the fall he and Ella took the train to California. He had some vague idea of making movies.

> "Making *Hell's Angels* by myself was my biggest mistake. I learned by bitter experience that no one man can know everything."
> —Howard Hughes, 1932

Installing his wife in the Ambassador Hotel, Hughes bankrolled a movie so bad it was never released. Rather than lose his own private fortune, he amended the charter of a subsidiary of Hughes Tool to allow it to make movies. He hired the son of a poor Wisconsin minister to head the new Caddo Rock Drill Bit Company of California. Noah Dietrich became invaluable to Hughes as an administrator who could take command of the business—and let Howard play.

At first all went well. In 1927 Hughes signed a talented director, Lewis Milestone, to a three-year contract and produced a spectacular box-office success, *Two Arabian Knights,* which won Milestone an Academy Award for best direction. One of the knights was played by William Boyd, who would go on to worldwide fame as Hopalong Cassidy. Milestone himself, no longer under contract to Hughes, went on to direct among other movies *All Quiet on the Western Front,* which won both best movie and best direction in 1930.

Hughes considered that he was a success while the rest of Hollywood thought of him as "the sucker with the money."

Nevertheless, he had absorbed the techniques of filmmaking. For his next project he settled on *Hell's Angels*. It was a subject close to his heart because he had fallen in love with flying. By 1928 he was an expert pilot. The story was about a pair of Royal Air Force aces and the woman they both loved. Marshall Neilan, Hughes's friend, was set to direct, but the two had a falling out. Another director was hired, but he too could not work with Hughes, who had his own ideas about how the movie should be made.

Hughes took over and directed and filmed all the indoor scenes in two months, a relatively easy thing to do since no sound was involved. He then moved into the really difficult part—and the part he relished the most—the aerial sequences.

He assembled props and manpower on a scale to rival D. W. Griffith. For more than half a million dollars, eighty-seven vintage planes were assembled from all over Europe. He bought Spads, Sopwith Camels, Fokkers, and SE-5s. He disguised a Sikorsky as a German Gotha, the terror of the Luftwaffe, to crash and burn in the last climactic scene. He hired World War I aces and daredevil stunt pilots to fly his collection of antiques.

As he watched the classic planes rocketing through the California sky, he couldn't resist the temptation to take one up. Without any experience and against the advice of the other pilots, he took up a Thomas Morse scout plane. Four hundred feet off the ground, he banked left and the plane flipped into a dangerous spin. He crashed.

The story for the newspapers was that Hughes crawled from the wreckage unhurt, "combing pieces of the motor out of his hair." The reality was that he was pulled unconscious from the plane with one cheekbone crushed. He spent days in the hospital and underwent reconstructive surgery. In that he was luckier than others attached to the project.

In those days the only way to film planes flying at targets with machine guns blazing was to have them fly directly at the cameras mounted on other planes. Three pilots died in fiery crashes during the filming. Still he went on and on, shooting scenes over and over, spending incredible amounts of money to put planes in the air to fly the scenes and planes in the air to film them. His direction and his vision were something Hollywood had never seen before.

Meanwhile, Ella led a "Caesar's wife" existence in Hollywood, almost completely neglected by her handsome husband, who spent twenty-four hours a day on his projects but wouldn't allow her to be part of the glamour and excitement of them because the people were "beneath her." Even trips to fabulous parties at San Simeon were forbidden. William Randolph Hearst loved to entertain Charles Chaplin, Mary Pickford, Douglas Fairbanks, Louis B. Mayer, Jack Warner, and, of course, millionaire producer-director Howard Hughes. But Hearst's live-in actress Marion Davies might contaminate Hughes's wife. Ella went back to Houston for a trial separation that ended in 1929 in divorce.

The filming of the last scene of *Hell's Angels* was an unmitigated horror. The crash of the Gotha was supposed to symbolize "the destruction of the Hun menace." For the big bomber to go down in flames, two men had to be aboard: a pilot to take it up to five thousand feet and a mechanic to work a series of smoke pots. Both men were equipped with parachutes. The pilot kicked the plane into a spin and bailed out—a dangerous stunt out of the side of spinning plane. From the fuselage and the tail, smoke billowed, but a second chute failed to appear. The mechanic never got out. Either he did not know what was truly happening until too late, or he could not get out of the spinning plane.

Hughes, who was flying a small plane watching the action, made an emergency landing in the field beside the burning wreck. The mechanic died in the crash.

In 1929 no one ever filed a lawsuit. People considered that any job had perils, and everyone took chances when he worked. Cecil B. DeMille caused four extras to drown while making the flood scene from the first *Ten Commandments*.

Though finished, the movie was already obsolete. The year was 1929, the year of *The Jazz Singer.* The American people were demanding "talkies." The battle scenes, which occupied the majority of the movie, could have a soundtrack added without trouble, but the actress hired to play the love interest had a thick Swedish accent. She was out and the scenes were to be filmed over again. Hughes held auditions.

An eighteen-year-old with "almost albino blonde hair" and a "puffy somewhat sulky little face" was tested at the end of the day. Her dress was too tight across the hips and bust. She didn't wear a bra. Her agent, Hollywood legend Arthur Landau, insisted that she was a perfect combination of "good kid and tramp." Though Hughes didn't care for her, Landau convinced him to hire Jean Harlow for $1,500 for six weeks.

The pre-release hype dragged audiences in off the streets. People whispered that Harlow didn't wear any underwear. Someone started the rumor that a man actually died in the crash at the end. On June 30, 1930, simultaneous premières were held on Hollywood Boulevard and Broadway. In California planes buzzed Grauman's Chinese Theatre while stunt men parachuted onto the street.

Inside the theatres the movie delivered even though it looked like two different movies. The planes roared and streaked through the skies and went down in spins that trailed smoke behind them. Audiences ducked and covered their eyes. Then they sat up straight to watch Jean Harlow, with her white hair, her blackened eyebrows and eyelashes, and her habit of caressing herself while she spoke her lines. Legions of ministers preached against her from their pulpits. People went back again and again unable to believe what they saw.

Hell's Angels set the style for Hughes's other movies—rich in entertainment, packed with sex and action, weak in the storyline. It set another style for Hughes as well. Because of his perfectionism the movie cost almost four million dollars. With movie audiences paying a nickel or a dime for a seat, it was a smash hit that earned only two million. Hughes's accountant Noah Dietrich was appalled at the loss that finally amounted to $1.5 million dollars.

A man of lesser means would have gone bankrupt. In this case the loss was easily recouped. Back in Texas in October a man named "Dad" Joiner brought in an oil well called Daisy Bradford No. 3. It set off another oil boom. While Caddo—the Louisiana part of Hughes's business that financed the movie—was in deep debt, Hughes Tool in Houston began to earn astronomical profits.

Hughes was the man with the golden reputation—a hit movie and a booming business. Yet he remained shy, "self-conscious with strangers and reticent with intimates." He was photogenic enough to be his own leading man with his dark hair and eyes and lean body, yet he hated to be photographed. The movie colony embraced all his eccentricities. They fit right in with so many of their own who "vished to be alone."

Hughes produced eight more pictures while he was working on *Hell's Angels.* One of the best would have been *The Front Page,* which would have starred James Cagney, except that Hughes nixed him, calling him "the little runt," and Clark Gable, whom Hughes rejected because "his ears make him look like a taxi-cab with both doors open." Another would have been better if Hughes had left the ending alone. *Scarface,* a thinly veiled story of Al Capone and his Chicago mobsters, was directed by Howard Hawks. It starred Paul Muni, whom Hughes had discovered at the Yiddish theatre in New York. George Raft played the bodyguard who flipped a silver dollar as he watched his boss from under his snapbrim hat. A young British actor named Boris Karloff also made his film debut. Hawks wanted the ending where Scarface turns into a coward and is gunned down by the police. Hughes wanted an execution. The New York censors considered both too violent. They suggested a reformation. Hughes wrote a ringing statement calling for "freedom of honest expression in America" and describing his film as "an honest and powerful indictment of gang rule."

In the end Hughes won the right to show *Scarface*, which was finally released with Hawks's ending. Hawks went on to directorial achievements. Muni won the Academy Award for *The Life of Louis Pasteur.* Raft and Karloff enjoyed long, colorful careers, but for Hughes, the movies were past history. Though he returned to the business for a few years in the forties, he never displayed the same vitality.

He had a new obsession—speed!

> "Money is trash, and he that will spend it,
> Let him drink merrily, fortune will send it."
> —Thomas Dekker, 1565

When Hughes was only twenty-seven years old, he began the pattern that would govern his life. He could focus on only one thing at a time. He had spent millions making movies. Now they no longer interested him.

He bought a new toy—a sleek little racing plane. Feckless as a teenager, he would hop into his Deusenberg roadster and speed down to Burbank in the San Fernando Valley to look at the new project housed in an oily hangar that eventually became one of the nation's largest and most powerful defense contractors—Hughes Aircraft Company, a division of Hughes Tool.

Charles Lindbergh's daring flight across the Atlantic had galvanized America's youth. Hughes was no exception. Everyone wanted to fly a plane. They were touted to replace cars as the main means of transportation. Howard had learned to fly before he made *Hell's Angels.* Now he became an expert pilot. He practiced looping, turning, banking, rolling, with dedication raised to the heights of obsession, which was swiftly becoming the ruling force in his life. He jotted copious notes of wind velocity, air speed, altitude, engine performance, and fuel consumption. He bought a silver racer from Boeing Aircraft and began rebuilding it to his specifications.

Lindbergh's pilot's license number was 69. Hughes's would have been 4223 except that he badgered the Aeronautics Branch of the Department of Commerce to give him a much lower number—80. He flew one trip as a copilot on American Airlines under the name of Charles Howard. When he was found out, he resigned. It was the only job he ever held.

The Boeing racer had a 580-horsepower Wasp engine that flew 225 miles per hour, a remarkable speed for that time. Hughes decided to enter a race. The All-American Air Meet was scheduled for January 1934, in Miami. The Boeing behaved spectacularly, averaging 185.7 miles per hour and nearly lapping its nearest competitor.

Flushed with victory, Hughes decided he could do better than the Boeing racer. He wanted to design and build his own plane. The secretive side of his nature asserted itself. He did not want to share his new obsession. To be fair, his obsession for secrecy was not unfounded. The world of aeronautics was in its infancy. Ideas on flying were everywhere, and everyone "borrowed" from everyone else.

Hughes put together the best team money could buy including Richard W. Palmer, a California Institute of Technology graduate, who was already known for his radical ideas. He brought with him his friends from Cal Tech. Hughes hired Glenn Odekirk, a mechanic and pilot from the *Hell's Angels* days. He leased a corner of Babb Hangar at Grand Central Airport in Glendale. He ordered it walled off and sealed from all inquisitive eyes. His instructions were broad to say the least. "...build a land plane that will fly higher and faster than any other in the world."

The men started with wooden models in the wind tunnel at Cal Tech. From there they began to build the H-I, a twenty-seven-foot-long racer. Its rivets were flush with the fuselage to reduce drag. Its wings were only twenty-five feet long to increase speed. The most outstanding innovation was a unique landing gear that retracted after take-off into a compartment under the wings. Many of its features were already described in magazines and some were even used elsewhere, but nowhere was there another plane built with everything in the package.

Hughes, of course, was getting the credit for everything while he actually did very little. He was not an aeronautical engineer. He was a brain-picker. He would call people up and talk them out of their ideas then incorporate them as his own. In 1935 in the depth of the Depression, with good old Hughes Tool bankrolling it, Hughes H-I was creating aviation history. Fortunately, he had the power of total economic freedom because creating aviation history wasn't making money. His plane was a very rich man's very expensive toy.

In the meantime, Colonel R. C. Kuldell, longtime successful manager of Hughes Tool, learned that Howard was going to fly this experimental craft. He fancied himself the "voice of Howard's conscience." He complained to Noah Dietrich, Hughes's financial advisor in Los Angeles, that Hughes needed to tend to business at home. At the very least, Howard must take the time to make a will. With the new inheritance bill passed by the Congress, if something happened to him, ninety percent of the company would belong to the federal government.

Dietrich wrote back saying that Hughes had revised his will and that it "generously provided" for all his top executives and his family. Actually, no will had ever been executed at this time. Hughes spoke of wills over and over without ever bringing himself to write such things. He was extremely annoyed at the "voice of his conscience" for bringing it up.

Kuldell's management of Hughes Tool had been exemplary. His had been the idea of operating a brewery on the tool company grounds at the end of Prohibition. Gulf Brewing Company produced Grand Prize Beer, the largest-selling beer in Texas at that time. It had saved the company.

Back in Hollywood, Dietrich had long wanted to be the sole manager of all Hughes's far-reaching properties. By annoying Hughes, Kuldell had opened the door. Within a few months, Hughes sent Dietrich to live in Houston. Kuldell was out in less than two years.

Kuldell had not been wrong about Hughes's danger, however. On August 18, 1935, Hughes decided—against the advice of both Palmer and Odekirk—to fly the H-I on its maiden flight. Both engineer and designer could not sway him. He flew it for fifteen minutes, accelerating to 300 miles per hour. He was supposed to bring it in to be checked over, but he flew on and on. The flight ended when the plane went down in a field. This time he was only shaken up. The danger had been real, and Hughes had been very lucky.

Undiscouraged, he knew he could easily beat the world's record of 314 miles per hour set by French pilot Raymond Delmotte. To contest it, he had to fly over an official three-kilometer course supervised by the National Aeronautic Association. He had to make four consecutive passes at speeds of more than 314 miles an hour. The test was scheduled for September 12, 1935.

He made seven passes of speeds from 339 to 355 miles per hour. So enraptured was he with his "beautiful little thing" he ignored the gas gauge. Suddenly, the H-I's engine died. Hughes considered bailing out, but he couldn't bear to lose the plane. He rode it down again into a beet field where it bounced to a stop. Hughes was unhurt and the racer had only minor damage. When he was told he had also set a new land-speed record, he muttered, "It'll go faster."

Fame was his and adulation. What more could he want?

He wanted it all.

More, more, more records. The transcontinental record of ten hours, two minutes, and fifty-seven seconds was his next sight. The H-I couldn't do it. But one pilot owned a plane that could—a single-seat, high-powered Northrup Gamma. She was a twenty-six-year-old blonde named Jacqueline Cochran.

Though she wanted the record for herself, she was out of funds. Hughes made her an offer she couldn't refuse, bought her plane, and flew the distance in nine hours, twenty-seven minutes, and ten seconds. (It broke her heart.) Then he broke more records flying from Miami to New York and from Chicago to Los Angeles. With nothing left to do at the moment, he sold the plane back to her for much less than he had paid for it.

Though he continued to fly the H-I, renamed the *Winged Bullet,* he had nowhere to go but up in it. In 1937 he made many flights of 15,000 and 20,000 feet equipped with oxygen. On one occasion his mask failed and his "arms and legs were practically paralyzed." With all his remaining strength, he nosed the ship down, shouting "to equalize the pressure within his head." At the same time he beat his own record for transcontinental travel. His new record would stand for seven years.

Howard Hughes beside the *Winged Bullet.* The inscription reads "To Jesse Jones, Without whose help my trip around the world would have been impossible. Howard." Jesse Jones, the millionaire owner of the *Houston Chronicle* and head of F.D. Roosevelt's Reconstruction Council, was one of the most powerful men in America. Center for American History, UT-Austin.

There was literally only "one world" left to conquer. It came in 1938 with his historic round-the-world flight. While all the world waited breathless, the lanky Texan flew as no man had ever flown before at a speed no man had ever thought to achieve. Hughes issued a challenge to aviators everywhere.

In those exciting days, wiser heads were becoming alarmed. Looming on the horizon was a horror that would accelerate the aviation world as nothing else could ever do.

> "We don't want to fight, but, by jingo, if we do,
> We've got the ships, we've got the men,
> We've got the money, too."
> —G. W. Hunt (1878)

In 1939 wars and rumors of war echoed on both sides of the two continents designated Eurasia. America had no will to fight. Nor did she have the weapons. Her armed forces had not been updated since World War I, when she had fought to make the world "safe for democracy."

More sophisticated political heads than the majority of the American people saw terrible prospects ahead. The air force set a goal of 5,500 military planes to be manufactured in 1939, then raised it to 10,000. It was a daunting task. American aviation was still in its infancy. Planes were by and large rich men's toys. Ordinary people traveled in trolleys, busses, and trains. If they had them, they used their motorcars for short distances.

American aviation had been practically brought to a standstill by the Depression, which hung on stubbornly all over the country. Then came the fateful attack on Pearl Harbor on December 7, 1941. When America's plane makers saw the footage of the Japanese Zeros sinking huge battleships, they knew—if no one else did—that the Aviation Age had dawned. They saw a chance and they seized it. Among others Boeing built the B-17 "Flying Fortress" and Consolidated, the B-24 "Liberator."

Howard Hughes believed he had the perfect fighter. It would be a plane that was already tested and proved. He would modify his H-I. Unfortunately, his attempt to sell it to the Materiel Command left him bitter and disappointed. Though he cried foul, Lockheed had simply built a superior plane, the P-38 "Lightning" with its distinctive twin fuselages and connected tail. It was extremely versatile with the capabilities of a fighter, a reconnaissance plane, and a bomber. It was as fast as its name. Though Hughes refused to recognize it, his H-I was outclassed.

Angry and sure that those in charge of selecting weapons and awarding contracts were prejudiced against him, he began a new project. Some quirk of his personality made him fly in the face of all reason. He came up with a design for a medium-range bomber to be built out of *duramold plywood*. He was infuriated when Materiel Command turned thumbs down immediately. They considered aluminum superior on all counts. It was impervious to moisture, it did not develop cracks, and it would not catch fire. Bullets could not shatter it, spraying lethal splinters into the men in the cockpit and cabin.

Nevertheless, Hughes became obsessed with building a plane out of wood and selling it to the government, but it was a relatively minor obsession. He was also busy acquiring a major share of the company that would become Trans World Airlines. But he was a man who enjoyed total economic freedom. The most important thing on his mind at that particular time was making a movie with a tall, bountifully endowed brunette named Jane Russell.

Undisciplined as always, Hughes focused on making a film based on a love story of Billy the Kid and a half-breed girl. *The Outlaw* was to have been made in Arizona and directed by Howard Hawks, but Hughes wouldn't leave him alone to do the job. Hawks quit after two weeks. Though Hughes remained in California, he directed the film with the idea of displaying Russell's breasts at every opportunity. He even sketched a bra that would, at the pull of a string, accentuate her already impressive endowments.

When *The Outlaw* was finished, the Hollywood censors moved to block its release. Hughes was in for another long battle.

Meanwhile, up in Oakland four hundred miles from Hollywood, during the hot summer months of 1942, Henry J. Kaiser was building 10,000-ton Liberty Ships in forty-eight days. Unfortunately, the Nazi submarine fleet was sinking them faster than he could build them. In May they sank sixty-eight ships. In June eighty-seven went down.

These were not only oil tankers and ordnance and equipment transports. These were troopships as well, carrying American boys. Naval convoys were incapable of stopping the losses. There were not enough warships to escort the cargo vessels to Europe. During the week of July 12, 1942, 100,000 tons of American shipping went to the bottom of the Atlantic.

In desperation Kaiser began to talk about building flying boats. He proposed that the nation turn over nine shipyards to their construction to ferry men and supplies over the Atlantic where "no submarines could shoot them down." Without any idea how his dream might be built, he sold the idea to the public, desperately concerned about the loss of thousands of American lives. Political suicide waited for any rational congressman who opposed him. In turn, President Franklin Roosevelt felt the pressure from them.

Kaiser boasted that he could turn out a flying boat in ten months. The best aeronautical experts protested that building planes was much more complicated than building Liberty Ships, but the public didn't listen. The head of the War Production Board gave the project the green light. Kaiser had his project, squarely in his lap. What to do with it?

Someone identifying himself as an engineer phoned in a "tip." Howard Hughes, holder of the record for round the world flight and creator of the H-1, had two hundred aeronautical engineers about to be available. Who made the call will never be known. Was it someone from Hughes's California offices? Perhaps Noah Dietrich in Houston had heard through Washington about the prospective deal. Perhaps one of the Hollywood agents such as Arthur Landau, who could persuade anyone to do almost anything, had been told to do it by Hughes himself.

No matter. Kaiser immediately began seeking the elusive millionaire producer. August 21, 1942, he found the man in a hotel suite at the Fairmont in San Francisco, just across the bay. How fortuitous! How coincidental!

Kaiser found Hughes stretched out on a bed looking wan and exhausted. He was recovering from a severe bout of pneumonia. Kaiser bounded into the room exclaiming, "Sit up! We want to talk about winning the war."

"I am very tired," Hughes said. "Besides, you're crazy."

Kaiser spent an hour explaining his idea for the huge planes. They were all pipe dreams, but Hughes listened. He was now thirty-seven years old. The last twenty years had been hard ones for mind and body. He had few friends, only associates and employees.

The only thing he had were his companies, deeply involved with government contracts for parts and making money by the millions. Among the items he manufactured were parts for B-25 and B-26 bombers. His plants made gun barrels for army machine guns. Still he was frustrated. He had been denied a government contract to build a plane. He did not like to be denied anything.

Kaiser wanted a plane in ten months. Hughes agreed to design and build the prototype. At the same time he was sensible enough to realize that he could not mass-produce them. Hughes Aircraft, unlike Lockheed or Boeing, was too small to mass-produce anything. It would be Kaiser's obligation to mass-produce the fleet. Kaiser agreed.

The next day a notice appeared in the newspapers coast-to-coast. "Henry J. Kaiser, West Coast shipbuilder, announced tonight he had teamed with Howard Hughes, multi-millionaire Hollywood airplane designer, speed flier, and film producer, in a program to build 500 cargo planes." No longer was Howard Hughes denied anything.

Then the worry began. His experience with H-1 and other individual projects had taught him there was no way to design and build even one flying boat in ten months. Such a plane had never been built, hardly conceived. It would have to be constructed piece by piece from materials that had to be tested endlessly.

When he failed, he would be blamed. His reputation and public image would be tarnished. Yet it was too late to say no. Everyone knew he had agreed to do it. On November 16, 1942, he signed the contract to build the HK-1, the Hughes-Kaiser One. Hughes planned to make it out of the spruce plywood he had championed so long. It was to be known as the Hercules. The name was quickly forgotten. The project quickly became a joke as the public and press dubbed it the "Spruce Goose."

As the months crept by, the project stalled for too many reasons to recount. Everything that could possibly go wrong went wrong. Materials were created but failed to pass standardized tests. Men came and went, unable or unwilling to do what needed to be done. To hold the monster plane, a new building had to be constructed—the largest building in the world made out of wood because all metals were being used for the war.

While things went from bad to worse, Howard Hughes and several men including a CAA observer took off in his rare Sikorsky S-43, the twin-engine amphibian he had bought for an around-the-world flight. When he tried to land it on newly built Lake Mead south of Las Vegas, he crashed it. Two men were killed; one was crippled for life. Hughes was only slightly injured. He paid all the medical bills and hired navy divers to raise the Sikorsky. It was his third plane crash. How much longer could his luck hold?

At least for the foreseeable future, or so it seemed.

Back in Washington a new type of plane was needed. Colonel Elliott Roosevelt, the president's second son, was surveying aircraft plants in the hopes of finding a photo-reconnaissance plane to provide accurate maps of the terrain and enemy positions before the invasion of Europe already being planned.

In August 1943 Roosevelt was entertained in Los Angeles by a publicist who was one of Hughes's cronies. He threw the president's son a party. He arranged for a tour of the studios—Hughes Productions in particular. While men died on the sands of North Africa for lack of information, Roosevelt attended a party where he met blonde actress Faye Emerson.

On August 11 Hughes personally led Roosevelt on a tour of Hughes Aircraft for a look at his wooden plane, the D-2, repeatedly rejected by the air force. Though it was smeared with grease, it was a thing of beauty. Hughes always made beautiful planes. Roosevelt was entranced. Whether with the D-2 or Emerson, no one was ever sure.

"I have never seen anything more magnificent that could do a better job." Roosevelt told Hughes. The president's son returned to the East Coast. Faye Emerson soon followed, wearing part of $132 worth of nylon stockings presented to her by the publicist. She and Roosevelt married four months after they were introduced.

Hughes was given another government contract to construct 100 XF-II's to be used as photo-reconnaissance planes. It was his personal triumph. Even with D-Day in the planning stages, he had not one but two contracts in his pocket. Though other manufacturers and their congressional representatives cried foul, the assistant secretary of war remarked, "Hughes has got very powerful friends in Washington."

Still, he did not have it all his own way. February 16, 1944, the order came from Washington to stop all work on the "Spruce Goose." Hughes flew east and lobbied so charmingly that Roosevelt allowed one boat to be built, saying, "...the experience to be gained...would be too valuable to throw away...The contract should not be cancelled."

Germany surrendered unconditionally May 7, 1945, without either the HK-I or the XF-II being finished. The European war was over, and Japanese surrender was expected within weeks. The next day the air force canceled the contract for ninety-eight of the XF-II's. Hughes was to finish the two prototypes, which the government considered were theirs. He intended to do so for his pride's sake.

The next month at a cost of $80,000 dollars, he moved the Hercules, now called by one and all the "Spruce Goose" to Long Beach harbor. Thousands watched the caravan of flat-bed trucks move the parts of the giant plane down the twenty-eight miles of narrow highway. There it would remain, costing millions of dollars, for over two years while its parts were put together.

> "Money:
> There's nothing in the world so demoralizing as money."
> —Sophocles

In 1945 *The Outlaw* was finally released after battling the censors since 1941 over Jane Russell's breasts. The movie ran for years because practically everybody in the United States had heard about it. Apart from the "breasts that won the West," it was a laughable effort that looked and sounded as if it had been directed over long distance. Even excellent character actors Walter Huston and Thomas Mitchell could not save it. Though thousands went to see it because of its notoriety, few were actually entertained.

July 7, 1946, Hughes was scheduled to test the XF-II. Contrary to air force procedures he made arrangements to test it from his own hangar at Culver City. Rather than flying the experimental plane over the desert, he was going to be flying it over heavily populated Los Angeles.

Even as he took off, the landing gear malfunctioned. Instead of immediately returning, he continued to climb, as he attempted to lower and raise the landing gear several times. At last he made the red light go off, leaving him to assume that the gear was up and locked.

At five thousand feet he cruised in ever-widening circles. Another plane took off and came up behind him to look at the XF-II in flight. He tried to radio it to find out about the landing gear, but their radios were tuned to different frequencies. When the second plane returned to the ground, expecting him to do likewise, he continued to fly, well beyond the forty-five-minute time limit set by the air force for testing.

Suddenly, the plane pitched right. Hughes felt a strong drag "as if someone had tied a barn door broadside onto the right-hand wing." The plane began to lose altitude. He tried everything he could think of including getting up from the seat and looking out the windows in an effort to see what might have happened. Nothing helped. He thought of bailing out, but he had ridden too many planes to the ground and survived. Lower and lower he roared over Venice Boulevard into the heart of Beverly Hills. As it crossed Wilshire Boulevard, the plane sounded as if it were falling apart.

For the fourth time, a plane Hughes was piloting crashed. A two-story house loomed in front of him just a block from the grounds of the Los Angeles Country Club. He plowed into the house, his right wing slicing into the second floor of the house and garage next door. The plane turned sharply right and sheared off a utility pole. Then it skidded through an alley and finally came to a stop between two more houses, one of which caught fire as a blaze started in the wreckage.

Hughes managed to crawl out onto the burning wing. A homeowner in the neighborhood dragged him off and smothered the fire in Hughes's clothing. Although by great good fortune no one on the ground was injured, the crash almost killed Hughes. His extensive and extremely painful injuries included many broken bones and second and third degree burns over much of his body. His heart was pushed to one side of his chest cavity. No one in the emergency room thought he would live through the night.

More than his body was burned that day. Perhaps something of his sanity was consumed as well. He became convinced that only fresh orange juice from oranges sliced and squeezed in his room had saved and would preserve his life. He became convinced that a germ-free environment was the only way he could live. The pursuit of this environment led in a very few years to almost total seclusion and strange obsessive-compulsive rituals. Furthermore, as a result of the extremely painful burns, he demanded and got increasingly larger doses of morphine. The doctor realized his patient was becoming addicted and switched to codeine, a weaker narcotic. Too late. It became the addiction that ruled the rest of Hughes's life.

Though Hughes recovered with the exception of some scars on his face, which he covered with a moustache, and some stiffness in his left hand, which had been badly burned, he was never the same.

After investigating the crash, the air force ruled pilot error. Hughes was furious. He was further forbidden to test the XF-II, which belonged by contract to them. He made a quick trip to Washington to the deputy-commanding general of the air force, Ira C. Eaker, who was easily persuaded to allow Hughes to fly the last plane. Nine months later Hughes hired Eaker to be a vice-president of Hughes Tool Company in Houston.

Almost a year later Hughes actually tested the second XF-II as a show for the press when he was about to be investigated by the special Senate committee investigating the National Defense Program. After a perfect flight, he turned it over to the air force without ever getting into the cockpit again. It was used for two years as a trainer. At Shepherd Air Force Base, Wichita Falls, Texas, it was cut up for scrap.

The Senate had needled Hughes about the "Spruce Goose," which had never flown. Stung again and wanting revenge on the committee, he pushed Hughes Aircraft to finish assembling it. On November 1, 1947, with the press gathered at Terminal Island in Long Beach, Hughes brought out the flying boat. Built to carry seven hundred passengers or a load of sixty tons, it was overwhelming in its size. The tail was eight-stories tall; the wings were so thick a man could stand inside them. With its eight powerful engines, it weighed 400,000 pounds. To this day it remains the largest plane ever built.

The next day Hughes decided to execute the taxi runs in the prescribed manner for test planes. A stiff wind was blowing. The reporters rode the course twice with Hughes. He then let them off in a small boat and began his final taxi run of the day. Slowly it gathered speed in the face of the wind, then dramatically, magically it lifted off. It cruised for a mile seventy feet above the water. Then Hughes set it gently down.

The Senate committee meetings closed just as gently three weeks later. Hughes had "flown in the face" of their strongest indictment. The "Spruce Goose" was towed to a dry dock on Terminal Island. Though he never flew it again, he arranged to keep it in proper condition in a permanent air-conditioned, humidity-controlled hangar. His cost was $1 million a year. Howard Hughes would live another twenty-nine years.

In 1948 Hughes took over RKO movie studios, then the third most profitable movie studio behind MGM and Twentieth Century Fox. With Hughes at the helm, revenue dropped twenty-three percent within a year. He did not care. He was interested only in taking another uninspired script and turning it into *Hell's Angels* of the Cold War. His latest venture into movie making was begun in 1949.

Jet Pilot starred John Wayne, who was already too old to be a fighter pilot. It was filmed with Hughes's usual overabundance of shots over a period of two years. When it was finished, Hughes had twenty-five hours' worth of film to reduce to a less than two-hour movie. The story goes that he could not make up his mind, an increasingly serious problem that also kept him from closing business deals and making a legal will. In his spare time between his many projects and his deteriorating physical and mental states, he wrestled with the thousands of feet of film for six years.

When it was finally released, the spectacular footage had been abandoned because the planes he had filmed were no longer in the air. They—like John Wayne, who looked embarrassingly young despite being too old for the part— were obsolete. One film critic called it "silly and sorry."

For the rest of his life, Hughes's personal playthings would cost him millions. His corporations allowed him to play as no commoner and very few kings had ever played before. In the hands of more than competent people, they ran smoothly and efficiently, garnering huge profits. If danger threatened one of them, he could be trotted out of his various dens like an ancient legendary lion. He would shake his black mane and roar and send senators, generals, and investigative boards fleeing in terror.

While RKO seemed doomed, the Korean War brought about a revival of fortune at Hughes Aircraft. Indeed in 1950 the aircraft corporation showed a profit largely because of the presence of Generals Ira Eaker (retired) from the air force and Harold L. George (retired) from the Air Transport Command. Hughes had always been extremely lucky in the men he had hired. These men knew whose buttons to push.

The air force turned to Hughes Aircraft to develop "an electronic weapons control system," a combination of radar and computer that could find and destroy enemy planes day or night in any weather. By plunging into a new field, the company got the drop on everyone. In June of 1950 Hughes Aircraft became the sole source of supply for the entire air force interceptor program. The work force grew to fifteen thousand and the money rolled in.

At the same time these workmen were settling in, Hughes was making decisions that would upset them. California had levied an income tax against him. He refused to pay it, declaring that he was not a resident of California—and neither was his company. He had negotiated a land deal with the United States government for 25,000 acres of desert in Nevada, which had no state income tax. The land, which cost him $3 an acre, adjoined Las Vegas.

Though everyone at the California plant was in turmoil, Hughes had spoken. They prepared to move while he pored over plans for the new facility; at the same time he descended deeper and deeper into aberrant behavior.

A thorough description of his mental and physical rituals would take many pages. A couple of examples should suffice to exemplify the situation. His paranoia had burst into full bloom. He imagined people were listening to his conversations. Therefore, he conducted business and legal conferences in cars that he personally drove to isolated areas, often in the middle of the night. If the talks were held inside buildings, they were invariably held in the bathroom where running water would thwart the listening devices or in large halls with the conference table in the middle of a huge bare room.

Terrified of germs, he required anyone handing him anything to first slip into thin white cotton gloves before passing the documents or objects to him. The doors and windows were sealed with masking tape. Aides bought three copies of a newspaper and extended them to Hughes who took the one in the middle. People who worked for him were instructed not to touch him, not to look at him, and not to speak to him directly. He began to neglect his personal appearance, going for days without shaving and wearing old, torn clothes.

He had been working on a will for approximately six years, ever since his first plane crash. The document had grown to thirty-four pages when it was finally typed up and brought to him. He studied it in silence, leafing through the pages, reading portions of it. He returned it to his secretary, Nadine Henley, and told her to place it in the safe-deposit box. He never signed it or looked at it again.

At the same time he announced plans for Howard Hughes Medical Research Laboratories to be built for the purpose of "scientific research necessary to accomplish the discovery and/or development of methods...for the cure of those diseases...dangerous to the people of the United States." In this case there was method in his madness, for it established a counterfeit charity pure and simple to receive his profits. He therefore had no taxes to pay.

It began with a debt to Howard Hughes, its creator, who sold the dummy corporation assets, receivables, stock, and liabilities from Hughes Tool and Hughes Aircraft Companies. It issued a promissory note for $18,043,300 with an annual interest rate of four percent. Without actually donating anything to it, Hughes had created a tax dodge whereby millions of dollars in interest payments would be collected from his own charity.

In a very few years, Hughes Medical proved more self-serving and sinister. It became an asylum of sorts for Hughes. Its one-man medical staff consisted of Dr. Norman F. Crane, a Beverly Hills internist, whose only patient was Howard Hughes. The good doctor did not treat his patient for mental disorder or physical ailments. He never gave him a physical at all. Crane prescribed Hughes's drugs. With a combination of codeine and Valium self-administered by syringe, Hughes kept himself tranquil. He watched movies on television during the evening and late night, ate his one meal a day around two or three A.M., and dropped off to sleep when most Americans were rising to go to work.

How he continued to be a presence in his various businesses was a miracle of his own strength of will when his flesh was weak. Though he left the running of the aircraft and tool businesses to abler hands, he continued to lavish his attention on Trans World Airlines and to a lesser extent on movie making with Jane Russell. TWA was now one of world's largest air carriers with twenty thousand employees. Hughes saw jet airliners, inaugurated by British De Havilland Corporation in 1952. Hughes was tempted to buy the British planes, but in 1954 Boeing began to build the 707. When the company came to Hughes at TWA, he hesitated again.

His inability to make decisions had reached critical mass. One executive described negotiations with Howard Hughes as "conducted by flashlight during the small hours of the night, out in the middle of the Palm Springs municipal dump." His paranoia almost crippled TWA. While he hesitated, Pan Am and United acquired 707s and DC-8s and moved to tie up gates at major airports for overseas traffic. Hughes's vacillation is not surprising considering the drugs he poured into his system, but flying was his first love. Above all things, he wanted a successful airline.

In the end he dealt with Convair to build a fleet of jets at a cost of $400 million. But where would the money come from? Hughes was adamant against long-term financing by banks or insurance companies who might try to impose conditions or offer suggestions on how to run his business. He refused to name a new president for TWA when the old one dropped dead of a stress-induced heart attack. He concentrated on the color of his fleet rather than how to finance it. Bad feeling was mounting between him and Noah Dietrich, his chief lieutenant who had managed so many of his properties including Hughes Tool so deftly for so many years.

In 1956 Hughes felt his years creeping up on him. One night in desperation, he called the one man he remembered as a friend—Dudley Sharp. He had not spoken to him in years. He poured out his anxieties ending with "I've messed up my life. I'm miserable."

Sharp tried to be upbeat, but Hughes was morose. "I've just messed it up so much there is nothing I can do about it."

He hung up.

How would Hughes's life have been changed if Sharp had only called him back, and said, "Howard, you need help. I'll come and stand by you and help you get yourself straightened out"? But Sharp did nothing. The years between had been too long.

It was the last time Hughes ever tried to communicate with a friend.

> "The victor belongs to the spoils."
> —F. Scott Fitzgerald
> *The Beautiful and Damned*

In what might have been his last serious bid for sanity, he married an actress twenty-one years younger than he. He knew her very superficially. (He knew everyone superficially by this time.) The marriage was probably a desperate ploy to keep Noah Dietrich from having Hughes declared mentally incompetent.

Hughes had to trust someone. Jean Peters, whom he had known off and on for ten years, seemed the least-dangerous person. Dietrich could not take control of the empire if Hughes had a wife.

In a secret ceremony on the morning of January 12, 1957, they flew to Tonopah, Nevada, and married under assumed names. Peters was a beautiful woman, the wholesome American girl-type, whose leading men had included Tyrone Power, Richard Widmark, and Burt Lancaster.

Three hours after they started out, they returned to the Beverly Hills Hotel, where Hughes lived in Bungalow 4 and Jean lived in Bungalow 19. Whatever she had hoped for, this was what she got. She remained totally discreet throughout their marriage. She had married one of the richest men in the world. She would never want for anything.

It is doubtful that he ever had sexual relations with her or that they slept together. They watched television together and sometimes they traveled together. She helped him when she could, but her influence was slight. She was Caesar's wife as his first wife had been. Sometimes he did not see her for months, though they talked on the phone often.

His personal situation had become extreme. He sat naked in a white leather chair in the center of the living room that he deemed a "germ-free zone." He watched one motion picture after another shown by a projectionist, who along with cooks and waiters lived in Bungalow I-C. Bungalow I-A was used for storage of cartons of Kleenex and cases of Poland water. Another bungalow was headquarters to all sorts of messengers, doormen, and assorted helpers.

His food was served ritualistically. The man would not approach until signaled to do so. He would walk down the right-hand side of the chair. When Hughes had looked him over, he would roll back the edges of the bag and bend over, holding the bag at approximately a forty-five degree angle. Hughes would reach in with Kleenex and take the food out one piece at a time.

He refused to touch doorknobs. He refused to let his aides clean the floor where he had urinated. Indeed, he ceased to use the commode, choosing to urinate against the bathroom wall. No one was allowed to clean anything. Paper towels were spread out over the mess. Paper towels covered his bed while his sheets went unchanged. The codeine constipated him. He once spent twenty-six hours on the toilet.

From 1958 on he ceased to care about the outside world.

While his fortune was left in the hands of others who did well or ill by it, he would spend hours methodically cleaning the telephone. He did not see his wife for months. His life was completely dominated by his obsessive-compulsive behavior. He existed unwashed, unshaven, and uncared for in any manner that would contribute to his well-being.

The men who controlled his fortune and his life preferred him that way. At the same time he began his odyssey to escape the rumors that his "disappearance" generated. A *Saturday Evening Post* writer called him "a modern-day Scarlet Pimpernel," referring no doubt to the hero's verse about his alter-ego. "Is he in heaven? Is he in hell? That damned illusive Pimpernel?"

Certainly, he was in hell and he didn't have any idea how to get out of it. His life was preoccupied with his fears. The most innocent things would generate insane terrors. Once Jean's cat somehow got into his room. He called Los Angeles animal control, comparing the emergency situation to a panther or a lion loose in his house. Once her nephew came for a visit and spoke to him. Hughes was not amused. He acted as if the child were an animal to be exterminated.

After four and a half years inside Bungalow 4, Hughes took a trip by train to Boston. He traveled 300 miles and spent $250,000 trying to decide where he would live next. Jean came and together they looked at maps of the area, but he was not serious. Finally after four months, he returned by train to Las Vegas and settled in the Desert Inn where he took up two entire floors. The penthouse was for himself; the floor beneath for his entourage. The manager was incensed. He needed those rooms for gambling guests.

In fact, no one in the entire world had the least sincere affection for him. Yet his money ensured that he would be kept alive. Indeed, it was imperative that he be kept alive. He was sixty-one and in fragile health, morbidly addicted to codeine and Valium. But so long as he was alive, his minions controlled one of the great fortunes of the world.

In his condition the world must indeed wonder how "he" sold his stock in TWA and used the $546 million dollars to buy properties to build a business empire in Nevada. Later in 1970 "he" bought Air West and was indicted for the purchase, but somehow the case was dismissed. "He" was the cover story for the CIA in the recovery of a Russian submarine from the ocean floor.

Perhaps unable to live any longer with her conscience and her complicity in the marriage farce, Jean Peters Hughes sought and was granted a divorce. She took a huge sum of money in the settlement and left him to the mercy of the minions. In 1972 "he" took Hughes Tool public, something he swore he would never do. His company was renamed Summa Corporation, distancing itself from his flamboyant, powerful image.

What is truly known is that for the next four years, Howard Hughes traveled, accompanied by a squadron of personal aides who took him to Panama, Canada, and London. Finally he ended up in Acapulco. During that time he kept a meticulous personal log of activities, which were limited to bed, chair, going to the bathroom, screening movies, sleeping, and eating one small meal a day. He also recorded the drugs he took, including abbreviations BB for Blue Bombers (ten milligram Valium capsules), 8 E for eight Empirin Compound No. 4s (a prescription drug containing codeine, which he took regularly), and BIG E referring to enemas that he needed because of the codeine.

His aides allowed him to inject himself with codeine and leave the needle hanging from his arm, depressing the plunger at slow intervals to prolong the feeling. An X-ray of his body post-mortem revealed three needles broken off in the flesh of his arms. His body deteriorated until he was an unrecognizable skeleton. Over six feet tall, he now weighed ninety-three pounds. When his aides decided he might actually be in danger of dying, they loaded him on a plane headed for Houston. He died just after he crossed the Rio Grande. Howard Hughes had died where he was born—in Texas.

The overall value of his estate at the time of his death will never be known. Estimates have run as high as $2.5 billion and as low as $600 million. Undoubtedly, many hands dipped into the till and absconded with what they deemed their share before any accounting could be made.

Howard Hughes exists today a quarter of a century after his death in the form of 626,000 sites on www.google.com. In February 2002 the *Wall Street Journal* reported a proposed merger between Hughes Electronics Corporation and Echo-Star Communications Corporation. The infamous Hughes Medical Institute exists today as a respected medical entity—quite different from the one-doctor operation with the sole purpose of imprisoning its creator's soul.

Perhaps the most appalling part of his miserable existence and death was the sheer sadistic cruelty displayed by his hired help during the last twenty years of his life.

No attempt was ever made to hospitalize him despite his desperate condition, to give him treatment for his addictions, or to give him psychological aid for his compulsions. Such simple mercies were denied him.

The most ironic and saddest twist is the latest development in the ongoing saga. It comes in the form of an announcement in the *Wall Street Journal,* May 28, 2002, concerning the sham entity that Hughes created as a cover for one doctor to give him the drugs that kept him imprisoned.

The Howard Hughes Medical Institute has chosen to pursue a combination of treating patients at the same time it does research to find cures for leukemia, hemophilia, AIDS, and heart disease. $120 million of Hughes' ever-multiplying wealth is earmarked for this initiative, plus $1 million each in the form of grants for twelve new physicians. The *Journal* further reports that the institute has an $11 billion endowment and expects to spend $450 million in support of biomedical science and education in its current fiscal year.

Had even a tiny portion of that incredible wealth been used to treat and cure his psychological problems and physical addictions, how different his last years would have been.

The incredible power of Hughes's wealth has passed beyond the power of the men who kept him prisoner. Like a runaway train it thunders on and on into the twenty-first century, long after the engineer has left it.

He was one of the richest men in the world. He possessed total economic freedom. Yet he could not buy his own treatment at his own institute. He most assuredly could not buy the one thing he needed most—a friend.

Oveta Culp Hobby
"The Best Man in the Cabinet"

Oveta Culp Hobby of Texas had hosted many parties in her reign as wife of William Pettus Hobby, former governor of Texas and owner of the *Houston Post*. None was more satisfying to her than the night when her two worlds came together. In early 1955 the Secretary of Health, Education, and Welfare invited her boss, Republican President of the United States Dwight Eisenhower, to an intimate party at the F Street Club in Washington, D.C. There Ike met informally and as friends with Oveta's old friends from the Democratic Party, Senator Lyndon Johnson and Speaker of the House Sam Rayburn. For her the meeting was a political coup made all the more triumphant because of the singular circumstances.

Oveta Culp was born in Texas in 1905. In other words, she was born a Democrat. Since the Civil War, the state had voted exclusively Democratic. No Republicans allowed. The politically savvy were flabbergasted when Eisenhower busted the Solid South.

Ike himself had been born in Texas and reared in poverty in Kansas. A graduate of West Point who had been in the military all his life, he was not a political person and scarcely knew what party he favored. Both parties courted him, sure that their best chance to win the White House was with the military hero of D-Day and the European Theatre of Operations. Finally, he made up his mind that he was a Republican and easily defeated the Democratic nominee Adlai Stevenson. His popularity carried Texas and swept enough Republicans into the Senate and the House to give him a majority for his first two years.

In November 1954 the honeymoon was over and the Democrats regained many of the seats they had lost with Stevenson's disastrous defeat. The House returned to the capable hands of Speaker Sam Rayburn of Texas. The Senate Majority Leader was Texan Lyndon Baines Johnson. Both were Oveta's friends.

She was a Texas lady who had Eisenhower's complete confidence. Now she was working to help usher in a new era for the president, one that would require all his tact and diplomatic skill. Used to giving orders and having them obeyed without question, Ike would be facing men nearly as powerful as he, who were in a confrontational mood. It would be war but with a difference he barely understood.

When Congress returned in 1955, Oveta planned the party. All the men involved were delighted. She was personal favorite of theirs as well as a rich, powerful woman with a heritage of breeding and culture. The executive branch met the legislative branch at the behest of Oveta, in a red satin dress, displaying her "vivacious style, grace and charm." In a room full of strong men, she dominated the occasion. At the same time she made every guest feel welcome, admired, and appreciated. No one else could have done it.

She had charmed Lyndon Johnson for years. He enjoyed beautiful women, and this one was the daughter of his father's friend. Sam Johnson's desk had been next to I. W. Culp's in the Texas House of Representatives. Sam Rayburn was even easier. As a bachelor he had always enjoyed the attention of refined, warm-hearted women.

In her presence and with her aiding and abetting, President Eisenhower met the two most powerful men in the Congress in a social setting. The bonhomie flowed along with the wine. His administration made a close connection with them. Johnson and Rayburn mellowed in the warmth of presidential attention they both loved.

Oveta was a woman who enjoyed total economic freedom. She did not even think of asking permission of her husband to stage this soiree. With her considerable personal fortune, she was able to use it as French and British noblewomen did in previous centuries to bring together various strong personalities with obdurate opinions. She would be an ameliorating presence, for no one would dare behave boorishly in the presence of such a lady. Consequently, they were perfect gentlemen.

Seeing themselves reflected in her eyes as worthy human beings, they took the first steps toward working together to change postwar America. Good humor, good food, good wine, and good company work more miracles for mankind than force ever did. As Oveta herself said, "If I have learned anything in business, in politics, in state or national government, it is that we can do nothing unless we work together as a team...able to make small compromises to gain the greatest common good."

Oveta had masterminded it all. What a personal triumph to help the United States to be governed well and co-operatively! She was absolutely radiant on the occasion. In fact, she had a ball!

> "Money is like a sixth sense without which you cannot make use of the other five."
> —W. Somerset Maugham

Oveta was named for a Cherokee heroine in a romance novel. Strange and exotic names were a charming fad of the literate class at the turn of the nineteenth century. Miss Ima Hogg, a governor's daughter, was also named for a romantic heroine.

Oveta's father was Ike W. Culp, whose grandmother Rachel Eaton Culp "rode horseback, dodging Indians in the darkness when called to aid the sick." As a child in Killeen, Texas, Oveta delivered baskets of food, clothing, and money her mother had collected for the poor.

Those were also the years when her grandmother insisted that Oveta come and live at her house to help take care of her. Her granddaughter fussed and fought at the idea, but she did as she was told. Only later did she acknowledge the advantages she received. Instead of being the second oldest of seven children, she was an only child in the home of a well-educated, lively woman who was interested in everything. Oveta credited her grandmother with getting rid of her atrocious West Texas accent.

Her father rode horses, practiced the law, and loved politics. On her way home from school, his daughter would stop by his law offices to listen, to talk, and to read whatever he had lying around. At ten she was reading the *Congressional Record*. At thirteen she had read the Bible three times. All this unusual education trained her for what would have seemed like an illogical step in any other family.

When Ike Culp was elected to the State Legislature in 1919, he took Oveta with him to Austin. She was fourteen years old, but no school could equal what she would learn at her father's elbow. Then as now, the governor convened the legislature on the second Tuesday of January in odd-numbered years. The representatives met for a short time—usually a matter of weeks—to do the business of Texas. Oveta sat in on the deliberations every day, everlastingly fascinated by what she heard and saw.

Though she missed quite a few days at school, she was still scheduled to give a speech at graduation. Proud and independent, she prepared her speech. When the principal would not approve it, she walked out of Temple High School without her diploma.

Undisturbed by her rebellion, perhaps even proud of it, her father sent her to Mary-Hardin Baylor College in Belton. She loved the freedom of the academic world. Instead of running wild as so many college students do, she became more and more engrossed in what she considered her work. She studied her subjects, taught elocution, put on school plays, and became a cub reporter for the *Austin Statesman*.

In 1925 she was asked by the speaker of the Texas House of Representatives to act as legislative parliamentarian. She served in her first government job for six years while she continued her education at the University of Texas. In 1928 she was released to work as a secretary of the Democratic Club in Houston. There she helped to plan the Democratic National Convention.

Oveta Culp at twenty. In 1925 she was parliamentarian of the state of Texas. To the far left is Governor Dan Moody. Texas State Library & Archives Collection.

The mayor of Houston was so impressed with her work that he offered her a post as assistant to the city attorney. She accepted with the understanding that she would have to return to Austin for the next legislative session. She reminded him she was their parliamentarian.

Fate played a joke on her in 1930. At twenty-five she ran for House Representative for Harris County. Her opponent defeated her by letting everyone know—as if he were imparting a shameful secret—that she was "a parliamentarian and a Unitarian." Since many people didn't have any idea what those two words signified, she lost by 4,000 votes.

She wasn't particularly unhappy over the loss because she was getting married. Her parents' good friend former governor William Pettus Hobby had become owner of KPRC radio and president of the *Post-Dispatch,* the newspaper formerly belonging to Ross Sterling, who had just been elected governor of Texas. Oveta was twenty-six and Hobby was fifty-three, but she loved him dearly. She never called him Bill or William. It was always Governor. She often said, "Everything...fell in my lap. And nothing in my life would have been possible without Governor."

Her parents were cautiously approving of the marriage. Her mother had campaigned for Hobby in his run for a second term in 1918. Her father was his close personal friend. In fact, her father warned Hobby, "Will, she'll embarrass you. She doesn't give a hang about clothes."

Up until then, Oveta really hadn't thought about how she looked. All she cared about was books, politics, government, and horseback riding. However, unwilling to do anything to embarrass her husband, she threw herself into a study of fashion as she had done everything else in her life—wholeheartedly with gleeful determination to be as fashionable as any woman in Texas.

The description of her dress from the *Temple Daily Telegram,* February 24, 1931, reveals how much she had learned. The bride "wore a Jeanne Patou spring ensemble of grey with long coat of basket weave material and collar and cuffs of pony. Her hat was a close fitting combination of grey gros-grain and felt, and all other accessories were to match. A touch of grey reptile trimming was noted on pumps and purse." Obviously, the *Temple* reporter was impressed. An exclusive French fashion house, then as now, commanded high prices. As her father's wallet lightened, his chest must have swelled with pride.

Thereafter Oveta never failed to impress everyone who met her. In January 1953 she was ranked sixth on the New York Dress Institute's list of the world's twelve best-dressed women.

> "She walks with the air of success."
> —*Time*

On the Hobbies' return from their honeymoon in February 1931, Oveta began to learn newspaper publishing. Governor changed the name back to the *Houston Post*, and they both became intensely involved in it. She barely took time to have a baby boy, William Pettus Hobby Jr. Dividing her time between home and work long before most women did such things, she reviewed books, edited copy, and wrote editorials. She also accepted the position of state president of the League of Women Voters.

In 1936 she was in a serious accident. She and Governor were returning from Dallas in a private plane that caught fire. The pilot crash-landed in a cotton field and Governor was knocked unconscious. Oveta pulled her husband and the pilot from the burning plane. She and the other passengers drove the injured to a hospital in an old car they borrowed from field workers. She promptly took charge of the emergency room and helped care for the injured. Only when everyone else was taken care of did someone inform the staff that Oveta had also been a passenger on the plane. She was hospitalized for minor injuries.

She thought of herself as mother, wife, and assistant to the editor and publisher—her husband, Governor. In 1937 their daughter Jessica was born, and in 1938 her husband promoted her to executive vice president. In her free time she wrote a book on parliamentary procedure called *Mr. Chairman*. The Texas Public Schools adopted it as a textbook.

The Hobbys continued to work as a team to pay off the huge debt he had incurred to buy the paper. While riding in the park, Oveta was thrown from her horse. Her leg and wrist were shattered. She edited the book pages from her bed. Returning on crutches, she resumed her newspaper work. She was never far from his side.

In July 1941 the likelihood that America would go to war hung over an unprepared and unfortified country. The depression of 1929 had kept the birthrate low for a decade. Military men perceived that as a problem. Who would answer the call to arms when so many men were essential for factories and farms? While Oveta was in Washington on Federal Communications Commission business, General David Searles asked her to head the women's division of the War Department Bureau of Public Relations.

She refused, saying that she must stay at home with her husband and her children. When Governor heard she had turned down the request, he told her, "Any thoughtful person knows that we are in this war, and that every one of us is going to have to do whatever we are called upon to do."

> "Hand me my sword."
> —Oveta Culp Hobby

She was thirty-seven years old, in excellent health despite two serious accidents. She did not expect the job to be physically taxing. A dollar-a-year woman, her first undertaking was to facilitate communication between men in service and their wives and mothers.

In less than three months, army chief of staff General George C. Marshall asked her to begin studying plans for establishing an auxiliary women's army. Most women would have been daunted or even overwhelmed. Not Oveta Culp Hobby.

She had never met a challenge she didn't relish. She flung herself into the task of creating an army from scratch. The task was monumental. The smallest details became problems. Glitches that no one had foreseen loomed large. Women had never served in any military capacity in the entire history of America. Hobby had to create an entire organization for which no precedent and little support existed.

Women's groups objected because the government was expecting women to leave their families. Oveta herself was criticized. She often thought about the time she was giving up to care for her family. She didn't feel "...a sense of guilt as much as a sense of regret, of dissatisfaction at being unable to be in two places at once." She was creating a group of women soldiers, no different from the men who were also giving up their time with their sons and daughters.

Men, particularly army men, resented and condemned the entire idea. Women were regarded as weak, frail creatures totally unsuited to regimentation and army life. Oveta faced that prejudice over and over for the entire time she headed the WAACs.

In May 1942, six months after the Japanese attack on Pearl Harbor, Oveta completed her proposal. The Women's Auxiliary Army Corps was officially authorized by an act of Congress. On the sixteenth, Secretary of War Henry L. Stimson swore her in as director with the military rank of major.

She accepted the appointment with these words, "You have said that the Army needs the Corps. That is enough for me."

Her rank was raised almost immediately to colonel. Patriotic women had heard what she was doing. Already more than 10,000 had made inquiries. Hobby's challenge was to recruit 12,200 volunteers immediately. The authorized force

Oveta Culp Hobby is sworn in as Commander of the Women's Army Corps by Major General Myron C. Cramer. Chief of Staff General George C. Marshall and Secretary of War Henry L. Stimson look on. Washington, D.C., May 16, 1942. U.S. Army Photo, Eisenhower Presidential Library.

was set at 150,000, although no men in Washington really believed that many women would ever appear or be needed.

Dissension came from another quarter. Because Colonel Hobby was a southern woman, the National Negro Council and the National Council of Negro Women asked Stimson to appoint Mary McLeod Bethune as assistant director. Mrs. Hobby solved the problem by announcing that Negroes would be recruited in proportion to their number in the population. In other words ten percent of the WAACs must be Negroes.

An officers candidate school was established at the Fort Des Moines Army Post. Old line military officers sneered when they referred to it as the "Women's West Point." When women's barracks first were requisitioned, the army engineers replied that they worked only for the army. The WAACs were not army. Hobby drew her own plans for the barracks. Her treatment from transportation was not much better. While sergeants had their own jeeps, she was told to call for a vehicle from the motor pool.

Men continued to sneer when she put out a call to fashion designers to create a uniform that would be attractive to large numbers of young women. When she presented her choice, the Army Quartermaster Corps vetoed the belt as a waste of leather and the pleat in the skirt as a waste of cloth. Fortunately, they allowed her to keep the distinctive pillbox hat with the brim. It swiftly became known (derisively in some circles) as the "Hobby Hat."

When the barracks actually went up at Fort Des Moines, the base commander was horrified. He ordered a fence built around the structures and allowed the WAACs to go to the post movie only two nights a week, while men went on other nights. Men were ordered not to look at a WAAC's legs. Later, as barracks went up at other posts, their commanding officers followed suit.

Faced with constant objections, Oveta worked all day and all night. She went home for a shower and came back to work. Since she had only one uniform—the only WAAC uniform in existence at the time—she washed it, blew it dry with an electric fan, and ironed it every night. Her thinking was that it had to have the spit and polish representative of the corps she was seeking to establish. She ordered khaki underwear to silence jokes about pink "unmentionables" and set a policy of limited makeup.

Even Congress gave her problems. Made up almost entirely of middle-aged and old men, they grudgingly decided that women could do fifty-four different military jobs. Hobby pushed and persuaded, charmed and bulldozed them into revising their thinking. In the end they agreed that 239 separate types of jobs—almost the entire scope of noncombatant duties—might be performed by women.

The comptroller general's office refused to pay for women doctors for the WAAC because it was authorized to pay only for "persons in military service." Women were evidently not persons. They were also not allowed to make a mistake. Oveta was furious when she learned that women were to be dishonorably discharged for "Pregnancy without Permission." She charged into the Pentagon and "reasoned" with the generals that male soldiers who fathered illegitimate children, must, in all fairness, get the same treatment and suffer the same loss of rights and pay. The regulations were promptly changed, and P.W.O.P cases were given medical treatment and honorable discharges.

Equipment and supplies were slow in arriving for many reasons, not the least of which was a male smugness that the women could wait. A great deal of her paperwork never got to General Marshall's desk. One day Katherine Marshall, the general's wife and Oveta's good friend, invited her to lunch. The general was there and wanted to know if the WAAC was having any problems. Oveta replied that the paperwork was crawling through military channels.

She barely got back to her office before she received a call from Lieutenant-General Brehon Somervell in charge of Services of Supply. He wanted to know what the problems were and promised to solve them immediately.

Later another general snidely remarked, "Well, you certainly went through the back door to get what you wanted."

She smiled sweetly. "Well, if you want to call Mrs. Marshall 'the back door' that's your privilege."

Perhaps impressed with her zeal and more impressed by the strong support she was getting from Marshall and Stimson, the army began to come round. Colonel Hobby was grudgingly invited to enter the all-male sanctity of the officers clubs, but "would she please use the back door?"

On a much "lighter" note, the military diet with its high percentage of starches and sugars was found to be too caloric. WAACs gained too much weight. The menus had to be adjusted. The women also had a hard time with the thirty-inch marching stride, something their colonel also admitted she could not perform. At the base where the first WAAC detachment was stationed, the commanding officer considered a beauty parlor an "unreasonable feminine frivolity" until Colonel Hobby reminded him that no one considered the base barbershop an "unreasonable male frivolity."

The first officer candidate class of 440 women began at Fort Des Moines on July 20, 1942. It was much more of an ordeal than it should have been because the army refused to bend or compromise on so many rules. Many women felt they had made a terrible mistake in the heat, the insects, the unfinished chaotic barracks, the ill-fitting clothes, and the often sarcastic, sometimes sadistic male instructors determined to fail as many women as possible.

The situation became more reasonable swiftly as Colonel Hobby gave notice that she was reporting for training. Her advisors were shocked. No less a person than General George Marshall told her firmly that such an action was impossible under the army's system of rank. Unable to do as she had planned, she nevertheless came to the fort the first day and observed the 440 officer candidates in training. They were the first of their kind on the continent of North America. On the fourth day, she spoke to them.

"You are the first women to serve. Never forget it…You have just made the change from peacetime pursuits to wartime tasks—from the individualism of civilian life to the anonymity of mass military life. You have given up comfortable homes, highly paid positions, leisure. You have taken off silk and put on khaki. And all for essentially the same reason. A debt to democracy, a date with destiny…"

One woman remembered that day vividly. She took comfort in Colonel Hobby's words. Her guilt at leaving her family was assuaged. If the "Little Colonel" was not afraid, then she would not be afraid. "I looked up to see one of those odd dappled cloud formations [that looked like] white faces crowded shoulder-to-shoulder in rows…I felt a little chill, and wondered if they were the silent ranks of our ancestors, of long-dead soldiers and patriots, watching us. We were entering history."

At first the army was interested only in typists, clerks, chauffeurs, and cooks. Oveta insisted that she was training "serious-minded women with a serious purpose, resolved to do a serious job."

When the winter uniforms didn't arrive, the WAACs nearly all got sick when an unexpected snowstorm struck in September. Colonel Hobby went back to Washington without her overcoat, since her troops had none. The winter uniforms arrived by the next shipment. The army had at last decided that the WAACs were there to stay.

In October 1942 Colonel Hobby flew to England with Eleanor Roosevelt to study the organizational structure of the British and French women's units. When she arrived in London the king and queen were there. A red carpet was rolled out for Mrs. Roosevelt, who introduced Oveta. Five minutes later the president's wife drove off with the royals, leaving the colonel standing there.

She had nothing to fear. General Dwight Eisenhower and General Walter Bedell Smith appeared to take her and her aide to lunch. "Ike," who was really an overgrown Kansas farm-boy, couldn't get over the two women standing back to allow him to enter the doors first. He laughed every time. Where he came from, a lady was a lady. Moreover, she was a beautiful woman with a chest full of military brass not the least of which was the helmeted head of the Greek goddess of war Athena—the symbol of the WAACs.

Still he treated her like an equal when he hauled out his cigarettes and tossed them into her lap and when he tried to trick her into buying drinks for the Short Snorter Club—a drinking club of crewmen who flew transatlantic flights. She had been initiated into the club but was almost caught without her membership card (a signed dollar bill). If she hadn't run to get it, she'd have had to buy drinks for every Short Snorter at a dinner given by the U.S. Ambassador at Claridge's in London.

She made quite an impression on Ike, who was remarkably free from prejudice against women in uniform.

The following year, 1943, "Auxiliary" was dropped from the organization's name. The WACs were given full military status. And about time. By then WACs were serving in non-combatant posts both in the United States and overseas. Eisenhower himself used a WAC as his driver throughout Europe.

Originally the commission had been for 150,000 women. Only 99,000 were actually trained, but by 1944 WAC headquarters had requests for 600,000 women from commanders all over the world. WACs, who had initially been cleared to handle 239 jobs, had assumed 406 in every area of military occupations.

Colonel Oveta Culp Hobby among her admiring troops, January 21, 1944, 6716 WAC Headquarters Co, Naples, Italy. U.S. Army Photo, Eisenhower Presidential Library.

The WACs had done their colonel proud. Moreover, they had done themselves proud. She was in Italy during World War II at a base hospital when the wounded began arriving. A colonel came to her and said, "You'll have to say something to your troops, or their rations will be cut back."

Aghast and puzzled at the same time, she asked what was wrong. "...they are giving their food to all those starving children outside the fence, and it's beginning to show in their work. You have to say something."

She called an assembly and told them that they had to stop. If they were not strong and healthy, they could not do their jobs. She was very stern, but when she walked away, she wept.

When she got back to Washington, she told the story to a meeting of Congressional wives. She told about the starving children, the typhoid, and the wounded Americans. She should have cleared the speech with the War Department, but she didn't.

The chief of staff was on the phone when she got back to her office the next morning. She went in and saluted (a trick she never got right no matter how much she practiced in front of the mirror).

"Did anyone in the War Department clear your speech...?" he began.

"No sir."

"Thank God! My phone rang all night and it hasn't stopped. Those women told their husbands, and the senators and representatives have been calling me asking what Congress can do about the war. And don't you ever let anyone in the War Department clear a speech for you in the future."

She had done more than most men had done. On July 12, 1945, thirty-five days before Japan surrendered, she resigned, pleading her husband's serious illness and her own mental and physical exhaustion. Her raven black hair had silvered. The lines had deepened in her forty-one-year-old face. She returned to Houston to her home and her children. Her husband, her beloved Governor, met her at the airport with a stretcher and took her to a hospital for a complete rest.

In January 1945 she received the Distinguished Service Medal for outstanding service. The citation stated, "Without guidance or precedents in the United States military history to assist her, Colonel Hobby established sound policies and planned and supervised the selection and training of officers and regulations. Her contribution to the war effort of the nation has been of important significance."

> "In general, the art of government consists in taking as much money as possible from one class of citizens to give to another."
> —Voltaire's *Dictionnaire Philosophique*

Working as if she somehow knew she would not have her family and her life to herself for very long, she returned to radio station KPRC and the *Houston Post*. Her years in the army had strengthened her belief that everyone should have an equal opportunity. Because of who she was and who she had been, she served on all kinds of committees and boards, was awarded countless honorary degrees, received endless opportunities to advance the causes she and Governor espoused. Together they created the Hobby Foundation to support religious, educational, and charitable organizations. Her increasing wealth allowed her the total economic freedom to do just about anything she liked, and the wealthy of Houston, an oil-rich boomtown called familiarly Petro-Metro, followed her lead.

On the eve of the Supreme Court decision to desegregate the nation's schools, Oveta and Governor gave the front page of the *Post* to Houston's religious leaders to state their opinions on the decision. Distinguished men of every faith declared themselves unanimously in favor of the decision. A few years later Oveta spoke of her strong opposition to prejudice, which she called "the reasonless dislike of a person, the proofless distrust of anyone from another race or religion, the rejection without trial of a new idea or thing…It has been a costly luxury. It is still a costly luxury…"

June 17, 1947, she and twenty-one other passengers took off on Pan American's first round-the-world flight in the history of commercial aviation. She later turned a series of articles for the *Post* into the book *Around the World in 13 Days*. In it the voice of the WAC colonel can be clearly heard as she writes, "The sight of Nagasaki and Hiroshima moved me no more than the devastation…in Tokyo. Modern warfare…is destructive beyond one's capacity to understand without… learning the number of casualties. Instead of discussing the ethics of the atomic bomb, we should be discussing the ethics of warfare itself."

In 1952 Oveta Culp Hobby was named editor and publisher of the *Houston Post*. She only held the office for four months. Dwight David Eisenhower had been elected president of the United States. The Little Colonel had never forgotten him and his acceptance of her as a fellow soldier. She was a key figure in the national Democrats for Eisenhower movement.

He had never forgotten her either. He summoned her to Washington to head the Federal Security Agency. She tried to refuse. Governor was not so strong as he might be. She had already given four years of her life to World War II. She and her husband discussed the summons. In the end they both came to the same conclusion. Her president had called her. And she went.

The position was not a cabinet post, but she was invited to sit in on the meetings. America's new social consciousness was awakening. A country aware of its richness was adopting a new national agenda, one that would address the problems of health, education, and the disadvantaged. Ike proposed her name to head a new department he was creating—the Department of Health, Education, and Welfare. The Senate confirmed her nomination in seven minutes. Senate minority leader Lyndon Johnson explained. "There's no disagreement on...Oveta."

On April 11, 1953, Oveta Culp Hobby, one of the richest, strongest, smartest, and most advantaged women in America, became the first secretary of a completely new department. Ike knew what he was doing. She was perhaps the most qualified person in America for the job. To paraphrase a World War II song, "She'd done it before and she could do it again." She would do for HEW what she had done for the WACs.

Her daughter said of her, "She walked the corridors of power with eagerness and commitment, a powerful love of learning, and a powerful love of country."

The first day on the job, she began as she meant to go on. She had a department to organize and a war to fight for the least advantaged people in America. Some major aides had not yet arrived at the appointed time. She ordered the doors to the chamber locked. When the "tardies" started knocking, she ordered that the doors remain closed. She said they'd be on time for the next meeting.

Again she was gripped by a feeling of urgency. A whole new America had been born since World War II. When the servicemen and women came home, they "walked in the front door and started their families immediately." The resultant generation (now old and graying in 2002) would require services that the country was incapable of providing, especially since the smallest generation in history had been born between 1929 and 1945.

Before she could get started with the new, she had to overhaul the distribution of $4 billion annually in pension and welfare funds to 67 million Americans.

Likewise, widespread epidemics of poliomyelitis had crippled and killed children for several years. At first it was called infantile paralysis because it struck mostly among the young and vulnerable population. The demand for a new vaccine was immediate. Parents were terrified to let their children out of the house. Swimming pools and movie theatres closed.

Dr. Jonas Salk had devised a vaccine. To hold back the vaccine before it was properly tested was to risk children's lives. To issue it prematurely was to risk infecting healthy children. She and her advisors worked with doctors to set up a program of voluntary distribution that promised maximum effectiveness and still allowed doctors to treat their patients rather than resort to a government-mandated program. Thanks to her efforts and the cooperation of everyone, millions of children were vaccinated and a terrible disease all but eradicated from the North American continent.

Up for her first appropriations request before the powerful House Ways and Means Committee, before which strong men quailed, Oveta had done her homework. She was ready to explain each request and answer all questions. She had brought a young gun with her that day, her new undersecretary, who had just received Rockefeller Center as his graduation gift from Dartmouth.

"Please, Nelson," she said, "do pull down the charts." While the audience and the illustrious committee waited, Nelson Rockefeller bounced up to pull down the charts. His presence and everything his name signified were not lost on a single person in that room. Neither was the fact that she commanded him. Wealth and power commanded more wealth and more power.

Billions of dollars were granted that day and at all the meetings afterward. Moneys were appropriated for expansion of federal-state-local hospital buildings and for chronic-disease nursing homes, diagnostic-treatment centers, and medical rehabilitation centers. More moneys were appropriated for a three-year emergency plan to pool federal, state, and local funds to build new school buildings already bursting at the seams across the country.

During her thirty-one months in the president's cabinet, she further improved the administration of the food and drug laws. That department was under her aegis. Four other health areas included mental health, nurse training, rehabilitation, and hospital insurance for people with no insurance or any

Oveta Culp Hobby, Secretary of the Department of Health, Education, and Welfare makes a TV broadcast from the White House on her Reinsurance Bill. On the far left stands Nelson Rockefeller, Under Secretary of HEW, along with members of the Rockefeller family. Eisenhower Presidential Library.

way to afford it. In her last year in office ten million people with no benefits at all were added to the Social Security rolls.

In 1955 Oveta was fifty years old and Governor was seventy-seven. She didn't feel she could stay away from him any longer. His health was growing more precarious. Likewise, he had been carrying the full load of the *Post*, KRPC Radio, and KRPC-TV. She resigned in July.

President Eisenhower told the other members of the cabinet first. George Humphrey, the secretary of the treasury, burst out, "But she's the best man in the cabinet." He was only half joking.

Later she and Eisenhower faced the nation in an unusual press conference with the two of them seated together at a table in the White House. He announced her resignation and then addressed her, "None of us will forget your wise counsel, your calm confidence in the face of every kind of difficulty, your concern for people everywhere, the warm heart you brought to your job as well as your talents."

> "Money begets money."
> —John Ray, *English Proverbs*, 1620

Over the next eighteen years, the dynamo that was Oveta Culp Hobby devoted herself to building the *Post* and all its various operations. Eventually, besides owning all the newspapers in Galveston and Texas City, it owned and operated six television stations in five states. The incredible organizational powers as well as the iron will to accomplish whatever she set out to accomplish raised the Hobby fortune to fantastic heights.

She managed to do this for the first nine years while never leaving Governor for more than a few hours. Did she feel that perhaps she had neglected him, particularly during her stints in Washington? Of course, she did. Did she regret what she had done? I think not. Did he resent the years she had spent away from him completely? Again, the answer is no.

For her beloved *Post*, she assumed the position of president and editor and director of KRPC Radio, while Governor became chairman of the board. During the ensuing years, seventeen educational institutions awarded her honorary degrees. She sat on literally dozens of boards in advisory capacity and lent her name to many more. But these were affairs that took her away for hours or days.

When Governor William Pettus Hobby died June 7, 1964, she set about ensuring that the people of Houston would remember him. Within three weeks, the Houston City Council was asked to change the name of Houston International Airport to honor him. On July 2 the change was made.

The next year Oveta took his place as chairman of the board of the *Post* while she kept the position of editor. At sixty, she wasn't ready to let others make the final decision as to what to print.

She acted as the driving force for the *Post*. She was almost always present for the editorial meetings. Every reporter had to clear his story ideas and his stories with her. Almost before the dawning of the computer age, she had investigated these new machines. Her newspaper was one of the first fully computerized papers in the world.

President Lyndon B. Johnson signs the Public Broadcasting Bill. To his left, fellow Texan and editor-in-chief of the *Houston Post*, Oveta Culp Hobby. LBJ Library Photo by Frank Wolfe.

Every three or four months, she made a ritual tour of the building. She would walk through various departments, say hello, and shake hands. She wore white gloves. When she finished, her gloves would be covered with smudges from the pressmen's ink. It was a source of great pride to work for her. The employees shared a sort of "Our publisher is prettier than your publisher" joke with the employees of the rival *Chronicle* across town. But in their hearts they believed she was the best.

The decision to sell the paper in July 1983 was the hardest decision she had made in her life. In October the Toronto Sun Publishing Corporation bought the *Post* for $100 million. The final papers were signed on December 2. On the last day, she went through the building checking cabinets, walking into rooms, and looking around. She hated so to let it go!

After her last look, she went down to face the photographers and reporters. She was, of course, beautifully dressed in a navy suit and coordinating hat. She smiled and smiled and shook hands. She shared a memory of stories with reporters and editors. She looked so animated. Only one photographer captured the reality—her face frozen for the flick of a shutter in an expression of grief.

She spent delightful hours adding to her collection of art. One of her first purchases had been in 1945, a modern oil by Modigliani. It was a fascinating choice by a woman whose art experiences in Killeen, Texas, were probably limited to Frederic Remington and bluebonnets. At the same time she bought a Picasso gouache and two ink drawings by Henri Matisse. Today the works of these artists are seen everywhere in the best museums. When she purchased them, they were virtual unknowns in Texas.

Her contemporaries had no knowledge of them either. She simply acquired what she saw as different, arresting, and exemplary of undeniable talent. She continued to collect art, furnishings, jewelry, beautiful things to please her eye all her life. Her taste has since been verified a hundredfold. In 1984 when she left her house to move to the Huntingdon, she donated Modligiani's *Caryatid* to the Houston Museum of Fine Arts. She later donated her *Barges at Chatou*. Vlaminck's masterpiece is recognized as the finest example of the Fauve movement in the museum today.

In 1991 *Texas Monthly* listed the Texas rich. She had already divided her fortune with her son and daughter. The three of them shared $525 million.

In her last years she was reclusive. Several different people who wanted to write a biography of her or help her write hers contacted her. She refused, saying, "it bespeaks a certain self-importance." It made her uncomfortable to think about it.

One women begged harder than the others, promising a motion picture or a made-for-television movie. "Can you think who might play you?" she asked.

Oveta's answer was instantaneous. "Madonna!"

After reflecting on her answer, one might say that the Material Girl and the Texas Lady were not that far apart in many ways.

At her death on August 16, 1996, she was buried with full military honors. Two of her former aides folded the flag and presented it to her daughter. The Honorable Eddie Bernice Johnson made a speech of tribute that was entered in the *Congressional Record*. Oveta would have been pleased at the feeling of her life brought full circle. The *Record* had been part of her preparation for her long life of service. Once upon a time, she had spent many long hours reading it in her father's office back in Killeen, Texas.

Glenn McCarthy
"King of the Wildcatters"

March 17, 1949, marked the beginning of an era. Upon that day a legend was born that half a century later has passed into the pantheon of Texas myth. It is extolled. It is satirized. It is accepted as a matter of course. It is taken as truth because in a very real sense it *is*. Texans came to be regarded as wealthy, powerful, and flamboyant around the world.

The legend began that St. Patrick's Day with a party to end all parties. That night Houston, Texas, the largest city in the South, entertained everyone who was *really* important from the rest of the United States. That night oilman Glenn McCarthy entertained Hollywood with a movie premiere. He entertained New York celebrities flown in for the occasion. He entertained Chicago luminaries of radio fame. He hosted a crush of the rich, the powerful, and the beautiful. He served them a "river of champagne" and his own brand of whiskey named "Wildcatter."

On that blessed saint's day, McCarthy's Shamrock Hotel opened in Houston with a $1.5 million bash that had been eagerly anticipated and publicized for months. Every step had been planned and choreographed to draw maximum attention to the event. The national press had photographed and written at length about McCarthy's purchase of the three top prizewinning steers at the Chicago Livestock Show for thousands of dollars. He just grinned and told everyone he was buying the best steaks for his party.

McCarthy had bankrolled the movie *Green Promise*, starring Walter Brennan and ten-year-old Natalie Wood. Its premiere showing would be that night, after which the VIP guests would return in limousines to the Shamrock for a stupendous party. Before the banquet Dorothy Lamour, at the height of her sarong-draped popularity as a Hollywood singer and star, would broadcast her popular weekly radio show *live* from the Emerald Ballroom. She would welcome the guests as they came in. Their excitement and appreciative comments would be aired nationwide in this world before black-and-white television was filmed anywhere but inside a studio.

Even transportation was cause for whistles and sighs of amazement. Celebrities from New York and Chicago were to be flown to Houston. Since Glenn McCarthy sat on the board of Eastern Airlines, swank new Constellations were chartered to bring them from the East Coast. The Santa Fe Chief drawing sixteen Pullman cars brought movie stars from Hollywood including Lamour, as well as Brennan and Wood. Van Johnson, Van Heflin, and Edgar Bergen also were attending. Houston, America's Petro-Metro, was hip-deep in Hollywood stars.

McCarthy himself came to his party in the only private Stratoliner in the country, piloted by his friend and fellow Texan Howard Hughes Jr. Along for the party and the ride were old buddies John Wayne, whose stardom had not yet reached supernova size, and John Carroll, a great personal friend and a handsome leading man currently slated by RKO for the "big push" to stardom. McCarthy is said to have admired Carroll so much that he grew his own famous moustache in imitation of the man who starred in a few easily forgettable movies before disappearing from the Hollywood scene.

The whole hotel was full of people including multimillionaires by the dozens. Fifty thousand gawkers, the hoi polloi of the city, thronged around the entrance and the grounds hoping to catch a glimpse of the celebrities as they arrived. Inside was such a crush that the host told the waiters to give up trying to sell drinks. Just move the whiskey out into the halls. Let 'em mix it with the champagne that flowed from fountains set up on tables all the way down to the lobby. Let 'em drink all they wanted was McCarthy's philosophic comment.

The man whom the press had named "King of the Wildcatters" was himself famous as a heavy drinker who believed that he could drink all night without showing the effects. That night he was never without a glass in his hand.

Even failures created media buzz that added to the excitement of the occasion. When the public address system failed, the master-of-ceremonies had no way to tell the VIP guests to move to the Emerald Room while others should take their seats in the Grecian Room adjoining. Of course, all the guests tried to crowd into the Emerald Room. By this time everyone was buzzing in an alcoholic haze. People became desperate. Then belligerent. Some who were more belligerent than others grabbed the metal stanchions strung with velvet rope to cordon off the entrance and began hitting each other with them.

An irate woman grabbed the microphone from Lamour's hand and announced, "I don't care about your damned broadcast. I paid to get in. I want my seat." An NBC engineer, thinking he was speaking into a safe line, complained that Houston was "fucking up on their end." Seconds later the broadcast was cut off. Too late. The F-word went out into Americans' living rooms where it was mistakenly believed to have come from Texas.

It was all too funny, too shocking, too much. Texas was rich. Texas was bawdy. Texas was where everyone secretly wanted to be that night. As Captain Eddie Rickenbacker, World War I flying ace and chairman of Eastern Airlines, remarked philosophically to McCarthy, "If there wasn't something like this happening, [your party] wouldn't be worth a damn."

In Texas famous for egregious behavior, in the United States just emerging as a world power and standing tall, none stood taller than Glenn McCarthy.

The Shamrock was a place dedicated to bad taste—or at least to a kind of taste that had been the special privilege of European royalty of the particularly decadent kind. In the case of the grand hotel, the price tag was a cool $21 million. Of course, at that time McCarthy's wealth was reputed to be $212 million. The hotel was hardly a drop in the bucket.

Its roof was green, as befits an Irishman's heritage. Its Shamrock Room was a nightclub scheduled to carry its own radio broadcast "live." Nationally known chanteuses of the time Hildegarde and Dorothy Shay sang there. Its swimming pool was shaped like an Irish harp. It was the largest hotel pool in the world at that time—fifty meters long and fifty wide at its broadest point. Every room had a phone and a television set, almost completely unheard of in this era that predated *I Love Lucy*. Instead of the usual single or double kitchen from which all of a hotel's food was prepared, it had three kitchens and two bakeries—one for breads and one for pastries.

The lobby gave new dimension to the term *nouveau riche*. It was paneled in 22,000 feet of Honduran mahogany, all cut from the same huge tree. The rest of the décor featured sixty-three shades of green marble. When the most famous of American architects Frank Lloyd Wright heard about the colors, he is reputed to have asked, "Why?" Later, when he saw the interior of the lobby, he was reported to have laughed.

World famous also was McCarthy's private club on the hotel premises. The Cork Club, named for the county in Ireland rather than the stopper of a champagne bottle, was opened for 500 members only. Demand was so great that by summer of 1951, they numbered over 800. Its Western Room was a Texas tradition. The walls and floor were made of hand-tooled leather. If someone should drop a cigarette, the management would furnish him with a branding iron belonging to one of the members to cover up the damage on the spot.

A Cork Club *quickie* was a shower, a nap on Western style bunks, a shave, and whatever might be necessary for members running late to appointments. The Cork Club lounge featured a McCarthy creation, the "Spindletop," a highball (with secret ingredients) served in a glass that fit inside a brandy snifter of dry ice. The ice was ignited by a dash of Coca Cola that resembled bubbling oil in the space between the two glasses. The ice chilled the drink. How many men actually drank this more than once is open to speculation.

But it was McCarthy's hotel. His incredible wealth guaranteed him total economic freedom. He could do anything he damn well pleased with it. Anything—up to and including riding a horse into the lobby. Of course, he had to do that. Didn't Texans love their horses and go everywhere on them when they weren't driving their Cadillacs?

> "The first guinea is sometimes more difficult to acquire than the second million."
> —Jean Jacques Rousseau

And McCarthy was everything that was Texan. Just more than most. He reveled in what he was. His enthusiasm for life and his total belief in himself had grown to megalomanic proportions. And why should they not? He had started with practically nothing.

He was born Christmas Day, 1907, in Beaumont, Texas, less than seven years after the eruption that was Spindletop, the phenomenal gusher that started the Texas oil business. His father worked sometimes in the oil fields, sometimes for places like Port Arthur Gas Company where he could make a living for his wife and sons until he could get enough money together to try the oil fields again. He tried and failed again and again, but failure never seemed to bother him or to discourage him.

He was a wildcatter—a reckless gambler for whom the excitement outweighs the disappointment, outweighs the responsibility to home and family, outweighs all future prospects.

The first wildcatter drilled a well in 1857 in the hope of finding oil where he had no indication that it might exist. Others had drilled before him without success. They were wildcatters too, but history doesn't record their failures. Before Edwin Laurentine Drake, men dipped oil from pools that had seeped to the surface of the land. They used it to heat their homes, to light lamps, and sometimes to concoct rare and usually dangerous medicines, snake oil prescriptions that frequently made their patients sicker. When no one was sick, they used it to grease shoes and saddles.

Superstitions arose about the flammable stuff. It was the devil's sweat and the fuel of the fires of Hell. It was the fluid nature put in the earth to lubricate the globe as it rotated on its axis. Men were warned against trying to remove it because friction on that axis, believed to be an actual pole of some sort, would cause the world to burst into flames.

"Colonel" Drake liked being called by that title. He was an ex-railroad conductor. Passengers on trains often called the conductor Captain or "Cap" because he was technically the man in charge of everyone for the duration of the trip just as if he were the captain of the ship. When someone mistakenly promoted Drake, he let the title stick. Not bothered by warnings of disaster and doom, he threw his entire life savings—two hundred dollars—into finding a substance that had to this point in time little market value. In 1857 he spudded in a well outside Titusville, Pennsylvania, drilled with water-well equipment through hard rock, and found oil 69½ feet down.

Drake's well opened new thinking. Men began to experiment to discover what might be done with oil when others found more of it. If there was oil under their feet to be discovered for a few hundred dollars, there must be some way to make money from it.

Drake wasn't interested in what might be done with the oil. He was interested in finding it. He envisioned what he called a "Southwest Trend," a river of oil running southwest through Pennsylvania, West Virginia, Ohio, Indiana, and Kentucky. He speculated that the river might run into or out of a great pool somewhere. Again he had no basis in science for his hypothesis.

He was a true wildcatter for whom the strike is the thing. Riches that might result are comparatively incidental. Likewise, the expenses involved don't matter. Few wildcatters ever die wealthy. Like a gambler at the poker table or the roulette wheel, the more strikes a man has, the more he wants. If he fails, he burns to keep drilling until the next strike. And the cycle repeats itself.

Glenn McCarthy grew up to be such a man. He watched his father and followed in his footsteps whenever he could. He got his first job working as a waterboy in the Spindletop field. At age six he earned a nickel a bucket on the same rig where his father earned fifty cents a day. The job ended only when school started. Both his parents were determined that he would have an education.

He finished San Jacinto High School with a reputation in football. At Warren Easton Prep School, he played fullback. The local press called him Five-Yard McCarthy. He went to Tulane University in Louisiana on a football scholarship. An ankle injury cost him the scholarship, but after some time at Texas A&M, he ended his college days at Rice Institute—later Rice University, academically the toughest school in Texas. He was in the backfield with Tom and Dick Driscoll and Jap Thrasher the only year in the nearly 100-year history of the Southwest Conference that Rice ever won.

McCarthy never finished college. Many young Texas men attended only to play football to make names for themselves. At the end of the first semester, they quit to go into business depending on "the good ol' boy network" to get them jobs with alumni.

Faustine Lee, the daughter of a well-to-do oilman, was only seventeen. She heard about McCarthy from Tom and Vic Driscoll, who offered to get her a blind date with him. Wanting to see him for herself, she drove into the service station where Glenn was working and let him fill up her expensive car. He hadn't yet come to the place where he could tap his friends among the Rice alumni, but he was good-looking. She was pretty with no more aspirations than her "MRS Degree." Furthermore, any girl whose father was an oilman knew the problems she was facing if she teamed up with a wildcatter.

She married him anyway.

McCarthy and his wife were no different from most other American couples. When they married he was twenty-two with a pretty wife and $1.50 in his pocket. He was expected to go out and make a living for her and the family that would follow. To his credit he is said never to have let his father-in-law, oilman Thomas P. Lee, loan or give him money.

He never doubted himself, never considered abandoning his ambition. He knew he could scrape enough money together to stake himself. McCarthy burned to strike it rich in the oil fields where his father had failed. He'd been raised in the business. Like his father, he knew the chance was there to make millions. He was smart as well as a famous athlete. He had friends among the well-to-do. The only thing lacking was the money.

Soon, he came to manage the service station, one of many owned by Harry Sinclair, whose green and cream signs with the dinosaur logo were everywhere in the Southwest. More than manage it, McCarthy constantly looked for ways to innovate, to make more money. In the winter of 1932, he was managing two service stations, one built on a spot he had himself selected. Dollars were scarce as the state and the entire country struggled to come out of the Depression, but his take-home profits from the two were $1,500 a month.

He had a future with Sinclair, but it wasn't the future he wanted. Instead, he took the profits and talked his father and younger brother into helping him drill for oil in Hardin

County. When he failed to find it and lost his shirt, he was undiscouraged. Nobody could be expected to find oil the very first time. If it were that easy, everyone would strike it rich.

The story goes that he set up his offices as drilling contractor in Houston across the street from the Post-Dispatch Building that later became the Shell Building. McCarthy wanted the top floor if possible, but he wanted to pay next to nothing for the space.

The building manager asked how big McCarthy's staff was. McCarthy nodded toward his lone companion—his office force—a combination assistant, receptionist, accountant, and general flunkey. The building manager sighed. "This will be $50 a month."

"Twenty-five is all I can pay now," McCarthy said, "but we'll be expanding soon. We've got it made, once we get off center."

The building manager wasn't having much luck renting his building. Things were very bad in Houston as they were in the rest of the country in 1932. He let his new tenant have the $50 office for $25 on the condition that he use only half of the room until he could pay rent for the whole thing.

A prospective client came in and immediately noticed the unbalanced arrangement. Alarmed, he wanted to know why.

Without blinking an eye, McCarthy explained, "That's for expansion. We're getting along all right. What can I do for you?"

That same year he got in on the ground floor at the Conroe strike though his well had proved very nearly a dry hole. Within months he struck oil at Anahuac on the northern tip of Galveston Bay. His fortunes were immediately reversed because people's perceptions of him were reversed. Everyone knew two strikes in two years were phenomenal for wildcatters.

The proverbial luck of the Irish wasn't with him although the reason for his failure had nothing to do with his discoveries. Fortunately, ordinary people knew nothing of his problems, only that he had struck oil twice in two years. The

An early oil well. The derrick and platform have been moved on, and the horsehead pumps when the Texas Railroad Commission says it can. From the Collection of the Texas/Dallas History and Archives Division, Dallas Public Library.

Anahuac well proved profitable, capable of producing 3,000 barrels a day. Who would have thought that an oil strike could have been bad timing?

Unfortunately, Texas was glutted with oil. In 1929 Daisy Bradford No. 3 had come in producing 6,800 barrels a day near Henderson. In 1930 Lou Della Crim No. 1 began producing 22,000 barrels a day at Kilgore. In January 1931 the Lathrop well came in outside of Longview. At that time no one even suspected that the three strikes were not separate oil fields. Only when more and more extensions kept coming in, did developers and contractors come to realize all the oil was actually coming out of the same huge field.

By the time of McCarthy's Anahuac strike, East Texas was engaged in a "hot oil" price war that made water more expensive than oil. A gallon of oil sold for a nickel; a gallon of water, a quarter. On one occasion one million barrels of East Texas crude sold for 2½ cents a barrel. The Texas Railroad Commission, the regulatory agency trying to keep the price up enough for big contractors to make a living, decreed that McCarthy's well was small potatoes in comparison to the mammoth field. He was allowed to pump and sell only twenty barrels a day. A lesser man would have quit the business in disgust.

Prices fell so low that the Lathrop well was eventually sold to the Yount-Lee Oil Company of Beaumont. Faustine Lee McCarthy's father and his partner were rich enough to offer $2.5 million for the discovery well and the 2,500 acres of leases around it. For them the timing proved to be perfect. When prices were on their way up at the start of World War II, Yount-Lee sold out its company to Standard Oil of Indiana for $18 million.

Meanwhile, Faustine's husband was having to make deals to rent half a room. A sane man would have gotten out of the business. Of course, McCarthy never considered doing so. With determination bordering on obsession, he struck oil thirty-eight times in the next ten years. Stories abounded of his phenomenal ability to smell it or hear it or see the lay of the land for it. He was rumored to make lightning-like decisions. Men told that he threw up a well on a hunch, and "the damned thing came in just like clockwork."

He was said to be intuitive about oil probabilities. Some told of his uncanny ability to interpret geological findings. Others who were inclined to be more generous described him as acting on a combination of scientific advice and practical information at hand.

Given the number of oil fields developed in Texas in the twentieth century, perhaps he really wasn't particularly lucky. Certainly all along the Gulf Coast, where the majority of his strikes occurred, probabilities were very, very high of finding oil. Robert J. Kleberg Jr., general manager of the King Ranch, sold Humble Oil and Refining Company of Houston on the idea of leasing his property by saying that he doubted that there was any million-acre-tract along the Gulf Coast between Louisiana and Tampico, Mexico, where oil was not present. Humble signed the leases and eventually brought in the Agua Dulce field.

Likewise, many of McCarthy's strikes were extensions of existing fields. Anahuac, his first big strike, was itself an extension lying between Jackson Pasture to the south on Galveston Bay and a big field later developed at Hankamer less than four miles away to the north.

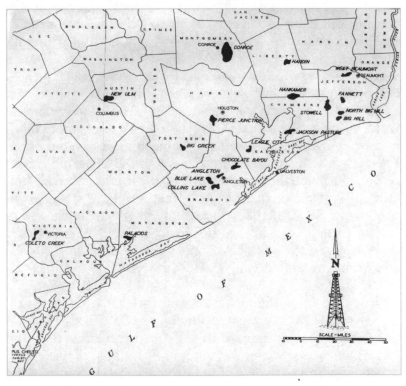

Extensions from existing fields and discoveries by Glenn McCarthy.

Of course, the Daisy Bradford No. 3 was the result of Dad Joiner's driller Ed Laster having to move the rig over a few hundred yards because the drill pipe had twisted off in well No. 2. Later exploration proved that Daisy Bradford Nos. 1 and 2 would have been dry holes. Glenn McCarthy's decisions as to where to drill on extensions were right on the money in thirteen cases.

At Hankamer itself, he pioneered a new way to extend fields. Many contracts read that a well should be drilled to a specific depth. The oil—if found, should be pumped out, the hole closed, and the rig moved. At Hankamer McCarthy obtained the drilling rights to the land *below* the existing production level of the field and around the flanks of the salt dome on which Hankamer sat. The extension went downward. From it he produced gas distillate that stretched his already proven oil production vertically rather than horizontally. The original developers cursed with frustration. Others laughed and shook their heads. It all seemed so logical—except that no one but McCarthy had thought of it.

McCarthy gave the impression to everyone with whom he worked that he was more daring, more masculine, more intelligent, and above all surer of himself than anyone else. Perhaps his arrogance was a natural result of his string of successes. However, the men who worked for him and with him thought he was magical. At one time he had two thousand employees. Most of them repeatedly swore to interviewers and reporters that they would go to hell for him. Some of them reported that they had come close to doing it.

In the early wildcatting days, workers came to him from the sawmills of the East Texas piney woods. Oil offered a wage only slightly higher than millwork, but it was vastly more exciting. A district superintendent of McCarthy Oil and Gas Company once reported that, "Things were double-rough back then, but we were all in the same boat. Glenn was living just like the rest of us. We didn't use the calendar for paydays then. We got paid when he got something to pay us with, and not until."

Men who worked a long time for McCarthy, especially in the early days, weren't above "borrowing" equipment when the boss needed it. McCarthy's rigs were generally leased. Since he couldn't afford the best of bad lots, they were the most run down. Sometimes they were abandoned outfits that he cannibalized for parts. Sometimes the parts couldn't be found. In that case some of his men would go out on "fishing trips." One told of driving over with a buddy and helping themselves to ten joints of drill pipe from a shut down rig. They had it back in three days and returned it to the rack. "The owner didn't miss it."

Before anyone gets impressed with McCarthy's rough-necks' loyalty, remember that they were all in the job together. They wouldn't get paid if some progress wasn't made or if the well didn't come in eventually. Helping themselves to what-ever would keep the operation running was standard oilfield procedure in the early days on those barren tracts of land in woods and fields when "the only law was outlaw" except when an occasional country sheriff or, more infrequently, a Texas Ranger paid a visit.

All the above sound very jolly and somewhat romantic, but the actual numbers required to pull every enterprise together show how close to the edge of disaster McCarthy habitually operated. Indeed, they show the way wildcatters lived their lives and why they so seldom died rich.

Seismograph crews were working in an area called South Strang, almost due east of Houston near the town of LaPorte on Galveston Bay. Seismographers exploded charges under-ground and recorded the vibrations. A geologist would then read the wavy lines and determine with limited accuracy the presence of oil, saltwater, or some other less dense strata than solid rock under the topsoil.

To the wildcatter's way of thinking, a seismographer was an untalented ignoramus who had to resort to machinery to strike oil. A wildcatter, on the other hand, observed all sorts of surface clues as well as called upon a healthy dose of experience and intuition. In his estimation the good guys should have won—but didn't.

A friend at La Porte told McCarthy about the South Strang exploration. Immediately, the oilman went into action. First, he took out an option on the lease and arranged with the contractor to drill. Next, he sold a major oil company the idea of putting up $12,000 worth of dry-hole money, that is, money pledged for payment for a crew to drill to a certain depth. Essentially, the major oil company gambled that the hole would come in—McCarthy was gambling that it would not but would come in at a greater depth.

As a safeguard against drilling solely for someone else, McCarthy blocked up additional leases around the drilling site. Landowners were willing to lease their land on the possibility that oil might be discovered nearby. The leases entailed royalties to them only if a producing well were actually drilled on their land. McCarthy promptly resold part of the block for a substantial profit. His name and his luck were golden in this respect because people leased or bought where he told them. One company took $15,000 worth, another $10,000 in leases. He sold some of his own property to put $12,000 of his own into the project.

McCarthy and his investors came out alike at the first South Strang well. They got nothing. When they reached the depth agreed upon, they got saltwater. So much for seismology. Undiscouraged at having lost thousands of dollars of his own and other people's money, he dug up more dry-hole money and started another hole, operating with a badly worn rented rig.

And so it went. Sometimes he made small strikes; sometimes he drilled dry holes. Sometimes he overextended himself and as happened at West Beaumont in 1936, the second well blew up in his face, caught fire, and burned for days while it threatened to ruin his own and the other properties around it. The story goes that while the well burned, he ordered an offset location staked out and sat in his car and entertained some potential investors with funny stories while he watched his equipment enveloped in a raging gas and oil fire.

His reputation grew. Men said he had ice water in his veins. By the end of 1936, he began plans for a $250,000 mansion in Houston that ended up costing $750,000. When creditors knocked at his office, he would show them the plans. His brash assurance convinced them to invest more money with him. When his mansion was finally completed in 1938, between it and his oil contracting, he *owed* $3,897,000.

When the Japanese bombed Pearl Harbor in 1941, the price of oil and the necessity for discovering it flooded the field with wildcatters. In the prime of life, McCarthy was considered the best because he'd been at it for ten years.

Glenn McCarthy in 1940. He was thirty-three years old with a solid gold reputation.

> "To think twice on every matter and follow the lead of others is no way to make money."
> —Ihara Saikaku in *The Millionaire's Gospel* (1642)

Richer by thirty-eight oil discoveries, in 1941 McCarthy bought land at $154 an acre at the future site of the Astrodome. He also purchased 4,800 acres of land where Sharpstown is today. He was no Gerald O'Hara desiring "the land, Katie Scarlett." He knew that Houston, like any coastal city, had a limited number of directions it could grow in. One was south. He sought to capitalize on future development.

Mostly on credit and the promise of his talent and his reputation for finding oil, he was able to make major moves outside the oil business. In 1943 he paid $2,225,000 for the Shell Building across the street from his original single office. He considered it a good investment since downtown Houston was booming. Six years later he sold it for a profit though he kept his operating headquarters on several impressive floors where they would remain indefinitely.

In 1945 he bought a 15,000-acre ranch west of San Antonio as a family retreat. His children were growing up while Houston grew bigger with less space available every day. He hired a staff and bought cattle. He hired experienced people to turn the place into a working operation. He built a house with six bedrooms and three baths when most people had only one bathroom. Like most Texans who hunt, he hung his mounted heads on the wall of his living room. He could have settled down to become a family man.

By car the ranch was five hours away. Of course, the distance gave McCarthy a perfect excuse to learn to fly a plane to take his family to their second home for their weekends. He bought a twin-engine Beechcraft for only $60,000. The more he had the more he wanted. In 1946 he bought a DC-3 to carry twenty-one guests with a full baggage load. In 1949 he bought a half-million-dollar four-engine Boeing Stratoliner from Howard Hughes. He used it to talk business with as many as eighteen guests at 16,000 feet at 250 miles per hour. If the business didn't drag on too long, his constituents could start a card game at an oval table in the lounge. By the time the game was over, they'd be in Los Angeles or Washington. A fully stocked bar kept them from getting thirsty while cruising along at a cost of only $76 per hour, more than most people's weekly salaries.

Everything now contributed to his spectacular image. Unlike Howard Hughes, he loved every minute of it.

In 1950 he made the cover of *Time* with an accompanying article. At the same time he was the subject of a *Life* photojournalism spread. Both writers criticized him for his display of wealth, for his seeming lack of seriousness and interest in the public good. The *Time* writer even criticized him for the way he shot goats that overran his ranch. While the rest of America might have been a little shocked, he never blinked, and his Texas friends couldn't find a single thing to criticize about the man.

Later Jim Clark, McCarthy's public relations man, commented on the cover story. In it the reporter stated that McCarthy drove a car with one hand at a hundred miles an hour with a bottle of whiskey sitting at his side. When people suggested that the oilman sue for defamation of character, he replied, "How in the hell am I going to sue him? The son of a bitch was sitting with me when I did it."

Conservatives and goat-lovers were doomed to disappointment. The world of gracious living did not turn its back on McCarthy. That same year the Duke and Duchess of Windsor paid a visit to Houston's Shamrock Hotel. The former king of the British Empire who had renounced the throne for "the woman he loved" was one of the most popular men on earth. They were dinner guests of Glenn and Faustine McCarthy. Also in attendance among several others were Charles Cushing, the eastern financier; Floyd E. Bates, vice-president of the Missouri-Pacific Railroad; Robert Young, president of the Chesapeake and Ohio Railroad; and the mayor of Houston, Oscar Holcombe.

What a triumph for a man who had carried water buckets for a nickel through the oily mud of Spindletop!

> "A man with oil fever will never tell you what he's worth.
> He's probably afraid he'll go broke before
> he gets back to the office."
> —Ernie Pyle

By 1950 the freewheeling days of the wildcatter, the independent oilman, and the big corporations all were numbered. Those in the business could see it coming. Moreover, some of the more thoughtful among them concluded that state regulatory bodies such as the Texas Railroad Commission would never be able to control oil production efficiently. "Buckskin Joe" Cullinan, who had been the first to discover oil in Corsicana, Texas, before the turn of the century, believed federal control was the only answer. He and others realized that price controlled production—not necessarily the other way around. When the demand for gas doubled, gas wells and reserves declined.

In spite of his perceived wealth, "Diamond Glenn" McCarthy, the "King of the Wildcatters," was $52 million in debt in 1952. As a result of his friends in high places, the government

Glenn McCarthy (right) with longtime Democrat Speaker of the House of Representatives Mr. Sam Rayburn. Center for American History, UT-Austin.

made him a private loan of exactly that amount to cover the debt.

In 1952 Edna Ferber wrote the novel *Giant*. During her research and writing time, she stayed as a houseguest of Robert Kleberg Jr. on the fabulous King Ranch, his million-acre spread where he conducted his fabulous horse and cattle business. Robert's wife, Helen Campbell, whom he had met and married in seventeen days, was the daughter of a Kansas congressman. From these Ferber pulled the characters of rancher Bick Benedict, later played by Rock Hudson, and his eastern-born wife played by Elizabeth Taylor in the MGM movie. In a book rich in Texas stereotypes appeared a third character—Jett Rink, the poor boy turned oilman, the portrayal that gave James Dean screen immortality.

Jett Rink was loud, boastful, and a heavy drinker. He was a brawler who drilled gushers and passed out over the banquet table at the opening of his fabulous hotel. He had built it because, according to Ferber, he had more money than he could spend. Many friends suggested to McCarthy that he sue the author for slander. Everyone knew McCarthy would never pass out at the Shamrock party. McCarthy could hold his liquor.

The oilman gallantly declined. He announced to all who would listen that Jett Rink was a sissy. He didn't see any similarities between them at all.

Whether Ferber meant the character of Jett Rink to be McCarthy or whether he was merely a composite of many characters she had heard and read about was unimportant. By her novel she enhanced and redrew the image of the Texas "zillionaires." To this day after Texas has settled into maturity as befitting a prosperous state in the twenty-first century, the old images of flamboyance, of unspendable millions, of irresponsible behavior lives on.

In 1954 the United States Supreme Court ruled that the Federal Power Commission should regulate the wellhead price of natural gas sold in interstate commerce. With a set price, the larger companies could wait for the smaller ones to decline to the point where they would sell their companies for a song and get out with the shirts on their backs. Oilmen everywhere prophesied that the big would get bigger and the small would get bought. The last half of the twentieth century has seen this prophecy come true everywhere with the production of gas, oil, coal, electricity, and atomic energy.

McCarthy's government loan was still to repay with less oil and gas to do it with. The new federal regulations, each one following the other thick and fast as hailstones, were crippling his business. One source of ready money was the magnificent hotel. He'd had his fun with it. In 1955 he sold the Shamrock to the Hilton Hotel family. His other various assets were in widely diversified large and small companies, which he owned part or all of. Among his still-retained interests were McCarthy Oil and Gas Company, the Beaumont Gas Company, KXYZ Radio, the Shell Building, and two banks. He was chairman of Eastern Airlines, whose president and general manager was his good friend Eddie Rickenbacker. He was president of the United States Petroleum Association. In 1957 he reopened his exclusive Cork Club in the Central Bank building where he had taken his new offices.

Still the best-known independent producer in the country, Glenn McCarthy was concerned about the regulations made by people who he believed did not really understand the expenses of the oil industry. McCarthy, on the other hand, understood them all too well. "With higher taxes on major companies, how are they going to get money to build $150 million refineries or billion-dollar pipelines? [The government isn't] going to get any new people in the business. Why is any young man with brains going to go into the oil business when he can see there is no possibility of success?" As the situation worsened, many people began to wonder whether the government would and should take over the oil business. Perhaps they wouldn't make such a mess.

A government with the best interests of its citizens might have helped, but a government where one party was bent on punishing an industry for supporting the other party would only contribute to the mess. And ordinary taxpayers and voters weren't sympathetic because of the flamboyant image. In part the legendary McCarthy had contributed to the problems of the industry he loved.

Drilling costs increased and the oil depletion allowance, a law since 1926, was eliminated for major producers in 1975. From 27½ percent it was allowed to decline to 15 percent by 1984. It had allowed oilmen to strike it rich and not pay all the taxes on the rich strike but save some to make up for the dry holes just as any other businessman would have done for his losses.

"We never bothered to talk to consumers," John Mitchell, a former president of Texas Independent Producers and Royalty Owners, explained. "We've never bothered to talk to the Chamber of Commerce in New England to explain the situation... Too damned late. I blame myself...we are to blame for most of our problems."

Oilman Bill Rudman of Dallas shook his head. "There's such a black name that we have. It's a shame that our country will have a catastrophe and that the price of oil will be impossible to buy...a quart of any kind of booze, it costs you from four dollars...to twelve dollars a bottle. A gallon of water that's distilled, it costs you a dollar. There's no liquid that can be bought as cheap as gasoline, and that's the energy of our country. You've got no right to buy energy that cheap, as hard as it is to find."

Glenn McCarthy was way down on his luck by the mid-seventies. He maintained that the industry couldn't continue without a depletion allowance. Offshore wells cost $85,000 a day to drill. If a well takes thirty days, that's $2.5 million. "It's gonna take a hell of a well to pay back that cost, let alone the dry holes. It they're going to take all your money away from you when you make one well, and you're not going to recoup those other nine that you drilled and were dry holes, how can you continue to operate?"

Disgruntled and much reduced in circumstances at seventy years of age, he said, "I can live on less than five hundred thousand dollars. Why should I go in and invest the hard-earned capital that I have now in trying to make [more]?"

His gambling fever declined as he saw the industry he loved ruined almost beyond recall. He shed more and more of his investments and gradually bought his way out of the business.

"The King of Wildcatters" spent the last thirteen years of his long life in a two-story house near La Porte in close proximity to the great fields he helped to develop. He died on December 26, 1988, the day after his eighty-first birthday.

Mary Kay Ash
"Power in Pink"

Mary Kay Wagner Rogers Hallenbeck Ash threw herself a party every year for thirty-nine years. At first no one outside her organization, originally named Beauty by Mary Kay, paid much attention. After all, in 1963 the partygoers were regarded as just little women earning a little extra money and celebrating the pennies they'd earned selling face stuff door-to-door.

Important men in the business world yawned and turned to the financial section.

Mary Kay ignored them as they'd virtually ignored her for the first twenty-five years of her professional life.

With each successive year, her parties got bigger. They spilled into the Dallas Convention Center. The excitement built. Lightning crackled on those klieg-lighted stages. Waves of emotional bedlam swept round the huge ballrooms. And the business world began to notice. The sheer exuberance of it! The brashness of it! The unmitigated gall of all those women having such a glitzy, cheering, laughing, crying-for-joy time!

Every year Mary Kay Cosmetics held three-day seminars for which Beauty Consultants and Directors came from everywhere in ever-widening circles. At first they came from Texas. Then from the Southwest. Then from all over the nation and the globe. Eventually so many women came that one seminar became four back-to-back. They were designated Ruby, Sapphire, Diamond, and Emerald. Every seminar was capped

Mary Kay Ash, Founder. Note the diamond bumblebee on her shoulder. Courtesy of Mary Kay Inc.

with an awards extravaganza that Mary Kay herself called "an Academy Awards, Miss America Pageant, and Broadway opening all rolled into one."

No single room was big enough to hold them all. The attendees spilled over into adjacent auditoriums where they watched on huge television screens. No expense was spared. Hundreds of Dallas dancers, singers, and musicians, lighting engineers, costume designers, and stagehands came to count on the Mary Kay shows for their rent money during the last two weeks in July.

After a spectacular opening featuring singing and dancing and flashing lights, Mary Kay herself would appear dressed in a gown worthy of Hollywood Oscar night. Sometimes she wore pink chiffon. Sometimes, black silk. Sometimes, red or blue sewn with thousands of rhinestones, sequins, and bugle beads, each one reflecting the hundreds of lights. Sometimes she would appear silhouetted in a circle of light. Sometimes she drove a pink Cadillac onto the stage.

Again the men in the business world, dressed like a convocation of crows in their black tuxedos with staid black ties and cummerbunds, shook their heads. She was so—so—Texas!

The excitement turned to cheers and tears of joy and adoration almost as if this short plump woman with her golden-blonde hair coiffed in an immovable helmet and her blue eyes heavily accented with black mascara were a sanctified being descended to earth.

After her words of welcome, the awards would begin.

They were world-famous. No one else had ever thought to give women such precious treasures. No one else had ever thought to give them (or any other sales force anywhere) diamonds, minks, and cars.

And Mary Kay handed them out. It was "Queen for a Day" with the contestants waving, giving each other high-fives, boogying on down, delivering the thumbs-up sign to the members of the cheering audience who, as Mary Kay reminded them, could be up on the stage next year. "You can do it!" she kept exhorting. "You can do it!"

The thing that really did it, the thing that made the world sit up and take notice, was the pink Cadillac. When she bought one for herself, quite a few people said, "How tacky!" Some even called her "Poor white trash!" But the next year she ordered her top five sales directors pink Cadillacs.

The public hullabaloo turned into accompanying national publicity that brought the company into the limelight as no advertising campaign could have done. While detractors continued to shrug their shoulders and raise their eyebrows, the answer to any criticism was "Oh? And what color was the Cadillac your company gave you?"

The cars also showed Mary Kay's independent contractors exactly what they are working for. To this day the big attraction for the newly recruited Consultants is the fabulous car. Even before they're awarded ribbons for their first $100 shows, they dream of pink Cadillacs. Without fail for the last thirty-two years, the seminars have resulted in ecstasy for enough people to give encouragement to tens of thousands of others.

A Consultant who recruits three other Consultants may wear a special red jacket. Her own Director may give her a small gold pin to wear as well. Shoals of red-jacketed women prance across the stage with tiny gold pins glittering on the shoulders of their jackets. They are greeted with cheers and applause. It's their turn to shine in the spotlight with perfect makeup, done by themselves, and elegant hair. The audience itself is dotted like paprika on a schnitzel with more red jackets.

After the red jackets have left the stage, the Directors come in their rhinestone-covered gowns, so heavy and glittering that they must rival Liberace's capes. Women gasp as each of their sisters, more dazzling than the one before, passes in front of them on their way to the throne.

Successful Directors, who have recruited successful Consultants, win diamond bees. The gold-and-diamond bumblebee is Mary Kay's personal symbol. She wears one as big as a man's thumb on her shoulder. It's meant as an inspirational symbol because with its weight and limited wingspan, the bee is aerodynamically impossible. It shouldn't be able to fly. But Mary Kay points out that the bee didn't know that and so became one of the busiest creatures in the world. Mary Kay's bees have twenty-one diamonds set in gold. Their retail value is close to $5,000. Queens of Sales receive them with kisses and embraces.

Countless diamond rings are awarded for sales and recruiting. As Mary Kay says, "Except for an engagement ring, most women never receive diamonds." She also reasons that if she gave them money, they'd be inclined to let it be absorbed into the house payments, the groceries, and the children's allowances. This way they have something to enjoy and more importantly show off. By wearing the rings, they display a very persuasive instrument to recruit more people to sell more products for which they get a commission. They are constantly reminded that they can win them more than once. In just a few years, a star performer can have a diamond for every finger.

Five-thousand-dollar Neiman-Marcus shopping sprees are prizes. Dream vacations are awarded. The audience is approaching hysteria as a pink Cadillac revolves on a turntable of the Dallas Convention Center, its chrome throwing off sparks of reflected light.

The mink coats come next. The symbol of ultimate elegance and luxury—what woman has ever looked at a mink coat on a mannequin in a Neiman-Marcus window and not tried to imagine how it would feel to wear it? With tears in their eyes, they allow Mary Kay to praise them and present their prizes. Her son Richard Rogers, the company's CEO, helps each recipient into a coat and settles it about their shoulders. (A gentleman should always help a lady into her wrap.)

Finally, the moment arrives. The adoring, dazzling National Sales Directors appear. Each earns anywhere from $100,000 to a quarter of a million dollars a year in commissions paid back to her by her recruits. Each one kneels at the foot of the throne. For the lower echelons there are Oldsmobiles. For the second tier there are pink Buicks. For the people whose percentages of sales amounted to $75,000 worth of wholesale products for four consecutive quarters, there are the keys to the coveted Cadillacs.

Then comes what resembles the laying on of hands. Mary Kay touches them all. She looks into their eyes and whispers words of encouragement. She says, "You can do it!" and "God bless you." She holds her hands down at the edge of the stage and her Consultants come to touch her, to promise her to do better, to vow to her that they will be on the stage next year.

When the show is over and the queen departs, when the lights go out, and the parking lot clears, the experience sustains enthusiasm for hundreds of people for a very long time.

> "Are you to pay for all you have
> With all you are?"
> —Edward Arlington Robinson

Mary Kathlyn Wagner was born in 1918 in Hot Wells, Texas, a spa town that Houston has long since sprawled over. Some question exists about the date of her birth because she refused to tell her age. She declared that a woman who told her age would tell anything.

The family situation went from bad to worse very quickly when her father became ill with tuberculosis. They moved to Houston where her mother went to work managing a restaurant for fourteen hours a day. Mary Kay's job from the time she was a very small child was to take care of her father whom she nursed in their home. When a household situation would arise that she couldn't handle, she would call her mother on the telephone. All her life she remembered the phone number—CApital-476W. When things were tough or Mary Kay was discouraged, her mother would tell her, "You can do it."

How she managed to stay home with her father and still go to school and earn exceptional grades is not revealed in her autobiography or any of the biographical material about her. Perhaps her inborn competitiveness simply drove her to achieve nothing but the best whatever she did. She won a typing trophy and placed second in a statewide extemporaneous speaking contest while still in junior high school. In high school she made straight "A's" and graduated in three years.

If she'd been a man, she could have pursued many avenues with a high school diploma. A woman required more education for a profession. College was out of the question, the family finances being what they were. Mary Kay had no thought but to do as most young women did in 1935.

She married Ben Rogers, a member of a musical group calling themselves the Hawaiian Strummers (in Texas?). They sang on the radio in Houston. Sure that she was secure for the rest of her life, she started her family immediately and had three children in quick succession. When the Strummers moved to Dallas, Rogers moved his family there and then left for the army even before the beginning of World War II. Presumably, Rogers didn't even take out an allotment for their support. Instead he "blew his entire eighty-dollar monthly pay on guitar strings and tuxedos."

In her early twenties with very little practical education, she was left as the sole emotional and financial support of her children.

She learned to drive her husband's car and sold books door to door for a while. Then she joined the Stanley Home Products sales force, selling directly to the public by persuading a hostess to put on Stanley parties for a dozen or so of her friends. The fact that the housewares were generally better than those sold in stores was well known, but the prices were a little higher too. The question that had to be in the minds of many customers was, "How much better can a mop or a broom or furniture polish be?"

So Mary Kay learned to be an entertainer. By sheer weight of her personality and her own marketing ideas, she increased her sales until she was making a thousand dollars a month in commissions. Her income was more than many executives in successful businesses. The census taker told her so. More important to remember was that she did it during the 1930s when a dime would buy a loaf of bread or a dozen eggs.

If Stanley had not been firmly entrenched in the male-as-breadwinner philosophy, she might have moved upward in the company. But they never really recognized how valuable she was to the company or gave her credit for the phenomenal amount of business she generated. When she was named the most productive salesperson in her region, her prize was a flounder light. She didn't even know what it was, let alone how to use it. She was devastated by the lack of thought or true appreciation the prize indicated.

Note to the puzzled reader: A flounder light was a sort of kerosene lantern that fishermen carried while they waded along in shallow saltwater at night gigging flounders.

Further note: A flounder is a flat saltwater fish the size and shape of a dinner plate. Both eyes are on the same side of its body. It lies flat in the sand of tidal pools until a tiny unwary fish comes swimming by. Then it flounders up, gulps it down, and settles back onto the sand.

Mary Kay quit Stanley and moved on to World Gift, another party sales outfit. She quickly devised her own strategy for selling. She would visit her hostess before the party, ostensibly to ask if her client had any questions. While she listened, she made mental notes about the living room. Then she would buy decorative items from World Gift to complement the hostess's décor. She would come back before the party to redecorate the living room with new candles, silk flowers in a vase, pictures on the wall, and other decorative items. Usually, the hostess bought everything Mary Kay put out if she didn't make enough "points" herself to get at least some of it for free. The guests were encouraged to buy similar items because they could see them displayed in a home like their own, rather than in a catalog or on a table display. Frequently they signed up to have parties of their own so Mary Kay could redecorate their living rooms as well.

With her highly competitive spirit, she approached her parties as events with the idea of turning every event into an exciting opportunity to make more money than she had the previous night.

The secret to direct sales, however, is not selling. It's recruiting others to sell for you and collecting commissions from their sales as well as your own. Mary Kay kept her sales lists and her contacts. She would call her former hostesses to tell them that her company was expanding in their area and she was sure they would make perfect salespersons. Rather than let them put her off, she would tell them that she would be out their way that very afternoon and she'd drop by around two o'clock to discuss their new venture.

Buoyed up by Mary Kay's relentless enthusiasm, hundreds of women took on new jobs while the children were at school. Every penny they could earn meant better food, better clothing, and more opportunities for them to expand their lives. Many women seized on her offer because opportunities were slim and none for married women in the late forties and fifties.

One year Mary Kay was responsible for fifty-three percent of World Gift total sales. She extended distribution to forty-three states in eleven years with the company. They made her their National Training Director at $25,000 yearly and gave her a seat on the Board of Directors, but they refused her any further promotions and raises. Though she sat on the board, most of her suggestions were passed over. She was accused more than once of thinking like a woman.

More humiliating was the fact that the men she trained were promoted above her to $50,000 a year. When she protested what she perceived as unfair, she was told that they were men who had families to support. She was unmarried at the time and the sole support of her three children.

More than likely her personal situation contributed to her job stagnation. Divorced women were regarded as slightly unsavory. Very little pity was wasted on them or their children as if the woman were the only one at fault for the failure of her marriage. At the same time, working married women with children were regarded with much the same disapproval. A woman's place was in the home taking care of the children. She shouldn't be encouraged to leave it. The prevailing attitude in the business community created a catch-22 that few women cared to brave if they didn't have to.

> "It seemed that a woman's brains were worth
> only fifty cents on the dollar in a
> male-run corporation."
> —Mary Kay Ash

Frustrated with having worked twenty-five years of her life only to encounter what the end of the twentieth century would recognize as the glass ceiling, she retired and married George Hallenbeck, a direct salesman in World Gifts. She was somewhere in her early forties, but with him beside her, she felt confident she could move forward with her dream. She had already begun a plan to start a company of her own, one that would involve direct sales, the type of business she understood and in which she excelled.

A business truism is that three types of business are depression proof—beer, cigarettes, and cosmetics. Mindful—as millions of survivors were—of the terrible depression of the thirties, she chose the business she considered most appropriate for her.

She had discovered a skin cream concocted by a hide tanner. It smelled bad and looked worse, but she had taken it to a cosmetic chemist who was able to radically change its appearance and odor. She had purchased the formula from the tanner's heirs, and the "secret ingredients" were born. Though she didn't particularly like pink, it seemed the appropriate color for a woman's cosmetics. Taking $5,000, her life savings, she ordered pink jars and boxes, had pink labels printed, and had the containers filled. Her initial five products—Night Cream, Cleansing Cream, Masque, Skin Freshener, and Day Radiance—were all in pink with the label "Beauty by Mary Kay." The initial prices for these products were $14.95. (Today they sell for $70.00.) She leased a storefront in downtown Dallas. She bought a $9.95 shelf from Sears and Roebuck to display her products. She was ready for the big push. The date was set for Friday the 13th, September 1963.

"Beauty by Mary Kay" storefront in downtown Dallas. Courtesy of Mary Kay Inc.

Her husband was set to take care of the administrative end while she handled the business of getting her direct sales force off the ground. In August, one month after their marriage and one month before her dream company was to open, he was going over their plans at the breakfast table when he suffered a fatal heart attack.

Her lawyer advised her to liquidate immediately—otherwise, she would be penniless. Her accountant agreed. Her commission schedule would never work. She would be bankrupt before she could get the business off the ground. What they didn't understand was that she would be penniless anyway. She couldn't go back, but she found she didn't want to. As her mother had so often told her, she could do it.

Her daughter Marylyn and sons Ben and Richard arrived from Houston for the funeral. They had been with their mother at the beginning of her career, helping her package her orders when they were little children. Their educations and personal successes were the products of her drive. Twenty-year-old Richard immediately volunteered to leave a $480 a month job to work for her for $250 a month in Dallas. Twenty-seven-year old Ben couldn't leave Houston because of his family obligations, but he gave her his savings passbook with its $4,500 balance. Her daughter Marylyn went back to her family in Houston. Later she became the first Mary Kay Director there.

On September 13, 1963, "Beauty by Mary Kay" opened on schedule. She had nine salespeople and her younger son, who never dreamed he was beginning his lifetime career as her business partner. Eight months later—with the business expanding exponentially—her older son Ben came to manage the warehouse. He gave up a salary of $750 a month to start at $250. Both men were quickly given raises. At the end of the first year, her sales reached a quarter of a million dollars.

May Kay's starting her own cosmetics firm was not really different from other women who were known nationwide. Helena Rubenstein and Estée Lauder had done it before her. What was different was her sales approach. She utilized independent businesswomen by recruiting a sales force where each woman worked for herself. In other words, Mary Kay supplied the product that her sales force purchased to sell to others—with a 100 percent markup.

The initial Mary Kay kit cost $95. A woman could pay for it with her credit card or write a check. The company has never extended credit. Business has always been strictly cash and carry. But what came with it was more important than what went into it. It was support. The sales force met weekly for pep talks, instructions on what to say, what to do, how to follow up on sales. Follow-up was the key to easy sales. Mary Kay cosmetics were disposable commodities. Women used them and needed more. If the formulas were right for them, the Beauty Consultant—as the saleswoman called herself—had a customer for life. As the customer told her friends, she frequently became a Consultant herself because the Mary Kay parties had to be small enough for every woman to sit around the table and give themselves facials under the direction and with the aid of their own personal Consultant. For every Consultant the original Consultant signed up, she received a commission on her sales.

Besides pep talk and support, Mary Kay offered a completely new idea in marketing. Her inspiration came from, of all things, the flounder light. The wildly inappropriate gift, which had so disappointed her, served as an example of what not to give. Likewise, ribbons and stars and contests for the top three most productive salespeople were rejected. Mary Kay knew that every company had a few hotshots. She'd been one herself. Likewise, she knew the world-weary boredom of receiving worthless things for hard work.

She planned to hold her first seminar on September 13, 1964, to announce that the company had generated $250,000 in sales. She wanted to give her independent contractors something to remember. No flounder lights ever. She wanted to give them a Golden Goblet if they sold $1,000 wholesale in a month.

Richard Rogers objected. "We're dealing with *reality*.

Our top people sell approximately $150 a week. And you're talking about selling $1,000 a month? Do you think they're going to do that to win a stupid [gold-plated] cup?"

If she had been rude, Mary Kay could have told him, "You're thinking like a man."

Six hundred dollars was good money for a woman in the early 1960s. But if women thought they could get Golden Goblets, they could increase their efforts. Why if they sold $1,000 worth of wholesale product for twelve months, they could have twelve beautiful Golden Goblets—and next a pitcher and a tray! What a beautiful and impressive table they could set for their guests, their families, and their in-laws who were probably critical of their working at all. The Mary Kay company soon had to stop inscribing the goblets because the women were winning too many. And too many women were signing up to be Consultants so they could win Golden Goblets too.

In January of 1966 Mary Kay married Mel Ash. All across the country people wondered if her marriage would signal a withdrawal from her business ventures. Would she step back and live on her wealth? Would she allow her husband and her son to support her? Certainly no one would have blamed her if she had. She was nearly fifty. She didn't need to work anymore. But she continued to establish a new woman's role model rather than step back and "enjoy life." As she once said, "Nothing wilts faster than a laurel rested upon."

She stayed actively involved in her firm and constantly devised ways to improve her direct sales force.

Soon too many women had too many goblets, so Mary Kay invented the Ladder of Success—a gold pin with each rung representing a different personal plateau. As a woman accomplished more, diamonds would be added to the pin. Furthermore, no one was competing with anyone else. Her only competition was her own sales record.

Moreover, Mary Kay Consultants didn't have territories. If a Consultant visited her sister in Omaha and recruited someone there, that Consultant belonged to her. Though the Consultant would attend the meetings of the Sales Director in Omaha, the commissions went to the one from Dallas.

Today the reciprocity is worldwide. Everyone helps everyone else. The sisterhood constantly opens new doors and makes new connections. The possibilities to make money and win prizes are limited only by how many hours a woman is willing to work.

And Mary Kay knew just how to make them work harder and harder. In 1968 her public offering of over-the-counter stock enabled her firm to open its first distribution center outside of Dallas.

With the added influx of money, she bought her first pink Cadillac from Rodger Meier, the most prestigious dealership in Dallas. A special color had to be blended at General Motors. Its name came to be Mary Kay Pink. Of course! Her license plate was Mary K-1. She wanted everyone to know about

Mary Kay, and she certainly turned heads in Dallas when she drove down Preston Road.

But the most spectacular event was yet to come. If General Motors thought they would do the special color only once, they were sadly mistaken. In 1969 she awarded five Mary Kay Pink Cadillac Coupe DeVilles to her five top National Sales Directors. The media buzz was instantaneous. No amount of money—surely not the money she spent to lease the five pink cars—could have bought her company and its products such nationwide attention. Sales exploded. Recruitment climbed.

She extended the color to her office. Her growing fleet of eighteen-wheelers rolling down the roads to and from her distribution centers were all painted pink with her distinctive Mary Kay logo on their sides. Eventually the centers were located in California, Georgia, New Jersey, and Illinois. No driver is known to have complained about the color being a threat to his masculinity.

On the other hand, when she bought her 19,000-square-foot mansion on Douglas Avenue in Dallas's exclusive Preston Hollow neighborhood, she painted it pink over the protests of her neighbors. Her sales representatives, invited for pink lemonade and cookies made by Mary Kay herself, had their pictures taken for luck in her round pink bathtub.

Eventually, the American Camellia Society registered the Mary Kay camellia, a large pale pink hybrid. Four years later a soft pink miniature rose was patented.

> "God first, family second, career third."
> —Mary Kay Ash

All of her life Mary Kay had insisted she ran her business and later her company by the Golden Rule. She was a devoted member of the Prestonwood Baptist Church—one of the largest congregations in North Dallas. At her seminars she told her Consultants and Directors, "I love you" and "God bless

Mary Kay Ash with a showcase of products in 1975. Courtesy of Mary Kay Inc.

you." Her speeches were filled with the Christian virtues and the importance of a woman's God and her family.

When Morley Safer interviewed Mary Kay for *60 Minutes*, he asked her, "Do you really think that's fair to inject God as though it were a religious experience in working for, marketing, and selling?"

Mary Kay thought about her answer. "God is using our company as a vehicle to help women become the beautiful creatures that He created."

"But do you think in a sense, you are using God?"

She looked right at him, her sincerity obvious. "I hope He's using me instead."

Certainly her friends and associates believed her to be sincere. Mary Kay was a devout Baptist who on a single Sunday was asked to address the congregation of the Prestonwood Baptist Church for their funding drive. That day she pledged to match their contributions dollar-for-dollar. The result was $2.3 million raised toward the new fifteen million dollar building.

No one could doubt her sincerity.

Part of the excitement of a Mary Kay meeting used to be the songs they sang. Hardly a person alive does not respond to music, especially pieces with strong rhythms and rising crescendos. Men have gone into battle and won with "The Battle Hymn of the Republic." Presidential campaigns have picked up steam with the marches of John Philip Sousa.

Early in the life of her company she organized a song contest. The Consultants were supposed to compose original words to familiar tunes. Mary Kay would select the best songs for them all to sing at the seminars. Prizes would be awarded for those that generated the most enthusiasm. "I've Got That Mary Kay Enthusiasm" sung to the tune of "Joy, Joy, Joy (down in my heart)" was only one of the results. The original song was a great favorite in vacation Bible schools throughout the South. It revived spirits at Mary Kay Seminars.

Directors were told to make every meeting for their Consultants as special as Mary Kay made her seminars. The secret was sell, sell, sell so that you can have all the beautiful things you want and so that every woman can have the same opportunities you have. And the more they sold, the more they made, and the more they made, the more Mary Kay made.

Mary Kay's husband Mel Ash, whom she had married in 1966, set the standard for support that many husbands came to emulate. He took a backstage position to his brilliant glittering wife and solved problems that she was not even aware of. Once a snowstorm closed all transportation in Chicago and two thousand Consultants and Directors were trapped in an expensive hotel. Mary Kay's business picked up the checks for their meals, and workshops were organized to fill in the gaps.

But many of the women were on very tight budgets. They were wandering around the lobby unable to pay for their extra nights in their rooms. Mel Ash moved through the crowd, finding those women and lending them money. They were his family, he said later—his "hundred thousand daughters." Later when he got back to Dallas, Mary Kay wanted to know why all these women were sending him money. He never told her.

At a typical meeting in Harlingen, Texas, at The Center, a building whose logo is a pink sign with a red rose, Pam Barrone, a Mary Kay Sales Director, conducts her meetings with her Consultants. The room is decorated with ruby, sapphire, diamond, and emerald stars. A table holds gifts including special ones for visitors. Consultants and Future Directors are hugged and congratulated for achievements. Refreshments are served.

Pam's husband accompanies her to the meetings and has a speaker system set up. Whenever someone walks down the short aisle to be introduced, to receive a gift, or to be awarded a special symbol of achievement, he plays triumphant music, just as it would be done at a Mary Kay Seminar. His support and the support of other husbands is a validation of the work of their wives. The family is together in the way that Mary Kay intended.

Equally as important is the fact that Mary Kay was right. All the extra effort and excitement generated at the meeting generates success. In Harlingen, Texas, population approximately fifty thousand, on June 2002 Pam exchanged her Buick for a Mary Kay pearl Cadillac.

> "I cried all the way to the bank."
> —Wladziu Valentino Liberace

In 1976 she took the corporation public. Mary Kay Inc. was welcomed to the New York Stock Exchange. Her stock opened at $10 and over the next seven years climbed by 670 percent. The little girl from Hot Wells, Texas, with the tubercular father and the mother who worked fourteen-hour days in a restaurant was a millionaire. And she'd done it all by herself against all odds and the advice of experts.

Her son Richard became one of the youngest company presidents ever to preside over a NYSE-listed company. That same year the American Marketing Association named him "Man of the Year." He was thirty-three. His gamble thirteen years before had paid off big time.

In 1978 Mary Kay received the Horatio Alger Distinguished Citizens Award reserved for Americans who by their achievements prove the fulfillment of the American dream.

In 1979, just fifteen years after the firm's inception, Dalene White, Mary Kay's dear friend and one of her original independent Sales Directors, surpassed one million dollars in sales commissions. Within two years, at the time Mary Kay wrote her autobiography, fifteen independent Sales Directors had become millionaires and three were double millionaires. Their achievements brought worldwide attention.

With such incredible success in her business, she suffered a great tragedy in her personal life. Her husband, Mel Ash, was diagnosed with lung cancer. He had been a lifetime smoker who had tried to quit many times. In 1980 he died. During the last two months of his life, she never left his side. Her career, as she had told her thousands of independent Consultants, took second place to her family.

When Mel died Mary Kay was sixty years old, though she would never admit it. She did exactly what her family, her friends, and her constituents expected that she would do. She launched herself into her business with astonishing fierceness.

Her numbers of Beauty Consultants jumped from 50,000 to 200,000 in two years. Probably the recession of 1980-81 drove many of them into the workforce. While Mary Kay was overseeing these legions of women and managing a major company, she worked with a ghostwriter to produce her life story. Besides her incredible life she described many of her sales secrets as well as her own personal philosophy. At the height of her company's popularity and her fame, Harper and Row published her autobiography *Mary Kay Ash,* subtitled *The Success Story of America's Most Dynamic Businesswoman.*

The book has sold more than a million copies and is now published in Harper and Row's Perennial Library.

When the economy improved in 1982, the company experienced a downturn though her sales in 1983 exceeded $300 million dollars. The sales force slipped by twenty-five percent. Its reduction was attributed to the fact that fewer women needed to work as the economy improved. The average income for a Mary Kay independent Consultant was only $1,600 a year—a supplemental income of about $135 a month. These women sold mostly to their families and friends and made little effort to go beyond their inner circle. When their $135 was no longer necessary, they gave up the job.

For the ambitious, the women's movement in America had brought about the new accommodations to allow women to join the mainstream of the workforce. While proficient Mary Kay Consultants could make more than secretaries or schoolteachers, they could not make more than young executive women upward bound. Government mandates required flextime, on-site childcare, progressive work schedules, and benefit programs. Computers and modems allowed women to work at home. The opportunities that Mary Kay offered younger women were no longer as important. Even when she offered them group benefits including health, life, and product replacement insurance, they still had to purchase those themselves rather than have them paid for by their companies.

As result of circumstances beyond the corporation's control, the stock, which had been at an all-time high of $45 a share, began to slip badly in 1985.

Mary Kay was disgusted. She came to realize that when her stock was public, her primary obligation was not to herself and her goals, but to her stockholders. They had no interest in the company beyond profit and loss. If the company stock went up because of its profits, frequently they would sell their stock because they wanted to make a profit as well. The result was the stock would go down and her company would no longer be an attractive buy until some analyst decided it had gone far enough down so he could sell it to new buyers.

She realized, as few people in America did, that the stock market too was a business. Analysts and brokers made their commissions by selling and buying stock—not necessarily the best stock, but the stock that went up and down. If more people buy and sell greater numbers of stocks, these professional stock watchers have fulfilled their obligations to *their companies.*

She discovered that when a company experienced ups and downs, i.e., Christmas season or summer doldrums when more people seek jobs or unemployment goes up, the stock brokers and analysts capitalized on those fluctuations to record a seven or eight million dollar profit one quarter as a downturn compared to ten million dollar profit the previous quarter. How a seven million dollar profit could signal a loss was beyond her comprehension. Yet they would advise their clients to sell and actually create a stock value loss in the market.

Her company was just as efficient as it had ever been. Mary Kay had *no overhead* for shops. She had no money laid out supplying drug and department stores. She had an eight-story Dallas office building and a low-rise laboratory. She owned three regional warehouses. That was the extent of her assets. Approximately 1,700 workers did their jobs in those buildings, but her sales force numbering a quarter million was made up of *independent* contractors. They offered the most viable opportunities in America for women. More women earned over $50,000 a year in commissions. No differentiation was made among white, Hispanic, black, and Asian women, so the same boast could be made for minorities as well. At the beginning of the eighties no one in America had even dreamed of empowering women to the extent that Mary Kay had done. "She...unleashed the talents of women. When she formed her company, women couldn't even sign their name to a bank loan," said Doretha Dingler, a Mary Kay Consultant who earned more than $9 million over the thirty years she was with the company.

In 1985 when her stock had skidded to $13.38, Mary Kay and Richard organized a leveraged buyout and returned her company to their hands. The buyout cost her $390 million. To execute it, she had to sell a 176-acre tract of land northwest of Texas Stadium where she had planned to put a $100 million "cosmetics college."

That was the year the *World Almanac* named her one of America's 25 Most Influential Women. Her list of honors and credits grew as she was named chairman emeritus in 1987. She was approaching seventy. Her son Richard was named chairman of the board.

Since she no longer had to watch the business end, she devoted many hours to charity. With the total economic freedom she enjoyed, she established the Mary Kay Charitable Foundation, a nonprofit organization that provided funding for research of leading cancers affecting women. Since its establishment, it has awarded twenty-one grants totaling two million dollars to fund research at leading medical facilities and universities. Of particular interest to her is cancer research, since Mel Ash died of lung cancer.

Always sensitive to national issues, in 1989 Mary Kay ordered a moratorium on the use of laboratory animals for consumer product development and safety testing. She formed a panel of experts to advise researchers on alternatives. Later the company shared its findings with groups such as Johns Hopkins Center for Alternatives to Animal Testing.

Richard Rogers, co-founder and CEO. Courtesy of Mary Kay Inc.

In 2000 she added violence against women as a corporate initiative, perhaps in memory of Sue Z. Vickers, one of her most enthusiastic National Sales Directors, who was kidnapped in 1978 in the parking lot of a Dallas shopping center and found murdered. The perpetrator has never been caught.

Mary Kay's techniques for setting up a business in direct sales are taught at the Harvard School of Business as a pure marketing plan.

In 1991 *The Dallas Morning News* listed her fortune divided between her and her son Richard at $600 million dollars. On the list compiled of the *Texas Monthly's* 100 club, she was one of only three women who had not received her wealth through inheritance or divorce.

She also took the time to write two more books. In 1995 *Mary Kay: You Can Have It All: Practical Advice for Doing Well* was published. In 1996 she published *Mary Kay: You Can Have It All: Lifetime Wisdom from America's Foremost Woman Entrepreneur.*

In February 1996 she suffered a stroke. To all intents and purposes her business career and her charitable work were finished.

She died at her home in Dallas on Thanksgiving Day, 2001.

In the Saturday editorial, *The Dallas Morning News* featured her picture and quoted her directly on her attitude toward her own life: "Most people live and die with their music still unplayed. They never dare try."

Earlier the editor had paid her high praise. "By empowering women and touching countless lives, Mary Kay really did leave the world better than she found it."

She died as the twenty-first century was in its infancy. It remains to be seen whether the women she trained will be able to maintain her legacy.

For now, the pink Cadillacs, their color softened to Mary Kay Pearl, still roll.

Haroldson Lafayette Hunt Jr.
"The Best Poker Player in the World"

The cheapest party H. L. Hunt ever threw was late, late, late in the night of November 26, 1930, in room 1553 of the Baker Hotel in downtown Dallas. He ordered a plate of cheese and crackers. He and Columbus Marion "Dad" Joiner shared the midnight snack after Joiner had sold all his oil leases (nearly 5,000 acres' worth) to the man that a seedier element of the population knew as Arizona Slim, one-time gambling hall operator and friend of the Hot Springs syndicate with ties to the Mafia.

Surely, this momentous occasion called for thick steaks and champagne, but Hunt had no wish to make Joiner suspicious about what he had signed. The Arkansas gambler played his cards very close to his chest. He was no stranger to highly suspicious dealings.

Joiner's Daisy Bradford No. 3, the first completed well ever drilled in the East Texas area, had come in on October 3. For five days it had spouted 6,800 barrels a day with oil selling for $1.10 a barrel. Joiner and his leaseholders were jubilant. The old con artist himself couldn't get over it. He'd never really expected it.

His delight was short-lived. His bad luck seemed to be holding true to form. The well began "flowing in heads," an oilman's term for giving up a few hundred barrels of oil, then falling dormant for half a day or longer. "Flowing in heads" generally meant that the well could not be counted on to produce for any length of time.

Dad Joiner on the left and Doc Lloyd shake hands in front of Daisy Bradford No. 3. Second from right of Lloyd with his tie blowing in the breeze, H. L. Hunt stands next to driller Ed Laster.

Indeed investors were saying that Joiner had fleeced them all. The amount of oil 3,500 feet down in the East Texas piney woods was thought to be negligible. The fabled Woodbine sand that Joiner's well had struck was another dry hole. A man couldn't make a living on 250 barrels every few days. Neither could his leaseholders, who were screaming for their money.

In fact, they had taken him to court within two weeks of the discovery. The judge in Henderson, Texas, just a few miles from the well, had refused to put Joiner's business into receivership, but "Dad" was sick at heart. In the last two weeks, two dry holes had been drilled south and east of Daisy Bradford No. 3. "Dad" himself was tenuously holding onto leases all around a well being drilled by Deep Rock Oil Company to the west. But nothing had been found so far.

"Dad" Joiner had a long history of dry holes. He had peddled oil leases in Oklahoma for years. Now he'd slipped down into Texas where he was doing it again for as little as ten dollars a lease. The leaseholders' money had gone to finance his Daisy Bradford Nos. 1, 2, and 3. And now it was gone. He had nothing.

Failing to get their pound of flesh in Rusk County, the howling mob followed him when he fled west. They took him to court in Dallas County. In that venue his lawyer presented the court with a petition of voluntary receivership. In the ensuing uproar, Joiner slipped out, perhaps fearful that he would be attacked and torn apart limb from limb.

H. L. Hunt was waiting for him. "Mr. Joiner," he said, "I'm offering to buy you out lock, stock, and barrel."

The old man shook his head and kept on walking.

But Hunt was not deterred. He had always believed in his luck, and he was feeling extremely lucky. More times than not, his hunches had been the making of him. He had already won and lost hundreds of thousands of dollars. They were fortunes as men counted fortunes in those days.

In this case he didn't have to depend completely on luck. He knew much more than Joiner did about what was going on in East Texas. Moreover, he had no respect for the old man's age and no pity for his ignorance. Hunt believed the strong and smart had the right to prosper. He had hired three men to keep watch on the Deep Rock well.

His own well on a south lease had a "showing" of oil, but when Daisy Bradford started flowing at the head, Joiner's lease prices had collapsed. Hunt was determined to seize the opportunity to buy those leases from Joiner before another well could blow in. He pursued Joiner to his ratty office in the old Adolphus Hotel. With the help of mutual friend H. L. Williford, whom Hunt bribed with a promise of $25,000, he dragged Joiner over to a much nicer room at the Baker, cater-cornered from the Adolphus.

To the poor old man, recovering from a bout with the flu, Hunt's corner suite decorated with gold drapes and a gold carpet was impressive. He came in and sat down on a much softer bed than the one he slept in at the Adolphus. He didn't know that in the second bedroom Hunt had set up a chain-call system to receive information on the Deep Rock well where the crew was taking core samples.

Hunt had also bribed the drilling superintendent, Frank Foster, with a promise of $20,000 to allow Robert Johnson, one of "Hunt's men," to be on the platform when the core samples were taken. Johnson was to drive at top speed to Henderson where another "Hunt man," Charlie Hardin, was waiting by a telephone. Hardin, in turn, would call Hunt in Dallas.

Joiner came in prepared to put up a show of a fight. Hunt had offered him $25,000 in cash and $975,000 in oil payments for his 5,000-acre lease block earlier in the day. Now Joiner had had time to think. He countered with $50,000 in cash and an unspecified amount of money in oil payments. Here his imagination failed him. He couldn't bring himself to say $1 million. It was too far beyond anything he had ever expected to possess. Indeed, $50,000 was more cash than he had ever seen.

For the next thirty-six hours, Joiner spent his time in consultation with Hunt. He too was supposed to receive information on the Deep Rock well. Whether a messenger arrived or a phone rang in his room will never be known. He couldn't receive either because he wasn't in his room in the Adolphus. He later claimed it was Hunt's fault that he never received any information. He refused to acknowledge that it was his own fault he didn't go back to his hotel.

Meanwhile, news hit the lobby of the Baker Hotel that Deep Rock had hit a pocket of natural gas. Joiner would later swear he knew nothing about it.

That same morning November 25, the negotiators called over J. B. McEntire, Hunt's lawyer, and a pair of legal stenographers and began dictating an agreement. As it was finally hammered out, the deal would be worth $1.335 million to Joiner.

At 4:30 in the afternoon, Hunt received his call from Charlie Hardin. "Mr. Hunt, I think they're right on top of the Woodbine sand now."

Hunt hung up in disgust. "On top" meant nothing.

Four hours later Hardin called again. "Mr. Hunt, they've cored sixteen feet of material from the Deep Rock well, and ten and a half feet of it is saturated with oil."

Only a gambler of H. L. Hunt's experience could have kept from raising his fists to the heavens and cheering. But he kept his poker face. According to his story, he immediately informed Joiner of the news.

According to Joiner, he was never told anything of the kind. Later he even claimed that Hunt had told him the telephone call had been from Hardin, but the Deep Rock well had drilled through the Woodbine—and come up dry.

Whatever the truth, no one will ever know it. Both men now are dead as are the witnesses to the historic signing.

A little after midnight November 26, Joiner and Hunt put their signatures on the agreement. Joiner sold his rights to billions for $30,000 cash and $1.335 million in oil payments. Hunt bought it all including the payments to his scouts and to Williford for $75,000—which he did not have. The gambler had run his biggest bluff.

He ordered the aforementioned plate of cheese and crackers and they celebrated. Since Hunt was strictly a non-drinker, he probably didn't even order any beer. Hunt said later that Joiner said to him, "Boy, I hope you make fifty million dollars."

Why did Joiner not check his messages at the hotel? Why did he accept the $1.335 million when the very amount of it should have rung alarm bells in his mind? Why was he so eager to sell?

Probably, he seized a chance to come out of East Texas with something. He quite possibly feared that it would be taken away from him as everything else had. He probably trembled with fear as he pushed Hunt up to one and a third million, fearful that at any minute the offer would be withdrawn and he would be left standing beside a dry hole.

The next morning he found out the truth. The news of the Deep Rock well was all over the streets. One man offered

Joiner $3 million cash. Men stopped him in the lobby and on the street and begged to pay him thousands of dollars for just a few of his leases. Too late! Joiner no longer owned any part of the field he had discovered.

By November 30 Hunt's name was in the headlines and his picture beneath them in every paper from Dallas to El Dorado, Arkansas. He had pulled the business coup of the decade.

Rather than be upset, at least at first, Dad Joiner was actually relieved. He did not have the strength or the stamina to handle all the demands that would come rolling in from his leaseholders. He'd received more dollars than he'd seen in a long, long time. He was seventy years old with a wife and seven children in Ardmore, Oklahoma, and a pretty young secretary in Dallas. He spent lavishly on food and entertainment. Like many a boomer before him, he set out to have the time of his life while his money lasted.

And H. L. Hunt got the headaches of dealing with hundreds of leaseholders.

He didn't mind a bit.

> "Make money, money by fair means if you can,
> if not, by any means money."
> *Epistles* of Horace (68-5 B.C.)

Haroldson Lafayette Hunt Jr. was the youngest of his parents' eight living children. He was born February 17, 1889, on a farm outside Vandalia, Illinois. He was given his father's name perhaps as a sign that his mother and father intended to have no more children. His father had decided, as so many men did in those days, that he had enough strong backs to successfully operate the family farm.

In many ways June, short for Junior, was the most unusual one of the lot. He could read the newspaper before he was two years old. His father enjoyed having his clever son come out, unfold the newspaper, and read the hog prices aloud in his piping baby voice. June also had a remarkable memory for numbers. When he was only a little older, he could fan a deck of fifty-two playing cards, look at them, close them back up, turn the deck over, and call out the number of each card *before he turned it face up.*

The boy was never sent to school. His mother preferred to teach him at home where she could reward his mental feats by allowing him to nurse at her breast. He continued to do so until he was seven years old, when his father caught them together. June ran out of the room. What passed between the parents is unknown, but June's mother never allowed her son to touch her again. Still, he wrote in his autobiography *Hunt Heritage* that his "mother was the wisest and smartest person and the best teacher I ever knew."

No one can doubt that he was exceptional in every way and determined almost from the beginning to make money. His father in particular used June to do the tedious job of weighing the produce wagons when they came in and when they went out. The family money and prosperity depended upon the accuracy of those computations. Hunt Sr. trusted his near genius son above all his other children to record those figures correctly.

The father also taught June a popular philosophy of the time—"social Darwinism," which Hunt espoused early and never replaced. It was "survival of the fittest" carried into the framework of society. In society "strong" meant mentally and psychologically strong. Those gifted with strength of will and brains became the leaders of society because they were strong enough to utilize, manipulate, and exploit the weak. Capital-ism was a natural extension of this philosophy because it allowed the strong to grow richer and richer. Capitalism was essentially amoral. The strong could do anything to the weak because to do anything else would be against the law of nature.

Certainly in the days of the ruthless robber barons of American industry and banking, June Hunt could see the examples of the strong and the weak. He was to practice this philosophy in both word and deed all of his life. Nowhere was it more evident than in his dealings with "Dad" Joiner.

Hunt was smart, and his intelligence made him confident. He undoubtedly felt contempt for those not so smart and felt no pity for them when he bested them or exploited them. His dealings with other human beings including his siblings, his wives, and his children were always tinged with contempt for their inherent weaknesses. Later in public life, he was adamant in his refusal to contribute to charities because "they sapped the will [of others] to succeed."

Toward the end of his life, he wrote a novel about his vision of a utopia. *Alpaca* portrayed a society in which votes were apportioned according to the amount the citizens paid in taxes.

After he could no longer be as close to his mother as he would have liked, he became almost a dual personality. On the one hand he was exuberantly childlike—showing off his intellectual abilities in front of the rest of his family and their friends. On the other he was a secretive, cold person—distant, authoritative, and stubborn—holding himself above others whom he consciously or unconsciously labeled as inferiors.

Not surprisingly, his father came to regard him as the "black sheep of the family," but in the end he respected June and raised him above the others. His older siblings saw their spoiled kid brother alternately as a freak and a pest. The situation could easily have turned into a twentieth-century version of Joseph and his coat of many colors.

But June was no Joseph. He cared no more for his brothers than they did for him. In 1905 when he was sixteen, without so much as a goodbye, he packed up a few clothes, went down to the station, and caught a freight train for Kansas. His ticket was "ship, ticket free," meaning that he had to work his way for his fare. He had not one cent to his name.

But he had a deck of cards in his pocket.

In his very first job as a dishwasher, he was taken under the wing of a woman whose husband owned the café in the depot. When he left she passed the word to other women to look out for June and take care of him. Rather than be grateful, he later said that her attentions embarrassed him. Given his later predilection for pretty women, his story lacks credibility. At sixteen he was six feet tall, well built, and handsome in a fresh-faced way. Women liked the look of him. Undoubtedly, he used his looks to his own advantage.

He earned his first dollar by escorting a shipment of sheep from Utah to Los Angeles. Bankrolled, he headed for the huge Irvine Ranch in Santa Ana, California. There he drove teams of mules and horses and generally learned ranch work. He wandered along the west coast until the San Francisco earthquake scared him back toward Texas. All along the way, in mining camps, in bunkhouses, in passenger cars, and in cheap barrooms, he played cards. His ability to remember pips at a glance allowed him to hold his own against men who made their extra money by fleecing strangers. By this time he'd left the name June or Junior far behind.

He had chosen for his "moniker" Arizona Slim.

About this time he won a pot off a man who sized him up as somebody extraordinary who was wasting his time. The man suggested that Slim go to college with it. Hunt laughed and said he'd never been to school at all, but somehow the idea stuck. With the money he'd won, he went to school at Valparaiso University in Valparaiso, Indiana. He took the usual courses—Latin, algebra, and rhetoric—but mostly he played cards and took the other students' money.

Occasionally he'd send word home to his mother. In 1910 he got a telegram that his brother had died. He went home for the funeral but left immediately. He felt little affection or obligation for his family. The next year he had to return when his father died. H. L. Hunt Sr. managed to leave his children well fixed, but the best share went to June, who inherited the family house with eighty acres attached and $5,000. Whether his father made the decision to do so alone or at the insistence of his wife is not known.

If the father expected that his youngest boy would play the biblical tale of the prodigal who becomes good and true after a long absence, his body must have spun in his grave for many a long night thereafter. The youngest Hunt wanted no part of that. He had no intention of settling down to run the family farm and support his mother.

Devoid of family sentiments, he took the money and went to Lake Village, Arkansas, on the Mississippi River. There he bought 960 acres of bottomland of the kind his father had owned originally. The old man had often spoken of the success of farming there.

June planned to become a cotton farmer. The first year when the river backed up and flooded the place, he lost his entire investment. While he might have contempt for people, he had nothing but respect for the Father of Waters. So much for farming.

He had discovered richer pickings. He discovered he was a better poker player than the Mississippi cotton farmers, who were merely gentlemen gamblers. He took a great deal of money from them. Arizona Slim, the railroad bum and king of the bunkhouse, had spent six years in the West taking money off desperate men. Gambling seemed what he was suited for. Why farm when he could make money sitting at a table, turning over pieces of pasteboard?

Besides, gambling was so exciting. He was flush one day, flat broke the next, and through it all he remained unruffled. Stoic whether boom or bust, he developed the face that would become his fortune.

> "You pays your money and you takes your choice."
> —*Punch*

Eventually, the gentlemen learned to exclude him from their games. With a shrug he went over to the racetrack at Greenville where he could always find a game. There he spent a great deal of time in Frank's Café run by Frank Ciolino, whose nephew Frank Grego was from Chicago. Grego operated as the local don at the track. Hunt and Grego became such good friends that Ciolino would carry him on a tab when he was busted. Both Italians understood the gambling life and recognized Hunt as a truly exceptional player.

Whether they were friends or merely partners is unknown. Hunt supplied the "talent." He was the gifted card shark with all the guts. Grego was the "management," the procurer with all the contacts. Together the two traveled up and down the Mississippi participating in high stakes games all the way to New Orleans.

In Lake Village Hunt was regarded as something of a mystery man—a loner to watch out for. If he got into a poker game there, while the others joked and drank and complained about luck, he would watch the play and players like a hawk. He knew what bets they would make and why within a very few hands. Because he could remember what had been played and the order in which the cards might come up if they were lightly shuffled, he sometimes knew the cards they held. While he attributed his success to his luck, he knew most of it came from his intelligence. He always maintained that he "learned by listening."

Though he was no longer really serious about his farm, he used it to settle himself into the community. He used his good looks and ready money to enjoy the company of young ladies in town. He had a good-looking horse named Spirits that he'd trained to buck and rear so the women would be impressed by his mastery of the big animal.

That same year, 1914, his mother died. He had lost his strongest advocate. Perhaps in his heart of hearts he needed another woman to center his life. At twenty-five he decided to get married and start his family. His choice was Lyda Bunker, a local schoolteacher just his age. She was five-foot-two with brown eyes and curly brown hair. She tended to be plump, but plumpness was fashionable in those days, and her college education, her accomplishments, and her well-respected family made her infinitely desirable.

He married Lyda, and the next year their first child, daughter Margaret, was born. Two years later he and Lyda had their first son named Haroldson Lafayette Hunt Jr. whom they called Hassie. Hunt was delighted with his beautiful new family and the respect it brought him.

But he was not reformed.

World War I sent cotton prices up to $625 per bale. Suddenly, owning a farm was not such a risky proposition. Hunt discovered or uncovered his natural talent for trading land. The money he earned at the poker tables he used to make small down payments with large promissory notes on farms. For a small outlay, he could own title to a great deal. The idea was to sell what he owned for more. It was a sweet deal so long as land prices kept rising. He managed to get several hundred thousand dollars ahead.

Sensing the war was about over and the land boom with it, he sold short. That is, he bet that the market would go down immediately. Eventually, it did, but not soon enough to cover his bets. He lost everything. A few months later when the recession hit, he had no stake left to recoup what he had lost. To make matters worse, he was stuck with a very large land deal, a 2,500-acre plantation in Louisiana. When cotton prices fell from $625 to $50 a bale, Hunt had only one resource left.

He went back to the poker tables.

The game that saved his family fortunes is legendary. It also probably saved him from going back on the railroad as Arizona Slim as so many men were doing across the depression-ridden country. If he had not won it, he might have felt as they did that he had no choice but to leave his very unhappy wife and small children to fend for themselves.

He got into a high stakes game at the Grunewald Hotel with some of the fabled players of the region. Jinks Miller, White Top, Indian Jack, and John Crow faced Arizona Slim. He had $100 to his name, just enough to buy his way into the game.

His facility for watching and listening came into play. In the first round he watched Jinks Miller stay but not raise. Hunt stayed too. When all five cards had been dealt, Jinks raised on a king and an ace showing. Hunt reasoned that he was bluffing; otherwise Jinks would have raised early to increase the pot if he had anything in the hole. Hunt himself had a small pair. He called.

And won the pot.

And kept on winning. Within a couple of minutes, he observed Jinks Miller suddenly sit up straight. Their eyes did not meet, but Arizona Slim knew that Jinks knew the mistake he'd made. And Slim knew that Jinks knew that he knew. One and all the gamblers stiffened their play. The game became as serious as only poker played by professionals can be. At the end of the evening Hunt got up from the table with $10,000 in his pockets. Arizona Slim had done it again.

He went home with the money, but he quickly dissipated it on more land deals and losing hands. When Lyda asked him to get a job, he looked at her as if she'd lost her mind.

He came out of the depression with 15,000 acres of cotton land and faced the possibility that he might indeed have to go to work. Then, through another gambler, he heard about an oil boom in El Dorado, Arkansas, a hundred miles west.

He had land, but he had no money. The banks wouldn't loan him a cent, so he managed $50 from three friends. With Frank Grego and two other men, he took the train to El Dorado. Needless to say, it was already packed with passengers who had the same idea. He played poker all the way. Oil be damned! Here was opportunity.

> "There are strange things done in the midnight sun
> By the men who moil for gold."
> —Robert W. Service, "The Cremation of Sam McGee"

When he stepped off the train that January day in 1921, H. L. Hunt saw that El Dorado had turned into one of the "biggest crap shoots in American history." Its population had risen from 4,000 to 10,000 in a few weeks with hundreds arriving on *twenty-two* trains daily. It was a gambler's paradise.

Men were desperate for some place to sleep. Barber's chairs were renting for two dollars a night. The town was filled with automobiles. One group of boomers had flown in from Oklahoma City in a three-seater airplane. They all came despite the spring rains. The streets beyond the town's original five paved blocks were quagmires. The bogs were so deep they swallowed up teams of mules and wagons. Skinners and helpers had to swim for their lives.

Besides the incredible hardships associated with wet, cold, filthy conditions, the town was full of vice. Hustlers (such as Hunt), con men, prostitutes, moonshiners, thieves, and murderers were everywhere. The chief centers of lawlessness were the barrelhouses, so named because drunken customers poisoned with cheap whiskey had to be hoisted into a barrel and rolled away.

On Pistol Hill these establishments had names like Dago Red's and Smackover Sal's. The moonshine was so raw it generally came from a still out back. In addition to gambling and drinking the barrelhouses pimped for two classes of prostitutes. The ordinary hookers worked the streets and the tents. The "oil-field doves" worked the barrelhouses by night and were trucked out to the rigs to service the workers by day. They charged $2 a trick, and the man who ran the barrelhouse got a dollar of it.

The place reeked of sin and vice. Only one thing would have made a decent man slide into a sinkhole like El Dorado.

OIL!

America was producing 442 million barrels of oil per year to supply the nine million automobiles now chugging down the roads across the country. Even at $2 a barrel, oil was instant riches and El Dorado had it. Black gold had blown out of the top of the Busey-Armstrong No. 1 just a few days before Hunt and his party arrived. The great plume of oil, gas, and water shot through the top of the derrick. The wind carried it across the town, painting it black.

One night in El Dorado was enough for two of the four fellow travelers. They left the next day. Hunt and Frank Grego stayed on to gamble. Three times Hunt sewed up the biggest game in town. His competition knew all there was to know about cheating, but he saw through their every ploy. They swore he was cheating them, but they couldn't catch him at it. Instead of drinking and allowing distractions to interrupt his play, he watched and listened. He was simply too good a gambler to need to cheat. In quick time he and Grego had enough money to open a gambling hall of their own. From there Hunt was unstoppable. He was "the house."

He chose an old hotel in the heart of the boomers' tents and shacks. He filled one big room with card tables and chairs. He provided no bar, no food service, no whoring, and no dancing. What he did provide was poker, blackjack, and dice. His establishment was such a success that he later opened another one in the neighboring town of Junction City on the Louisiana border.

Never once did he consider moving his wife and children to El Dorado. The place was dangerous day or night. Free-lance outlaws roamed the streets, not to speak of the Little Rock and Hot Springs gambling syndicates, all with ties to the Mafiosi on the East Coast. Frank Grego cleared the path for Hunt in many of his dealings with these people.

Interestingly enough, because Hunt provided gambling only and ran fairly honest houses, he became a respected man in the community. Arkansas has always allowed gambling within its state. The law enforcement came to maintain order and safety. No one ever broke up one of his games.

Until one night the Ku Klux Klan arrived.

Part of Christian conservative revival in the 1920s, the KKK had started riding again. White-sheeted horsemen galloped around the countryside burning crosses on lawns of Catholics and Jews, immigrants and lords of vice. Blacks were persecuted as a matter of course with signs like "Nigger! Read and leave!"

One night in 1921 a white-robed leader walked in the door of Hunt's gambling hall. Outside on the streets were twenty or thirty white-robed marchers. The leader waved his torch. "Shut this place down!"

While his customers cowered, Hunt stood his ground. His poker face in place above his broad shoulders and heavy muscled arms, the six-footer stared at the Klansman. The silence grew in the tense room until the hooded figure backed away and fled into the night.

The gaming continued that evening, but Hunt knew he'd better get out while the getting was good. Though he continued to run his gambling games for a while longer, he decided the time had come to invest in oil.

An oil trader named "Buckshot" Coleman was selling half-acre leases on a plot of ground near Busey-Armstrong No. 1. Bankrolled by his considerable poker winnings and his excellent reputation, Hunt bought one. He'd found an old drilling rig sitting on the side of the railroad depot, a hostage to unpaid freight charges. He paid the charges and hired some men. As with Glenn McCarthy, going into the oil business was just that simple.

Again Arizona Slim's luck ran true to form. Hunt struck oil on his very first well. His friends and family in Lake Village were not surprised. They had expected no less. Though the well didn't gush long enough to make a profit, it established Hunt's reputation. He had found oil. He was in the business.

He decided that he liked the land better to the south. He managed to take out a 40-acre lease on the Rowland farm some distance away from Busey-Armstrong. There with the help of Grego and another friend, Old Man Bailey, he struck oil in January 1922. By March he was producing 5,000 barrels a day.

He closed down his gambling hall and began buying and selling leases. Because of his success rate, he had plenty of takers. Not a millionaire yet but very well off, he had eight wells going in the El Dorado field. Shortly thereafter, he bought leases in Smackover, Arkansas, about fifteen miles away. Those wells too came in, though Hunt had trouble with his crew. His first well, Lou Ann No. 1, struck oil just below

2,000 feet. Hunt was "poor boy drilling," that is, he used old pieced-together equipment and promised to pay everybody when the well came in. With oil flowing over the sides of the platform, his crew went on strike refusing to cap it off until they were paid.

According to the story, Hunt rode out on horseback, dismounted, and rolled up his sleeves. Whether he meant to fight or was merely threatening, no one really knew. He was well built, strong, and tough. No fight broke out, because he talked to his crew. What he said was that they were "Hunt men" and they could always count on being paid. Hunt and his oil-soaked crew then went to work to cap off the well with a "Christmas tree" valve. He could run a line off it to attach to a pipeline close by. Again the Hunt luck held. His well had come in near a conduit, so he didn't waste any of his precious oil.

Well after well, the Hunt men drilled around Smackover and El Dorado. They were being paid. They had money to throw around. They bragged about who they were and whom they worked for. H. L. Hunt was an honest man and everybody knew it, most of all the men who worked for him.

In 1922 he'd moved Lyda and the children down to El Dorado into a little bungalow. (The Klan had calmed the town down considerably.) In 1924 he moved her into a three-story brick house covering an entire block in a residential section. By that time he had accumulated close to 400,000 barrels of oil reserves. At $1.50 a barrel, he was worth $600,000, a princely sum in those days.

He was still a loner, even cool toward his children and his wife. Lyda managed the house and family and made a place for herself in El Dorado by herself. Her family however was beset by serious problems and a real tragedy. The Hunts' son "Hassie" continued to be a "handful" that even Hunt despaired of ever controlling. Then Lyda gave birth to their fourth child, a daughter, who died the next month from a gas leak in the new house.

Lyda was devastated. Hunt was stunned. El Dorado looked on with sympathy and approval when he took her to New York City for their first real vacation and promptly got her pregnant. His family job done as he saw it, he went back to his life in the oil fields and the gambling halls.

> "All I need is a deck of cards and some poker chips."
> —H. L. Hunt

He was equally alone in his business dealings. He never had an office. Instead, he made his deals in hotel lobbies, in bank offices, and in cafés. He never talked to people to socialize. He entertained himself playing poker and going out to his oil wells, carrying a sack lunch each day. To the end of his life, he continued to carry a sack lunch to work.

Because Hunt continued to gamble, he frequently lost a great deal of money. Alarmed and determined to preserve her own stake, Lyda took over the fiscal responsibilities for the family and began to manage the money, setting aside savings and investing in safe securities. Hunt later credited her with "about 90 percent of our financial success."

Hunt was then thirty-six years old and everything seemed set for life. Except that he wasn't happy with being safe and secure. He wasn't happy with collecting oil money for years. He wanted another boomtown where he could make another fortune.

That summer he sold off his Arkansas and Louisiana holdings for $600,000 and informed Lyda that he was going to Tampa, Florida, to cash in on the real estate boom.

Frania Tobruk came to Tampa from Buffalo, New York. She was a twenty-one-year-old Polish immigrant who changed her name to Tye. She had made frequent trips back to Poland and spoke English with an accent. She was a beautiful girl with little formal education who had come with her father to get over a broken engagement.

Tampa was in the midst of a real estate boom. Developers were building subdivisions on reclaimed swampland. People were retiring to these subdivisions, which were all built around golf courses. They were the *nouveau riche* middle-class emergent in America.

Frania's father gave her $800 and told her to make her way while he shuffled back to Buffalo. She bought a tearoom for $400, operated it for a few weeks, sold it at a profit, and began selling real estate. By accident H. L. Hunt got her phone number. The next day he called.

She showed him the property. He propositioned her. She slapped his face and refused to come to his hotel room. Hunt accepted the challenge. He left Tampa for several weeks, but when he returned he engaged her attentions in a "whirlwind courtship." He said his name was Major Franklin Hunt. He told her the title was honorary. "Everybody in the South is called major or colonel."

His coldness for the feelings of others and his certainty of his own superiority made a strong combination. He set out to charm her. He told her he couldn't work properly because he had his mind constantly on her. She never suspected that he might already be married much less the father of four children.

> "It's the rich wot gets the pleasure,
> It's the poor wot gets the blame,
> It's the same the whole world over.
> Ain't it all a cryin' shame?"
> —Anonymous "Song"

They didn't have to have a marriage license to get married in Florida. Hunt bought a gold band in a pawnshop. Despite her Catholic upbringing and her stated desire for her children to be reared in her faith, she married him before a justice of the peace. Her wedding took place in the Cuban quarter of Ybor City with its restaurants, nightclubs, gambling halls, and speakeasies. She signed her name in a ledger. He signed also, though she didn't see what name he wrote down. No proof of the wedding has ever been found.

He went back to Louisiana soon after the wedding. When she joined him, she was pregnant. They went to Mardi Gras together, then he installed her in a small apartment in Shreveport, less than a hundred miles southwest of the big brick home he shared with his wife in El Dorado, Arkansas.

In the years to come, Hunt would deny that he and Frania were legally married, but he never denied that her children were his. She and Lyda were pregnant at the same time and delivered babies within five months of each other. Lyda, of course, had his name and access to all the family accounts. She had the respect and support of her neighbors, friends, and family.

To Frania he would give cash money, as much as a thousand dollars from his pocket. She never saw him carry a billfold. Once he came home and threw $15,000 on the table. She continued to believe that he was an oil field worker and a gambler. All the explanation he ever gave her was, "I was playing poker."

Like the typical "other" woman, she and her children were deserted on holidays. He spent those with Lyda and his children in El Dorado.

In December 1925 he pulled out of real estate in Tampa in favor of putting all his time and effort into his oil business. He incorporated his first operating company, H. L. Hunt, Inc., and began building a real organization. Frank Grego and Old Man Bailey continued at his side. They might have been his troubleshooters or bodyguards. He found however that he needed other men who actually had experience and knowledge of the oil business. One by one, he hired them. Not one of them was a qualified geologist, however. Hunt trusted his own luck and his gambling sense too much to weight it down with scientific "stuff."

"It either looked like oil land or it did not look like oil land," was his famous statement. However, he didn't actually discover any oil fields for himself. His play was to jump into the lease-buying action immediately after the discovery had been made. With timing, good sense, and great luck, H. L. Hunt gradually became one of the biggest oil operators in the Ark-La-Tex area. By 1929 he had more than one hundred wells producing. Still he had little financial security. Oil had fallen to $1.29 a barrel.

At about this time, rumors of bigamy were circulating around Shreveport. The oil community was a small society. Hunt himself was known everywhere. His own men traveled freely back and forth from El Dorado to Shreveport to East Texas. The two Mrs. Hunts were sure to be discovered sooner or later—especially since they looked nothing alike. Though they both had baby children, the one in El Dorado was nearly twenty years older than the one in Shreveport. Which one was the legal wife was never in question. Hunt realized he had to get one of them "out of town."

In 1930 he moved Frania to Dallas's exclusive Highland Park community. The two-story brick house on a corner lot at 4230 Versailles Avenue was definitely a step up from a tiny bungalow. For years afterward, Frania pretended she knew nothing about any other wife. She protested that her husband merely wanted her near his work, that he wanted her to have nice things, that their children should have good schools and a nice neighborhood. Had she cared to look, she would have found the deed to the house was not even registered in her name but in her sister's.

In September 1930 Hunt left her alone a month before she was to give birth to their third child. Word had come to him that a big strike was close in East Texas. A wildcatter was about to run a test on a poor boy well. The old man was trying desperately to sell enough leases to keep his operation going. His name was Columbus Marion Joiner, but everyone called him "Dad."

The two eventually came together in the corner suite of the Baker Hotel to strike the biggest oil deal in the history of this or any other state. And H. L. Hunt became a millionaire overnight. His picture and his name appeared above the fold on the front page of the Dallas papers for days.

Still, Frania Tye maintained she didn't know she wasn't married to Major Franklin Hunt.

> "The greater the wealth, the thicker will be the dirt. This indubitably describes a tendency of our time."
> —John Kenneth Galbraith

When the Daisy Bradford No. 3 blew in October 3, 1930, no one could know that it would still be producing in 2002. To this day the East Texas Oil Museum in Kilgore, Texas, passes out tiny souvenir bottles to its visitors. The East Texas field that Daisy Bradford tapped proved to be the greatest discovery of its time. People literally could not fail to make money in the giant field discovered to be forty-two miles long and from six to fourteen miles wide. It covered 140,000 acres in five Texas counties.

So dependable was its wealth that 32,000 wells were drilled. Fewer than five hundred came up dry. The cost to drill a well was about $32,000 in twenty-five days. And H. L. Hunt owned 5,000 acres inside it with 229 wells producing 60,000 barrels a day. In fact, after World War II, he boasted that his production alone was more than the Axis Powers' combined total of 276 million barrels of oil.

In actuality East Texas produced 500 million barrels, 100 million of which were H. L. Hunt's. Though his statement was exaggerated, he certainly did his part.

Unfortunately, in 1934 the situation was dire for the oil producers. So much unregulated oil was in itself a financial disaster for the producers, refiners, wholesalers, and retailers. When oil prices fell to two or three cents a gallon wholesale, consumers loved paying seven or eight cents a gallon at the pump. The state governing board, the Texas Railroad Commission, was helpless because it had no enforcement ability. Governor Ross Sterling, himself an oilman with the Humble

Company out of Houston, vacillated wildly between aiding producers and winning votes from consumers.

At this point H. L. Hunt made his first major entry into politics. He stepped forward to lead the prorationists, who believed whole-heartedly that oil production must be regulated. Prorationing would limit the amount of oil drilled per day from every well. IPAT men, independent oil producers with only a few rigs, would be closed out until the price of oil rose high enough to make a living off 250 barrels per day. But the big producers and state conservationists joined forces. The alternative was that the great East Texas oil field would be as depleted as Spindletop in the early part of the century and more recently Smackover and El Dorado. It was already showing the effects of over-drilling by producing 50 barrels of saltwater for every 100 barrels of oil drilled. The field was being drowned.

In the midst of all the problems in his business, Hunt had woman trouble. One of his friends told Frania point blank, "Your husband is not Franklin Hunt. His real name is H. L. Hunt and he has another family living in Tyler."

She could no longer salve her conscience with her sordid little game of "let's pretend." Heavily pregnant with their fourth child, she confronted him. When he didn't offer to divorce Lyda, she left with their children for Great Neck, New York, where he bought her a house.

Whether Lyda knew anything about her husband or remained in ignorance is unknown. Because her oldest daughter, Margaret, had actually met Frania at a party in 1934, the chances are good that Lyda knew nearly everything. The woman who had secured her husband's enormous fortune when he would, in all likelihood, have gambled it away had too much sense to rock her own boat. Secure in her status as his legal wife, she kept her mouth shut.

Hunt tried several times to woo Frania to return and even tried to persuade her to become a Mormon under the mistaken impression that Mormonism would allow him to take two wives in Texas. She insisted she was Catholic. When she announced that she was determined to remain in Great Neck, he began to make arrangements for his various children.

In 1935 he established the Loyal Trusts for his six children by Lyda. To fund the trust, he established Placid Oil Company (a name he selected because he believed names beginning with "P" and containing six letters were lucky) and transferred some of his best oil properties into it. It became the cornerstone of the family's fortune. The children were able to spend only the income—not the principal. The trust was set up to pass tax-free from generation to generation probably at Lyda's insistence. Knowing well his gambling tendencies and probably knowing that he had other heirs, Lyda tied him hand and foot.

The leases that formed the basis of the trust were producing as never before. Prorationing required the best efforts of the Texas Rangers to take effect, but when it did oil prices began to climb. By 1936 they were over a dollar a barrel. Even the independent producers could make money on that. Hunt was grossing over $3 million per year.

Rather than having peace and a feeling that he could lie back and enjoy life as he approached fifty, he believed his success resulted from his "genius gene." The money galvanized him. He loved the challenge. The true gambler always wants more money. He can never stop gambling. He always wants the next big pot. Like a true social Darwinist, Hunt set out to use his brains, courage, cunning, and luck to win the next one.

He bought out his partner Pete Lake for $5 million. Hunt Oil Company was then worth $20 million. In six years Hunt's bribe money to take Dad Joiner's leases had shown quite a rate of return on investment.

Hunt Oil was a multi-faceted corporation. First he sent Hunt men to West Texas, Louisiana, and Arkansas to scout for wildcat locations that he could own. His men had a specially devised questionnaire to collect information about local landowners much faster than the major oil companies could do it. He created Penrod Drilling, his own drilling operation with eleven steam-powered land rigs to start drilling immediately. He then forced the owners of Excelsior Refining Company to sell him a half interest by telling them that if they did not do so, he would stop refining his oil with them and set up his own refinery next door. For $150,000 he bought it and renamed it Parade Gasoline Company.

Unfortunately, one of the worst disasters in Texas history happened as a result of Parade. The New London Consolidated School in the heart of the East Texas field had illegally tapped into a Parade pipeline to heat their classrooms. The tap had leaked natural gas within the walls of the brick building. On March 18, 1937, the school blew sky high killing 294 people—the schoolchildren, the teachers, and members of the PTA that were meeting there that afternoon.

The radio carried the news across Texas. Within hours Hunt was on the scene, visiting relatives of the victims. For a man who loved his own children, this was a particularly tragic event. At his orders Hunt Oil employees came in pairs from the Joiner leases to aid the victims. Hunt himself helped load a casket into a funeral van and went everywhere stuffing hundred dollar bills into the pockets of grieving fathers. No one ever tried to bring suit against him. Tragedy was something men lived with in those days.

At that time one of his greatest disappointments began to manifest itself. Hunt's first son began to develop severe mental problems. Young Haroldson Lafayette (Hassie) looked enough like his father to be taken for him on occasion. There the resemblance stopped. Although Hassie was undoubtedly smart, he was emotionally unstable. Hunt refused to see anything wrong with his son and gave him every opportunity to learn the oil business. Since he himself had been a defiant youth, he laid Hassie's violent temper and sometimes illegal activities to youthful rebellion. Yet he had no idea what to do with him.

When Hassie went to court to have himself declared an adult and started buying oil and gas leases without his father's knowledge, the Hunt luck seemed to hold for him too.

He was a millionaire before he reached the chronological age of twenty-one.

While Hunt was furious that his son had beaten him to the leases, he was secretly certain that his son was a chip off the old block. Hassie was proof positive that Hunt was passing on his "genius gene." Unfortunately, the father-son relationship grew colder and more strained.

On January 1, 1938, Hunt moved Lyda and his children to a replica of George Washington's Mount Vernon on a ten-acre tract overlooking White Rock Lake in Dallas. It was located in a rustic setting eight miles from downtown Dallas, and the contractor was delighted to unload it for $69,000 cash. When the Hunts moved in two weeks later, *The Dallas Morning News* announced, "Quite the nicest family has come to Mt. Vernon...." It listed the names of Lyda and the children and noted that Margaret had been queen of the Tyler Rose Festival.

It was all the introduction the Hunts would have needed to be taken to the bosom of Dallas society, except that Hunt would not donate a penny to civic drives. R. L. Thornton, who would one day be mayor of Dallas, was determined to create an ideal metropolis on the prairie. Symphony, opera, parks, and theatre were all to be subsidized by donations from the wealthy. Hunt, with his aversion to charity, would not donate to any of these causes.

Besides the fact that he was a tightwad, he was also an amateur social planner. "The greatest good one man can perform for his fellow man," he wrote much later, "is to create gainful employment and opportunities for personal progress through constructive work."

He never bothered to explain any of this to any of the numerous charities who came to his office. He simply turned them away. As a result his application to the Brook Hollow Golf Club, the most prestigious in the city, was voted down. Later he joined the Dallas Country Club. He was never invited to join the social clubs that the wealthy sponsored.

Lyda went her own way, quietly donating to worthy charities as part of her membership in the Highland Park Presbyterian Church and various women's clubs. She was accepted everywhere, the feeling being that even if her husband was a barbarian, she was just exactly what she acted like—a thorough lady.

While Hassie went his own way, the other three Hunt boys, Bunker, Herbert, and Lamar, grew up and joined their father's far-reaching enterprises. Margaret married a Hunt Oil accountant named Albert Hill. She went to work as her father's business aide and confidante, acquiring business knowledge far superior to almost any other woman of her time. Caroline's husband, Lloyd Sands, also went to work for Hunt Oil. Everything looked to be coming up roses.

But in 1938 the international community was beginning to see signs of unrest. Whether Hunt was aware of problems arising in Germany and Japan was unknown. He started dealing with them. In Germany he traded oil for steel drill pipe. He exported oil to Japan through a California trading company. Later those deals would come back to haunt him even though he was not alone. While these countries were the world's principal aggressor nations, no one suspected what they would do in just three short years.

Meanwhile, the saltwater encroachment in East Texas was on the verge of destroying one of the world's great energy producers. Pumping it out into streams and fields was environmentally disastrous. Hauling it to the Gulf polluted with oil was equally unacceptable. At last a team of geologists developed a method of simply re-injecting the saltwater back into the ground. Operators could thereby maintain the pressure of the field and solve waste-disposal problems.

Hunt was one of the first operators in East Texas to use the process. Within four years the oil wells were producing only slightly more saltwater than oil, and the field pressure had ceased its precipitous decline. And Hunt continued to make money hand over fist.

> "Lyda was a very gracious woman,
> but she was not dumb."
> —Hunt family member (1940)

Meanwhile, Frania Tye decided she missed Hunt. Great Neck was too far away. Even though he was supporting her, she knew she could get more if she were closer to him. She was right.

Hunt was delighted to see her and installed her in a fine new mansion in the exclusive River Oaks section of Houston. Whether or not she truly believed that Houston and Dallas were too far apart to create a problem, she applied for membership to the exclusive River Oaks Country Club as Mrs. H. L. Hunt.

At a River Oaks party to introduce her to society, she received a disturbing phone call. The female voice threatened to expose her as a bigamist; $5,000 was the price of the blackmailer's silence. Frania returned to the party, but for her the party was spoiled forever. At least fifty people tried to blackmail her in the next few days.

When she complained to H. L. Hunt, he had no real solution to her problem. Worse, he did not come to Houston to help her. Distraught and furiously angry, she packed the children in her car, drove to Dallas, and checked into the Adolphus Hotel. Then she called him and said, "These are your children as well as mine. Come take them off my hands."

While he was hesitating, she put fourteen-year-old Howard in charge of the other three and drove back to Houston. When she got home, H. L. was on the phone begging her to return.

Back the next day, she found him with the children accompanied by his daughter Margaret. What Hunt and Margaret said to her did little more than leave her despondent and unhappy. She took the children and drove back to Houston.

A bit later she was summoned back to Dallas to meet not just Hunt, but the mother of his legal family, Lyda. What an unsettling meeting that must have been! Hunt talked while Frania and Lyda looked at each other. Lyda saw an exceptionally beautiful thirty-five-year old. Frania saw an older woman —plump and gray-headed—the fifty-two-year-old wife of her fifty-two-year-old lover, who was also portly and gray-headed. She must have known that her position as "the other woman" gave her very little leverage.

With Frania's future still up in the air, Lyda suggested they meet at a restaurant for a woman-to-woman talk. Whether Hunt's ears burned is unknown. Lyda offered to adopt the children to leave Frania free to do as she liked, but the second Mrs. Hunt refused to give up her children.

Embarrassed and upset that Lyda had found out, Hunt moved Frania to Los Angeles. He enrolled her children in private schools and set up the Reliance Trusts for them. Each trust provided a yearly income of $6,000 for each child. Lyda probably did not know about them since the money was to come from the Joiner leases. Had she known, she probably would have objected strenuously. East Texas was an old oil field. Its reserves were not endless.

In 1942 Frania came back to Dallas to arrange a settlement for herself. Since no marriage license had ever existed and she could find no trace of the ledger they had signed before the justice of the peace, she had really little chance of proving herself his wife.

Hunt offered her a million dollars to sign a statement saying that she had never married him. Torn between fury and tears, she screamed at him, "I'll never sell my children for all the money you have."

She ran out of the room. Hunt followed her and pacified her.

On January 24, 1942, she signed a sixty-two-page agreement denying she was married to him and a blanket release that she would make no future claims again him. He paid her $300,000 in cash and $2,000 a month for the rest of her life.

In February he arranged for her to marry an army colonel who was employed by Hunt Oil. The colonel was called back into service, but at the end of World War II, they moved to Atlanta and raised the four children in peace and quiet.

Meanwhile Hunt had decided to further complicate his life. He began dating a secretary, Ruth Eileen Ray. She was twenty-five and pregnant. He was fifty-three and more married than ever.

While others might believe he lacked a sense of responsibility, part of Hunt's reason for having children with Ruth was his own inflated opinion of himself and his "genius gene." According to the principals of social Darwinism, he believed he was doing the world a great service by having children. He talked about future presidents and future leaders in all fields. Six months before he became a new father, he became a grandfather. His oldest daughter, Margaret, gave birth to Hunt's first granddaughter, Lyda Hunt Hill. His patriarchy of "geniuses" included three generations.

Ironically, Hassie Hunt's strange behavior had turned increasingly violent. After the young man went berserk in boot camp, he was immediately discharged from the army. Hunt had to subject his oldest son to a lobotomy, shock treatments, and a prolonged stay in an institution.

At the same time Hunt's oil profits were growing. World War II demanded increased production, and prices increased accordingly. Hunt was able to supply over 100 million barrels of oil for the Allies from the Joiner leases. Thanks to the Noble Trusts insisted upon by Lyda, most of the profits went to her children rather than to H. L., who was spending now for land.

In 1944 he bought farms in Texas and ranches in Montana and Wyoming. None was a paying enterprise. The oil money constantly subsidized the properties, and the Hunt children and grandchildren enjoyed their vacation trips.

Hunt also went back to gambling, always his favorite thing. He claimed that his racetrack bets could break East Coast bookies and bragged that he was winning close to a million a year. The truth was that he won and lost fairly evenly. About this time he gave up smoking. He was not interested in his health, but he decided that the time he spent lighting cigars and smoking interfered with his concentration on the cards.

> "If you know how rich you are,
> you aren't very rich."
> —H. L. Hunt

In April 1948 *Life* and *Fortune* magazines ran simultaneous stories about the richest man in the United States. According to *Fortune,* Hunt was "the biggest of the Big Rich, and thus also probably the richest single individual in the U.S." It reported, "The Hunt Oil properties have been valued at around $237 million and their daily production of crude estimated at 65,000 barrels. At last year's average price of $2.25 a barrel, this would have given him a gross weekly income of more than $1 million."

Life ran a photograph of Hunt on a Dallas street corner over the caption, "Is this the richest man in the U.S.?"

Probably Hunt was not. Although he was exceptionally rich, he couldn't compare with Rockefeller or the Mellon family of Pittsburgh. Texas's own Howard Hughes was on his way to becoming a billionaire, as was J. Paul Getty. But Hunt had something none of them had. He had public recognition. And he loved it. Arizona Slim, whose first bankroll had been $1, was now worth upwards of $600 million. Furthermore, he was on his way to becoming one of the nation's largest landowners.

Shortly after his elevation to national prominence, he transferred ownership of Penrod Drilling to Lyda's sons, Bunker, Herbert, and Lamar. At the same time, he set up Secure Trusts for Ruth's family. The value of the Secure Trusts was $1 million, quite a nest egg for an average family, but like the Reliance Trusts for Frania's family, it was a pittance compared to the Loyal Trusts for Lyda's children.

The news of their father's wealth came almost as a shock to all his various families' members except perhaps Lyda herself.

Suddenly, their own future changed before their eyes. Were they ready for what lay ahead for them?

At the same time, Hunt's upper echelon employees and former associates cringed. He was growing more strong-willed and more self-deluded than ever. "He never changed his mind once it was made up," one said. "He thought he was a second Jesus Christ," said another. "He believed the world was the way he wanted it to be, not the way it is."

Uppermost in his delusional thinking, Hunt believed that the world was being taken over by the Communists. Joseph Stalin and Mao Tse-tung were threats from outside, but worse was the threat from within. The Democrats were leading the country down the road to socialism. Government should be limited in every area except national defense.

He published a pamphlet "A Word to Help the World." It advanced his belief that he was not a conservative in the real sense of the word. He was a constructivist. He called his philosophy of constructivism "the trademark of wholesome government." He noted that a person can be too conservative, but he can never be too constructive.

He was disappointed that the world did not immediately rally round his constructivism or buy his pamphlet. ("Everything I do, I do for profit," he insisted.) He needed a way to reach more people, to spread his ideas. In June 1951 he founded *Facts Forum,* a fifteen-minute radio commentary show and a subscription newsletter. It was not a group for discussion though it certainly began a great deal of that. As it turned out, it was probably the most effective private propaganda organ ever created in the history of the United States at that time.

"Democracy is a political outgrowth of the teachings of Jesus Christ. This is Dan Smoot for *Facts Forum.*"

"Korea: Police action or war? A question for all Americans. This is Dan Smoot for *Facts Forum.*"

"...everyone in the Dallas-Fort Worth area now has an easy opportunity to hear Senator Joe McCarthy in person.... This is Dan Smoot for *Facts Forum.*"

H. L. Hunt on the right with Dan Smoot, spokesperson for *Facts Forum*. From the collection of the Texas/Dallas History and Archives Division, Dallas Public Library.

Dan Smoot, the program's spokesperson was the Hunt ideal made flesh. Broad-shouldered, handsome, a former FBI agent and former college English teacher, he presented both sides of all their controversial opinions, though the liberal side was presented with much less enthusiasm than the conservative or constructive side.

Hunt was in his heaven, all being right with a world that was listening to his opinions. Although he ran afoul of the equal time campaigning laws by having a senator expressing his views on his program, he was saved because McCarthy's opponents declined to speak on his program.

Hunt added a "free circulating library" to his program. Hundreds of copies of books such as *We Must Abolish the United Nations*, *Iron Curtain over America*, and *Hitler Was a Liberal* were made available to people who loved to read and digest them.

The program later opened with a song to the tune of "Buckle Down, Winsocki." "Wake us up, *Facts Forum*, wake us up. We can win, *Facts Forum,* if you wake us up." It conducted what it purported to be polls but were really a random sampling from *Facts Forum* listeners. The results of these "polls" were sent out to 2,300 newspapers and radio stations as well as to every member of Congress. A number of legislators accepted them as true polls and allowed themselves to be guided by them in their votes.

True to his stated goal of profit, H. L. Hunt did not spend the estimated $4 million necessary to keep the program on the air. Radio stations all across the country and commercial sponsors came up with $3 million. Enough rich men contributed the rest. Many of Hunt's board of directors encouraged the others. They included Texas governor Allan Shivers, Norman Vincent Peale, General Robert E. Wood of Sears Roebuck, and actor and avowed McCarthyite John Wayne. The world's greatest gambler had pulled off his biggest win.

One of Hunt's great coups occurred in February 1952. It was the passage of the Twenty-Second Amendment to the Constitution, limiting the presidential tenure to two terms. Although his influence was unmeasured and probably negligible given the short time required to pass the amendment, Hunt was sure he had done it. "I alone and single-handed, by telephone, letter, and personal talks whipped the legislatures into ratification," he claimed. "It took me only seven weeks to do it."

At sixty-three he felt his body began to age and became concerned for his health. He became vitally interested in what he believed would be a wholesome diet. He also began to chase women again with his wife and his mistress in town only a short distance from each other and another woman in Atlanta, raising his other children.

Lyda continued to be his mainstay, but she was wearing thin. Hassie's mental condition and Hunt's strange fantasies and infidelities were becoming more than she could endure. She would frequently call friends to go to a movie with her.

One day she broke down in tears in front of one of Hunt's beautiful young secretaries. The girl asked why Lyda didn't get a divorce.

"Because I have children to be considered," the distraught woman replied, "and as long as I live, I'm going to protect them from what's going to happen when I'm gone."

About this time his sons found out about their father's infidelities. Margaret had known for years and had told Caroline. They had agreed to keep it from their brothers, who admired their father. Hurt to the quick, the boys were also angry. Hunt was a hypocrite who'd preached to them and then sinned himself—and not just once. Herbert found both the Reliance and the Secure Trusts. Caroline shrugged her shoulders and came up with the truth. "He just likes children until they get to be about six or seven years old. Then he isn't interested anymore."

On May 6, 1955, Lyda Bunker Hunt died at the Mayo Clinic in Rochester, Minnesota. She had had a severe stroke. Hunt had rushed her to the airport where all her children and their families were waiting for her. Unable to speak, she had shaken her finger at Nancy, Herbert's wife, who was due to give birth to her third child. Nancy stepped back and stayed home at Lyda's command. The baby girl was born three days later on the day of her grandmother's funeral. They named her Lyda Bunker Hunt.

Hunt showed no reaction at all. He never wrote, never talked, never memorialized his wife with charitable contributions or bequests. Instead, he invited Ruth Ray and her children to Lyda's house. Though she didn't move in, the first family didn't like her presence at all. Things might have rocked on indefinitely had not fourteen-year-old Ray Lee confronted his father. The spittin' image of Hunt, he said, "You *will* marry my mother. She is a good religious person, and you *will* marry her."

On Sunday, November 24, 1957, Hunt married her at the home of her pastor. He had told no one of the impending nuptials. His children had to read about it in the *Dallas Times*

Herald. For years he was estranged from them, while Ruth exerted more and more influence over him. Less than two years short of seventy, he gave up gambling.

Of course, he credited his reformation to Ruth, but in reality, a federal grand jury began a probe of a gambling syndicate based in Terre Haute, Indiana. It allegedly involved high-stakes wagers on college and pro football by such prominent persons as Zeppo Marx of the comedy team; Tobias Stone, the gubernatorial candidate for Indiana; and Texas oilman H. L. Hunt. Hunt managed to get out of a grand jury testimony by pretending illness. Only by avoiding the grand jury did he get out of paying the $11 million in gambling profits the IRS claimed he owed.

He joined Reverend W. A. Criswell's First Baptist Church, the largest Baptist congregation in the nation. It claimed Billy Graham as a member. Criswell wanted the "richest man in the world" also.

Inspired by religious fervor, Hunt resurrected *Facts Forum* under the name LIFE LINE. It was the same old propaganda organ, except it no longer even pretended to offer both sides of the question. It also provided an excellent tax dodge in the name of religion.

As Hunt grew older, he sought to extend his life by founding HLH Products. He bought a food-processing plant near Nacogdoches and set about canning products that were mistaken for "health foods" because his interest in his own health was widely known. In reality they were ordinary stuff, purchased and eventually canned everywhere throughout the South. He cared so little about the contents that he never used top-of-the-line products. LIFE LINE advertised HLH products, and people bought until they found out what they were.

In 1959 Criswell preached a sermon that gave Hunt a new crusade. The Baptist minister flatly stated, "The election of a Catholic president would mean the end of religious freedom in America."

The presidential candidate at whom the sentence was directed was, of course, John F. Kennedy. How Criswell managed to enlist Hunt will remain a mystery. Perhaps Hunt believed the "dump Kennedy" campaign would leave the way open for Texan Lyndon Johnson to be nominated. If so, Hunt clearly showed his own ignorance of the political situation. Though Johnson played down his political leanings, those with savvy knew he was even more liberal than Kennedy.

LIFE LINE distributed 200,000 copies of the pamphlet containing Criswell's sermon. It created a small stir because it violated campaign election laws by not stating who had paid for the printing. A Senate investigative committee was hunting for Hunt, who decided to drop out of sight for a time.

When the Kennedy-Johnson ticket was elected, the heat was off. Hunt went back to politicking but was never to see his chosen candidates make much of a showing thereafter. He also wrote a novel, *Alpaca,* which he self-published. The size of the print-run is unknown, but no more than a hundred copies were sold. Many complimentary copies were sent to critics and media, who one and all attacked it viciously.

While Hunt diverted himself with his constructivist crusade and his children by Ruth in particular, his first family grew up and began to run his business as well as their own. The Joiner leases continued to produce at the rate of 36,000 barrels a day, amounting to $50 million a year in their trust.

In November of 1963 Kennedy and Johnson were on the campaign trail along with Governor John Connally of Texas. H. L. Hunt and his LIFE LINE organization, having completely reversed their position, ran a steady diatribe in paid advertisements in the newspapers and on television and radio against the projected visit to Dallas. What happened in Dallas that day shocked the sensibilities around the nation and the world. People said that the advertisements, which ran in the ultra-conservative *Dallas Morning News,* had influenced Lee Harvey Oswald and later Jack Ruby. So dangerous was the situation and so inflammatory that an FBI man came to H. L. Hunt's house and insisted that he go into hiding. If he didn't, the FBI believed people would retaliate against him.

Hunt refused to go under cover. He insisted he wanted to go to Washington to "help Lyndon." Then Ruby shot Oswald. The national press accused Hunt of creating the "climate of hate" that had bred them both. The results were threatening telephone calls, threatening letters, and shots fired at Hunt's home. More telling was a widespread boycott of HLH Products of all kinds.

Deserting Lyndon Johnson when he dedicated himself to ramming through Kennedy's liberal agenda, Hunt backed Barry Goldwater, a man almost as conservative as he was. True to his philosophy of never giving charitable contributions, he did not contribute money. He merely created a disruptive presence at the Republican Convention. Goldwater lost badly.

Throughout Johnson's administration, H. L. Hunt continued to write more and more unreasonably. Rumors circulated that Hunt himself and his family were behind the assassination of Kennedy. He suffered not nearly so much as his family, who had to go out and deal with people every day of their lives, while their father sat at home writing political tracts and generally making an embarrassing spectacle of himself.

> "If he had more flair and imagination,
> if he weren't basically such a damn hick,
> H. L. Hunt could be
> the most dangerous man in America."
> —A. C. Green, the *Dallas Times Herald*

In 1965 the empire of H. L. Hunt expanded again. The Placid Oil Company discovered the giant Black Lake field in south-central Louisiana. The strike produced 25,000 barrels a day and made the Hunts bona fide billionaires at last. Added to the other Hunt interests, the Hunt companies' total average output was 100,000 barrels a day with oil prices at $3 a barrel.

The plaque reads:

TEXAS

THE JOINER NO. 3 DAISY BRADFORD

DISCOVERY GENIUS WAS C.M. (DAD) JOINER, 70-YEAR-OLD OKLAHOMAN WHO FOR YEARS BELIEVED THERE WAS OIL IN RUSK COUNTY. DRILLER WAS E.C. LASTER. CREW: DENNIS MAY, DAVE CHERRY, GLENN POOL, JIM LAMBERT, AND DAVE HUGHES. JOINER'S 2 EARLY EFFORTS FAILED – ONE WITH A JAMMED BIT, ONE WITH THE DRILL PIPE STUCK. THE RIG WAS NEXT SKIDDED 300' DOWN SLOPE. "THIS IS AS GOOD A PLACE AS ANY," SAID LASTER. THEN ON MAY 8, 1929, JOINER NO. 3 DAISY BRADFORD WAS SPUDDED IN. EQUIPMENT CONSISTED OF AN OLD ROTARY RIG POWERED BY A SINGLE-CYLINDER ENGINE, ONE 45 HP BOILER, ONE OLD COTTON GIN BOILER FIRED WITH SOGGY OAK AND PINE CHUNKS BY ROUSTABOUT DAN TANNER. THE DEPRESSION WAS ON AND MONEY SCARCE. THE CREW OFTEN WENT WITHOUT PAY. JOINER SACRIFICED MUCH OF HIS 10,000 ACRE BLOCK OF LEASES. FINALLY, ON ... 30, A DRILL STEM LOGGED AT 3536' INTO THE ...ORMATION SHOWED OIL. A BETTER RIG HAD TO ... IN ON OCT. 3, 1930, THE WELL BLEW IN AND ...ER THE CROWN BLOCK. THE BOOM WAS ON. ...MPER-TO-BUMPER ON ALL ACCESS ROADS. ... IN ALL DIRECTIONS. IN ITS FIRST 30 ...REAT FIELD PRODUCED MORE THAN 3½ BIL... OF OIL. IT NOW COVERS SOME 200 SQUARE ...ARGEST IN THE WORLD.

H. L. Hunt, second from left, with other dignitaries at the dedication of the Joiner well Daisy Bradford No. 3 in 1965. From the collection of the Texas/Dallas History and Archives Division, Dallas Public Library.

In the midst of all this prosperity came financial difficulties. HLH Products had initially lost money at the rate of a million a year. Every year since it had been founded, it had lost more.

When the children led by Herbert tried to close it down, Hunt found out about it. He literally grabbed his son by the collar and dragged him to the elevators shouting, "You're no son of mine." He further instructed his son to tell the rest of the family, "You're not running things anymore."

In the end his age and strange turns of mind kept him from interfering with his sons' running of the Hunt Oil business. Hassie was brought home to Mount Vernon on White Rock Lake. His lobotomy had muted his violence. With round the clock nurses, he could walk around the grounds with his father and take part in family "singalongs."

Hunt continued to be the center of media attention. For his eightieth birthday, he appeared on *60 Minutes* interviewed by Mike Wallace. At that time he said he had no idea how much money he was worth.

In 1973 he published two autobiographies, *Hunt Heritage* and *H. L. Hunt Early Days.* In 1974 his health continued to slip. His hair was wispy and white, his spine and shoulders badly hunched because of back pain that he refused to see a doctor about. His complexion had lost its ruddiness. He was extremely susceptible to colds. He had had to give up driving himself downtown because of failing eyesight. Around him his children fought for power. He knew it but could do nothing about it. Like King Lear he was regarded as old and foolish.

On September 13, 1974, he collapsed at his desk at Hunt Oil Company. He was rushed to Baylor University Medical Center in Dallas, where he lay for two months getting steadily weaker until he could no longer speak or move. On Friday, November 29, he died. The most reliable reports were that his heart had simply stopped.

One of the wealthiest men in the world was also one of the luckiest. None can doubt that he had been extremely lucky and daring all his life. However, his cherished belief that he was a genius is suspect. He had no critical skills, no self-understanding, no deep understanding or sympathy for the people in his life, and no understanding of political and economic processes. His money and what other people did with it created problems that he had no idea how to solve.

In the end he remained the sum of his parts—a wanderer, gambler, oilman, polygamist, health nut, and propagandist.

> "I know of no country, indeed, where the love of money has taken stronger hold on the affections of men…"
> —Alexis de Toqueville
> *Democracy in America*, 1835

In April 2002, the children, grandchildren, and great-grandchildren of H. L. and Lyda Bunker Hunt were invited to a dinner at the newly renovated Mount Vernon, which they sold in 1999. John and Teresa Amend had bought the estate on White Rock Lake. For those who grew up there, it was a chance to see it again and remember what had been their home place from January 1938 until November 1957.

At the close of the dinner, John Amend declared that he and his wife were custodians of the property. "I want to tell all …that no matter how long we live here, this will forever be the H. L. Hunt estate. It's a great legacy.…"

To be sure, Amend's sentiments are polite and respectful. However, the story in *The Dallas Morning News* makes no mention of the children of his last wife, Ruth Ray Hunt, who died there in 1999. Perhaps those children did not attend because they never really felt as if it were their home. Certainly the children of Frania Tye, wherever they might be, were not included.

A legacy Mount Vernon might be, but it is a fractured one, with hurt and shame staining it so long as it stands. The imitation of George Washington's beloved home is the sad legacy of a man best called Arizona Slim.

H. Ross Perot
"Mr. Super Patriot"

The best party H. Ross Perot ever threw began at 11:45 P.M. on Thursday, February 15, 1979, only a few yards over the border crossing between Sero in Iran and Yusekova in Turkey. On that night Perot's "eagles," five EDS executives, all veterans of Vietnam, managed to smuggle out two more EDS executives held for ransom in Gasr Prison in Teheran. The seven plus one loyal Iranian had made their way to freedom in spite of unbelievable odds.

On December 5, 1978, Paul Chiapparone, the head of EDS Corporation Iran, and Bill Gaylord, EDS Manager of the contract for the Iranian Ministry of Health, had been thrown into an Iranian prison. No official charges had been made against them. They were simply questioned, searched, and jailed. Their bail was set for almost $13 million. The astronomical amount just happened to coincide with what the financially strapped Iranian government on the brink of revolution owed Ross Perot's Electronic Data Systems for laying the groundwork to set up the country's first social security system.

Perot was willing to pay the highway robbery if he could have been certain that his men would be allowed to leave the country. To his dismay when his other executives lodged protests and inquiries, government officials maintained that Chiapparone and Gaylord would not be allowed to leave the country even if the ransom were paid.

A rescue by legal means if possible—illegal means if necessary—seemed in order. To effect it, Perot hired his old friend retired Colonel Arthur D. Simons. He was a decorated Green Beret whose troops called him "Bull." At a Hollywood party, John Wayne had once shaken Simons's hand with tears in his eyes when he said, "You *are* the man I play in the movies."

The daring rescue included the revolutionaries' riots that broke all the prisoners out of Gasr Prison when the city of Teheran seemed about to go up in flames. With the smoke rising behind them, the team made a hair-raising drive across five hundred miles of some of the roughest terrain in the world to the Turkish border. The details read like fiction in Ken Follett's best-selling book *On Wings of Eagles*.

They crossed the border to be greeted by Ralph Boulware, another EDS executive, who shook hands all around and produced a bottle of Chivas Regal from his overcoat pocket. The party began with cheers and a celebratory drink before they spent the night in the frigid guardhouse only a few feet from the border chain.

The next morning a bus arrived, hired by Perot and containing three more Vietnam vets whom he had chosen to be members of his rescue team. They produced another bottle of Scotch and started a poker game with the thousands of dollars they had brought out of Iran if bribes for the guards had been necessary. The party lasted for days as the group overcame still more obstacles.

After an all-day drive through mountains more beautiful than the Alps, they arrived at Van, where Perot had a charter plane waiting for them to fly to Ankara, the Turkish capital. From there they flew by commercial airline to Istanbul, where Perot met them, and the real party began. In Perot's suite at the Istanbul Hilton, Paul Chiapparone and Bill Gaylord got to speak to their wives and small children for the first time in over six weeks.

Meanwhile, the three "eagles" remaining in Teheran were in danger. The *Dallas Times Herald* broke the story of the escape, and the U.S. Embassy, eager to curry favor with ever-changing governments, asked for their passports. Perot was faced with the possibility that he might have exchanged three prisoners for two. Rather than go to the embassy, the eagles went directly to the airport where they were able to board an overloaded plane. Only when their jet cleared Iranian airspace did they relax.

Joe Poché, who had spent two years designing the enrollment system for people eligible for health-care benefits, got the pilot to send a message to EDS in the U.S. It read: *"The eagles have flown their nest."*

The gathering of eagles did not occur until they all landed in Frankfurt, Germany, which had no extradition treaty with Iran and therefore would have no reason to arrest Chiapparone and Gaylord or those who had abetted their escape. On board a chartered Boeing 707, they popped the corks on champagne. Thirty super deluxe meals had been ordered, including fish, fowl, and beef as well as six seafood trays, six hors d'oeuvre trays, six sandwich trays, six dip trays, three cheese trays, four pastry trays, four fresh-fruit trays, and four bottles of brandy. Soft drinks and mixers of all kinds had been stocked along with two cartons each of Kent, Marlboro, Kool, and Salem Lite cigarettes and two boxes of chocolates.

Unfortunately, the party had just begun when the charter developed engine trouble. They were forced to land at Heathrow Airport in London. They were immediately surrounded by a van of airport police, customs men, and immigration officials who were suspicious of the men who deplaned. With the exception of Perot, they were dirty, scruffy, smelly, and unshaven. More suspicious was the fortune they were carrying in various currencies. At last they were all admitted to the country except Rashid, the Iranian who had been so invaluable in getting Gaylord and Chiapparone out of Gasr Prison. British customs was going to imprison him since he had no passport.

When Perot protested, the agent asked if he knew anyone in Britain who could vouch for him. Perot thought a minute, then said, "I know Earl Mountbatten of Burma."

Rashid no longer had a problem.

When they boarded a 747 at Gatwick, Perot asked to rent the entire upstairs lounge for his party. Although a private rental was against policy, none of the other passengers seemed eager to join the dirty, smelly eagles for their nearly hysterical jubilation. Halfway across the Atlantic, the villainous-looking group got down on their hands and knees on a blanket on the floor and fished wads of bank notes out of their pockets, their boots, their hats, and their shirtsleeves. At the direction of Keane Taylor, whose job in Iran had been to computerize the Shah's bank, they began to organize their money. What a party with several hundred thousand dollars on the floor, some of it filthy from being carried out in a gas and oil can!

But Dallas saw the best party of all when their wives and children met them. The kissing and hugging, the squeals of delight at the sight of the returned daddies, the joy that everyone was home and safe made this day one of the happiest for these men.

On a final note, "Bull" Simons leaned over to Perot to whisper in his ear, "Remember you offered to pay me?"

"I sure do," said Perot.

"See this?" Simons nodded.

Paul Chiapparone was walking toward them carrying his littlest daughter Ann Marie. Both her arms were around his neck, and her head was on his shoulder.

"I see it," said Perot.

"I just got paid," Simons said.

> "Eagles Don't Flock—You Have to
> Find Them One at a Time."
> EDS recruiters motto

Henry Ray Perot was born in 1930 and named for his uncle. The Perot's first child had been named Gabriel Ross Jr. He died of spinal meningitis in 1921. In the fifth grade the parents changed their surviving son's name to Henry Ross, so he would be a namesake for his father.

In 1988 he was reported to be the third richest man in America after Sam Walton, who founded Wal-Mart, and John Kluge, the Metromedia tycoon. In 1991 *Texas Monthly* placed him at the top of its list of "100 Richest Texans" with a net worth of $3 billion. Contrary to most of the other Texas rich, he had not made his money through cattle ranching or oil and gas. Nor had he inherited it. Instead, he had earned it himself by recognizing a niche in the emerging world of computers and stepping boldly into it. In so doing he provided a vital service to other millionaires and billionaires. He developed systems to process and keep track of their paper promises for them. He was their money man.

Furthermore, he had done the job largely without a fancy, expensive education that would have provided him with "connections." Instead of an eastern private, preparatory academy, he was educated in the Texarkana public schools. He took pre-law courses at Texarkana Junior College and joined the United States Naval Academy at age nineteen.

The story of how he got into the Naval Academy reads like a work of romantic fiction. He had no congressional sponsorship by which all appointments are granted. Because he wanted the appointment, he wrote and kept writing for two years to Texas's two senators.

In 1949 when retiring Senator W. Lee O'Daniel was clearing his desk, an aide told him he had an unfilled appointment to the Naval Academy. The senator asked if anyone wanted it.

The aide remembered the boy from Texarkana who had been trying for years.

Incurious even as to the boy's name, O'Daniel said, "Give it to him."

Four years later Perot was commissioned an ensign and served on the aircraft carrier *Leyte*. In 1957 he left the navy to go to work as a salesman for International Business Machines. Within three years he saw clearly that the people who bought the machines didn't know how to use them. He was in the best position to tell them how to make the most of them because he had sold so many of them. He was a phenomenal salesman. In 1961, his last year to work for IBM, he had earned his maximum yearly commission by *the third week in January*.

Taking to heart the plaintive voices of his customers, he learned how disappointed and frustrated they were with the equipment they had bought with such high hopes. Furthermore, they didn't particularly *want* to know how to use it. What they paid such fabulous prices for was the fast, cheap information the machines could provide. Perot reasoned that the banks, the insurance companies, and the manufacturers would be willing to pay someone else handsomely to process their data and supply it to them in a format they could immediately use to increase their banking efficiency, to create the best and most profitable policies for the people whom they sought to insure, and to manufacture goods more cheaply and efficiently.

In the way of loyal employees, Perot went first to IBM with his observations and his plan to set up a unit to provide data to the people who bought the machines. (His idea for personalized service was in some ways similar to the one Michael Dell would capitalize on in his dormitory room at the University of Texas twenty years later.)

IBM wasn't interested. They were in the business of selling hardware—the big machines that were eighty percent of the data collection and dissemination business back in the infancy of computers in the workplace. They estimated that what Perot proposed at the time would represent only about twenty percent of their business. Software was not so important in those early days of computers because the machines themselves had so little capacity that multiple functions were beyond them. Essentially IBM told Perot that they didn't want to "chase pennies under the table."

On June 27, 1962, Perot left and drew out $1,000 from savings. Some accounts say the savings account was his, some that it belonged to his wife, Margot, who was teaching school at the time. No matter. With that small sum he founded

Electronic Data Systems to step into the gap that IBM did not care to fill.

Right from the beginning, the ex-navy man flew in the face of traditional wisdom for starting a business. He built his staff from honorably discharged military men from the war in Vietnam, with wounded veterans getting top priority. He considered rightly that they would be stable, conservative, and resourceful. In his opinion they might be twenty-five or twenty-six years old, but they would be more like forty-year-olds in terms of maturity and leadership potential. He also looked closely at their family history. A happily married man himself, he was reluctant to hire anyone who'd been divorced. He frequently said, "If your wife can't trust you, how can I?"

By setting standards for maturity and morality, he hired people who were content to go along with the long hours and the dress code that he had picked up at IBM: Women wore suits or low-key dresses. Men wore blue or gray suits, white shirts, conservative ties, black Oxford-type shoes, and no facial hair.

In his requirements Perot bucked a growing trend, which has frequently created workplace problems in the computer field to this day. The sixties saw the end of much formal dressing and the beginning of "do your own thing."

Although young "free spirited" people embraced computers with more enthusiasm than older workers, those who really understood them were in short supply. In order to get these exceptional people, bosses made exceptions for any quirks they might bring with them from their private lives. In many businesses where they worked away from the public, they were not required to adhere to a dress code. "Do your own thing" became a license to slap together outlandish outfits and ignore personal grooming.

Not at EDS.

Besides his own basic conservatism, Perot had a strong reason for instituting such a dress code. He was sending his men out on jobs that required conservative first impressions.

He believed most of his potential clients would be bankers and insurance companies, twin bastions of conservatism that in turn needed to display American home values of security and stability to their clients. Perot wanted his people to blend in with the other employees. A client in a bank must never suspect that the men and women working busily in front of blue computer screens handling his money were outside hired help. The banker who quoted the figures so glibly with regard to loans and collateral should never give the impression that he didn't uncover those figures for himself.

EDS offered what they termed "facilities management," at an economically attractive price—IBM's "pennies under the table." IBM's contracts as well as the contracts of other companies were written for a period of sixty to ninety days. EDS offered five-year fixed-price contracts. The company representatives would go into the customer's organization, set up the system, and then reassign employees to other jobs. Thereby they saved personnel costs, increased profits, and above all maintained a steady flow of business.

Even in the beginning Perot's style was conservative. (With only $1,000 start-up money, how could it be anything else?) For Collins Radio, his first customer, he purchased computer time discounted from an IBM computer at Southwestern Life Insurance in Dallas and sold it at retail prices. In 1963 he established a contract to process insurance data for Mercantile Security Life. Resulting growth was slow, but in thirty years data Perot processed for Mercantile made the firm the largest insurance data processor in the nation. His company's demonstrated efficiency there led to the multimillion-dollar deal of the century.

In the end the real business of EDS came from President Lyndon Johnson, a Texan himself, who chose a Texas man with an up-and-coming Texas company to design the computer systems for his Great Society. Perot's company designed the computer systems for Medicaid and Medicare.

When Perot took EDS public in 1968, he offered seventy-eight percent of the company, from which equal amounts went to himself and EDS. The initial public offering was $15 per share. Within days the offering was worth $1.5 billion. Perot was one of the richest men in America. In 1970 the shares rose to $160 per share.

His wealth fueled his ambition, and his sense of how things should be run, a product of his military training, became a compelling force in his life. Everywhere he saw waste and inefficiency. He became determined to use his wealth where it would do the most good for America.

> "Money alone sets the world in motion."
> Publius Syrus — first century B.C.

Uninterested in spending his money in a great show of personal wealth, he kept his salary at $68,000 a year and took no bonuses though he gave them frequently and unexpectedly to employees who had done good work. His message was clear for all to read. He was tying his personal fortune to his company's fortunes. When Richard Nixon was elected president, his well-known antipathy for Kennedy and Johnson's Great Society caused nervous sellers to bail out of the market. Perot lost six hundred million dollars overnight—more money in one day than anyone else in history.

At the same time that he was suffering business reverses, Perot never faltered in his staunch patriotism. At the request of President Richard Nixon, Perot became involved in activities that led to covert operations. Nixon asked Perot to seek to improve the treatment of U.S. POWs known to be imprisoned in Southeast Asia. The job was a political ploy. Because he had supported Lyndon Johnson, Perot was no friend of Nixon's. But Nixon had no interest in taking action on the POW issue. He merely wanted to give the appearance that he was taking action.

Perot was not supposed to succeed, but he tackled the problem from every angle, determined to "bring the boys home." He soon realized that he had no clout in the "military-industrial complex." EDS was a service organization. It supplied nothing directly to the military or the Central Intelligence Agency, with whom he began dealing. To gain clout, he determined to take control of his first client, Collins Radio Company, an important CIA and military contractor.

In March Perot announced he was seeking 1.5 million common shares of Collins to add to the 75,000 he already held. If he were successful, EDS would own fifty-one percent of Collins' outstanding shares. With the consent of the ten institutional shareholders who controlled another million shares of Collins, he would gain control of the company—and the attention of the CIA.

Arthur Collins, the company founder and president, regarded Perot's efforts as what would later become known as a hostile takeover. Pursuing an "anyone-but-Perot" attitude, he approached several rival companies seeking a merger. The large stockholders, including Chase Manhattan Bank, sided with Collins. Perot was forced to withdraw the tender offer. Disgruntled, he sought to help the POWs in other ways without the help of the CIA.

At the height of the Vietnam war in December 1969, he flew to Hanoi with a planeload of Christmas dinners for the American prisoners. The mission failed because he was refused landing rights. But it succeeded beyond his (and Nixon's) wildest dreams. It publicized the plight of the POWs and did much to win sympathy in mainstream America and the international community. Perot continued his work until the prisoners were released at the end of the war in 1972.

That same year Arthur Collins, who in 1971 had succeeded in merging his company with North American Rockwell, lost his job as president of the company he founded. Whether Perot would have forced him out if EDS had made the merger will never be known. Despite an agreement that Collins Radio should remain a separate entity, Arthur Collins was no longer listened to at the end of the first quarter, his company's name disappeared, and he left his thirty-nine-year-old company January 14, 1972.

Meanwhile, H. Ross Perot continued to rebuild his business. He had learned a painful but valuable lesson in the stock market crash of 1969. As the seventies dawned, he began to diversify. He stepped down as president of EDS and devoted himself to insuring that such a disaster would never occur again. How well he succeeded will be seen.

He diversified by buying Wall Street Leasing, a subsidiary of retail stockbroker Dupont Glore Forgan, Inc., and invested $10 million in the firm. When a merger was arranged with another brokerage house, Perot actually lost money, but the emergent company was stronger than ever.

At the same time, Perot recognized that the niche created by IBM in 1962 was disappearing from the American business scene. Hardware was much more sophisticated and affordable. Above all, small, relatively inexpensive machines had almost unlimited data capacity. Software had been created to run almost any program to procure any bits of data a company might want. Data of all kinds were being stored all over the country and were readily available for a small price. Companies no longer needed outside service providers. They could hire college or even high school graduates to do their in-house corporate data processing.

EDS evolved a new mission statement in the 1970s when it entered the sale of turnkey systems of hardware, software, and peripheral equipment. Every sale was geared to the specific needs of its users. Perot's clients were hospitals, small businesses, and credit unions. At the same time, he recognized the international market, particularly in developing countries.

In July 1976 EDS branched out into the Middle East. His first contract was with King Abdulazziz University in Saudi Arabia, whose rulers maintained iron control. The stable situation was perfect for EDS.

Unfortunately, the government of Iran was quite a different matter. The nation's petro-boom was about to run its course. The Shah headed a tottering regime. He had waited too late to share his billions with his economically deprived people. His efforts to set up a social security system, which might have sustained his people, were doomed by lack of funds.

Promised much but receiving little, the people were disillusioned. Their unease created a clear field for Muslim fundamentalists led by the Ayatollah Khomeini, who preached a return to the old pure days. He particularly targeted the evils of American capitalism, which he claimed had corrupted the country. Targeted evils were—among others—Bell Helicopter and Electronic Data Systems.

In 1979 Reza Pahlavi, the occupier of the centuries-old Peacock Throne, fled the country. The Americans along with the other Western enclaves were left to get out the best way they could. Perot moved heaven and earth to get his people out quickly without the loss of a single life. His "jailbreak" was greeted with cheers the length and breadth of the nation. His success, when President Jimmy Carter could not rescue his own embassy personnel, did much to bring down that presidency.

In 1979 Perot stepped down as president of EDS. His vice president and longtime friend Morton H. Meyerson became president, and Perot resumed his position as chief executive officer. With Meyerson as the president, the company sought and received extremely lucrative government contracts including one that streamlined and updated the United States Army's computerized administrative facilities and established a network nationwide.

The value of the company continued to grow. Perot could now enjoy the total economic freedom that truly wealthy people do. Rather than joining the rarefied ranks of wealthy dilettantes, he began to acquire objects of art that represented his great love for the United States of America and its ideals of individual liberty and universal education. He bought the Gilbert Stuart painting the *Spirit of '76*, one of the most popular images in American patriotic art. He bought one of Stuart's famous portraits of George Washington.

A navy man himself, Perot acquired Houdon's bust of Captain John Paul Jones, who uttered the famous words "Surrender, Sir! I have not yet begun to fight." With his ship sinking under him, the naval hero of the Revolutionary War went on to win the battle.

Ever conscious of the history of his native state, he bought John Neely Bryan's deed to the land that became Dallas as well as "the sublimest document in Texas history." Perot bought William B. Travis's February 24, 1836, letter from the Alamo. Written ten days before the fall, it asked for supplies and reinforcements and closed with the stirring vow, "I shall never surrender or retreat. Victory or Death."

Perot's greatest *coup*, however, was the acquisition of King Edward I's 1297 revision of the Magna Carta. He considered it the "basic document of all personal freedoms." He immediately loaned the document to the National Archives in Washington, D.C., for display alongside the U.S. Constitution and the Bill of Rights.

His lawyer Tom Luce brought the "Great Charter," the first statement that limited the power of a hitherto absolute ruler, out of London in a briefcase. When a customs official asked about it, Luce identified it as the Magna Carta. Since all Luce's papers were in order, the response was, "Very good, sir. Have a safe journey."

Perot loved to tell that story, which he considered an example of the attitude representative of a free society and a free world.

In that same year, 1984, he sold EDS to General Motors for what was then an unimaginable sum: $2.5 billion in cash, General Motors stock, and a seat of the board of directors. His already incredible wealth and power were doubled and re-doubled. Nothing that he could ever want was beyond his means.

Still he wanted to work—to put his boundless energy, brain, and body to good use. A provision of the GM deal was that EDS would remain in Dallas under its own name as a subsidiary rather than be absorbed into the other company. Perot himself saw the whole business as a merger whereby he would revamp the world's largest corporation. By using his computer systems, he would make it more competitive with Japanese auto manufacturers.

Unfortunately, his autocratic style did not sit well with the chairman of GM, who came to realize within months that he had a tiger by the tail. Instead of sitting quietly at the board meetings, Perot intruded into every element of the manufacturing process and began to criticize the company and its managements. According to interviewer Sandy Sheehy, "He seemed constitutionally unable to function in a bloated bureaucracy and equally incapable of keeping quiet about it."

His suggestions and criticisms rocked the GM brass to their foundations. Within two years they wanted him to shut up and go away. He became an embarrassment as well as an extremely costly mistake. To get rid of him, they agreed to buy back the 11.3 million shares of GM stock that he had received as part of the EDS deal. So eager were they that they paid him twice the stock market value—$705 million. For his part he had to resign from EDS and from GM and refrain from criticizing them thereafter.

Within a few hours Perot told seventy-five hundred people at the Detroit Economic Club, "There's something wrong. We just closed eleven plants and laid off thirty thousand people, and we just threw seven hundred million bucks at the guy who didn't want it."

> "We love mediocrity in this state. We'd rather have two hundred bad universities than one good one."
> —H. Ross Perot

For the first time since he was seven years old (almost fifty years), Perot had nothing to do. He was incredibly rich, but he was no longer earning a living by building a great corporation. He was no longer involved with POWs or protecting his people. His children were adults or nearly so. He was not a social person. He had no wish to impress anyone or to live the life of the idle rich.

What he chose to do with his life demonstrates his own boundless energy, his dedication to civic and social betterment, and above all his love of country.

In January 1986 Perot acquired the Pforzheimer Library of English Literature. Eleven hundred great books. New York investment banker Carl Pforzheimer had assembled the collection during the early days of the twentieth century. Among other nearly unique volumes, it contained the first book printed in English, Raoul Le Febre's *Recuyell of the Historyes of Troye*. Other works included fifteenth- through seventeenth-century volumes of Chaucer, Shakespeare, Donne, and Milton.

In the manner of people who enjoy total economic freedom, Perot wrote a check for fifteen million dollars the moment this single remaining private collection came on the market. While nationwide, museums and libraries were trying to find funding to make an offer for it, Perot donated it to the University of Texas.

Decherd Turner, director of University of Texas Ransom Humanities Research Center, received the books with the comments that he "would likely *crawl* to New York just to get a chance to look at that collection. Mr. Perot has changed bibliographic geography."

In response Perot said, "What does a guy who was trained as a sailor and worked all his life in high tech know about great books? The answer is, not much.

"Seeing documents has a special meaning for people. We couldn't have that spirit if Travis hadn't been able to write [his letter from the Alamo]. The worst mistake we could make is turning out large numbers of technological robots. The memory of the race, the rights of the next generation cannot be taught in high technology."

Perot's unprecedented donation was the culmination of his dedication to improving education in Texas.

As a result of his philanthropy accompanied by a certain element of control, communities on both sides of the Atlantic began to recognize Perot. In 1986 he was the third person (and the first American) to receive the Winston Churchill Award, whose recipients must demonstrate imagination, boldness, and vigor. Certainly Perot demonstrated those characteristics in abundance. He went to England to receive the award from the hand of Prince Charles.

At the same time he was the first recipient of the Raoul Wallenberg Award for a lifetime of service embodying spirit, courage, and dedication on behalf of POWs. The award was given in the name of the Swedish diplomat who saved 100,000 Hungarian Jews from the Nazis.

He was the first recipient of the Patrick Henry Award, an award created for a U.S. citizen for outstanding service to his country.

H. Ross Perot and his wife, Margot, are congratulated by President George H. W. Bush on May 23, 1990, the night of the first Patrick Henry Award. George H. W. Bush Presidential Library.

Personal friend Governor Bill Clements had asked Perot to head the Select Committee on Public Education to be known by the acronym SCOPE. Its goal was to improve public education to the point that Texas would rank better than forty-fourth among fifty states in percentage of its students graduating from high school.

Perot tackled the situation from a highly successful businessman's point of view. He assigned his EDS staff to work full time on the effort. After hundreds of hours of work and hundreds of hours of hearings in communities across the state, Perot produced the SCOPE recommendations, calling for the following changes:

1. Every teacher must pass a test of basic academic skills.
2. Funds for tax-poor districts must be equalized with those of tax-rich districts.
3. No student could participate in extra-curricular activities including football, the most sacred institution of Texas education and recreation, unless he passed. In other words—no pass, no play.

Faculties and teacher groups had little objection to the new rules. On the other hand, school boards in rich urban districts were incensed that they would have to share some of their taxes with poor rural districts whose children were getting the bare minimum in state funds. But the loudest screaming and protesting all across the state came from football dads' clubs and cheerleader and drill team moms whose children could no longer spend hours a day butting heads and prancing and dancing to the utter neglect of their homework in other classes.

Perot stood by his recommendations. He deplored the Texas attitude, which he described as follows: "Sports drive the school system, not education. You don't get in trouble teaching bad English. You get fired if you're not a winning coach."

When the SCOPE recommendations were implemented, schools slowly began to improve. Year by year more reforms have been added to the point where the president from Texas, George W. Bush, had cause to brag to Congress about the state's testing program and the real progress students are showing in 2002.

> "Knowledge—Zzzzzp! Money—Zzzzzp! Power!
> That's the cycle democracy is built on."
> —Tennessee Williams (1945)

Despite the sale of EDS, Perot still had plenty to do. His efforts at diversification had led him into Petrus Oil & Gas, his profitable energy company. He owned twenty-two thousand acres of real estate in growing cities. He and his son Ross Jr. were developing a huge acreage north of Fort Worth into an industrial complex and an airport. If that weren't enough, he founded a new company, Perot Systems, with money from a family investment partnership called HWGA. The initials stand for "Here We Go Again."

Perot Systems negotiated and eventually won the contract to design computer services for the Postal Service. To do so he began to raid the ranks of his former employees who now worked for General Motors. Of course GM sued, but Perot won the right to do both so long as he didn't show a profit for two years and the employees had worked for him before the merger.

HGWA saw another gathering of eagles.

Perot had become a keen observer of the Washington political scene and its impact on the New York stock market. He sold all his stocks during the summer of 1987, several months before October 19, when the markets went into freefall. He said later that he had watched the U.S. government doing stranger and stranger things. When he couldn't figure out why they were doing what they were doing, he figured it was time to bail out. Again he was proved right.

In 1992 the re-election of President George H. W. Bush, the first of that name to occupy the White House, seemed certain.

He had achieved a ninety-one percent popularity rating as his generals Colin Powell and Norman Schwarzkopf won Desert Storm before the eyes of the entire world.

Fought in the desert of Iraq over Saddam Hussein's appropriation of oil-rich Kuwait, the war had been a matter of a colossus against a poorly trained, poorly supplied, primitive army. The U.S. Air Force bombed Baghdad while the media photographed it through brilliant green night goggles. The Iraqi pilots flew their planes to Iran rather than fight. Iraqi troops, pulled off the streets of Baghdad and given weapons for which they had no training, surrendered to anyone who would take them.

When the army tried to curtail media access to the front lines, one national news team went out and found their own soldiers to photograph their surrender. When the team turned them over to the U.S. Army, the Iraqis still had their guns with them and hadn't considered using them. It was highly entertaining and practically bloodless—America's all-time favorite nighttime reality TV. Parents woke their children to see "the bombs bursting in air."

Even though Republican Bush had raised taxes after vowing, "Read my lips. No new taxes," there seemed little chance that he would be defeated. The Democratic candidate was a pitiful nobody from some nowhere state west of the Mississippi—Arkansas (for heaven's sake). What intelligent man would vote for a former Rhodes scholar with a former girlfriend who sold her story to the tabloids—a nerd with a checkered past?

Then Ross Perot went on Larry King's CNN talk show and changed the mix. He announced he would consider running if volunteers would send around petitions to get his name on the ballots of all fifty states. Millions of citizens responded, perceiving Perot as a refreshing outsider, different from the usual run of Washington insiders. He had never before sought an elective office. The other two candidates were obviously "politicians," a name that was synonymous with "crook" in many people's dictionaries.

The media believed incorrectly that Perot had indeed declared himself as a presidential candidate, when he had done no such thing. Then came a "dirty trick" as Perot characterized it on *Larry King Live*. He received a fake photo of his daughter posed in the nude. Accompanying it was the threat that it would be made public if Perot ran for president. With his daughter's wedding in the offing, he postponed his announcement.

Many people believed that he had withdrawn from the race. When his daughter was safely married, he announced his candidacy. Some damage had been done both by the media, who accused him of vacillating, and by voters who didn't know what to believe and chose someone who appeared more stable.

Still, his popularity was enormous. Whether people intended to vote for him or not, they watched fascinated. His Texas twang and his straight talk accompanied by pie charts demonstrating businesslike solutions were setting a new direction for politics. He spent fifty-seven million dollars of his own money in his race and changed the way campaigns were conducted. For the first time presidential candidates sought to attract voters through the entertainment world rather than through political ads and statements on news broadcasts. Bill Clinton, a quick study if ever there was one, went on the *Arsenio Hall Show* and played the saxophone. His wife was an elegant blonde with a feisty tongue who created controversy whenever she appeared.

Again it was all highly entertaining. Politics had become a show rather than a serious business. Conservative and comparatively colorless George Bush had come into his first campaign with the endorsement of Ronald Reagan. The polished Hollywood actor, who had been dubbed by the press the Great Communicator, had loved the idea of putting his hand on the man to follow him in office. Now Bush was in trouble. His understated air left voters lukewarm. His wife looked like everybody's mother. And he couldn't play a musical instrument.

H. Ross Perot makes a point against President George H. W. Bush during the first debate in Richmond, Virginia, October 15, 1992. George H. W. Bush Presidential Library.

Few could doubt that politics were changed forever. The media had won. The presidential debates were moderated by television commentators who asked the questions and limited the answers. Even the great party conventions ceased to be about platform, delegations, and floor business. They became media circuses with balloons and sweeping spotlights, confetti and dancing on stage in front of all the cameras.

On Election Day Perot received nineteen percent of the vote, more than any other third party candidate since Theodore Roosevelt. William Jefferson Clinton of Hope, Arkansas, won by receiving forty-three percent of the popular vote, a plurality of not quite six million votes. Political pundits declared that Perot's nineteen percent had been drawn from supporters of the conservative George Bush, who managed in

H. Ross Perot looking very presidential with President George H. W. Bush in the background, October 19, 1992.

the end to poll only thirty-seven percent of the popular vote. Whether they were correct is unknown, but George Bush fell from a height of ninety-one percent popularity to approximately thirty-nine percent in a matter of months.

Was it possible that Perot, who could not be "king," had instead been a "kingmaker?"

He ran again in 1996 carrying the aegis of his Independence Party, which became the Reform Party. Again strange things happened. Although he accepted contributions and matching government funds, he was refused a spot on the presidential debates, ostensibly because his low poll numbers disqualified him as a serious candidate. Though President Clinton wanted him in the debate, the Republican candidate Bob Dole, whom polls showed far behind the seated president, did not want any more competition than he absolutely had to have.

On Election Day Clinton's number from the previous election improved to forty-nine percent. Bob Dole bested George Bush's percentage by only one percentage point, giving the lie to the pundits who declared that Perot had cost Bush his second term. Perot won eight percent of the vote. Whether he would have won more or lost more by his appearance in the debates is open to speculation.

He did not run again in 2000.

Now seventy-two years old, he remains busy with his five children and his many grandchildren and totally involved in the things he does best—making money and spending it for charity and for civic betterment. Estimates are that he and his wife, Margot, have given over $100 million to various causes.

In recognition of his efforts for U.S. POWs, the Department of Defense presented him with the Medal for Distinguished Public Service, its highest civilian award. He has received many other awards for his support of business, for his support of the military, and for his service to his country and his state.

> "A feast is made for laughter, and wine maketh merry;
> but money answereth all things."
> Ecclesiastes 10:9, *The Holy Bible*, KJV

Comer Cottrell
"Education and Access"

On November 7, 1999, Comer Cottrell threw a fabulous party for his new bride Felisha. The Adolphus was the scene. Dallas's famous Beaux Arts hotel was built in 1912 by Adolphus Busch, brewer of one of the best-selling beers in the world. Even in a city with an ever-widening selection of first-class hotels, the four-star Adolphus offers every luxury the traveler or in this case celebrator could imagine. Located in the center of downtown, the hotel opened its ballrooms to guests from all over the state and the country. The beautiful people that were Cottrell's friends came in limousines and taxis to help him celebrate his wedding.

Felisha loved flowers, particularly their scent, so her indulgent groom had the place decorated with $30,000 worth of her favorite gardenias and roses. She loved music. Two bands were hired to play, so the guests were always entertained. Her gown, made expressly for her from her own design, cost $28,000. Nothing was too extravagant for the Dallas social season wedding where everything is a little bit bigger and a little bit more than most other places in America.

Champagne flowed and the menu featured both exotic and "down home" dishes in keeping with the groom's Alabama roots. No amount of money was spared to make the evening memorable. In all, the wedding cost a quarter of a million dollars.

It was not an outrageous price considering that the groom was the founder of the largest black-owned firm in the

Southwest and one of the most profitable in the United States. To please his new bride, to return invitations from countless wealthy friends and associates, and to anticipate the sale of his hugely successful business, the celebration might be termed restrained.

But for Comer Cottrell it represented another peak in his life—another step upward from his modest beginnings.

> "Oh, Lord, won't you buy me a Mercedes-Benz,
> My friends all drive Porsches,
> I must make amends."
> —Janis Joplin, 1970

Comer Cottrell was born into a middle-class predominantly white neighborhood in Mobile, Alabama. Though he wasn't able to ride the bus or go to school with some of the same children he played with, he never felt slighted, different, or inferior to anyone. He was happy with the way things were. He had no intense desire to change anything.

Comer Cottrell, founder of Pro-Line Products. His lapel pin signifies he is an honorary Texas Ranger.

His mother, Helen Coleman Cottrell, instilled a sense of self-worth and pride in both Comer and his brother, James. She always said they were just as smart as the other boys. She encouraged them in their studies and in their adventures around the neighborhood.

Not uncomfortably poor but not well-to-do by any measure, Cottrell did what hundreds of other boys like him did across the South in 1931 when jobs were scarce and the Depression was sapping the economy. He went to school and he followed his father on his job, learning how to work at different tasks. Learning has always been the most important part of his life.

In those days when so many men were out of work, few people had bank accounts or the ability to write checks. Most workmen were paid in cash. They brought it home and gave their wives household money. Every penny had to be saved and doled out carefully. The family business was done on a cash and carry basis. They paid their bills in person at the offices of the utility companies. Few people afforded even the price of a three-cent stamp and an envelope to mail the payment in.

When he was eight, Comer accompanied his father on visits to clients. Cottrell Sr. sold insurance door to door. To ensure that his clients kept up the payments, he returned each week to collect cash money. Salesmen selling everything from Bibles to vacuum cleaners operated in that way in 1939 because direct collection was the only way for most people to make payments.

Cottrell recalled those visits that gave him a sense of business and its possibilities. "It gave me a lot of pride to see him walk into those people's homes, sit down in the living room, and talk to them about when they die and how he would give them money to bury them. At that age I didn't think people ever died. He [Cottrell's father] gives them a receipt, a little piece of paper, and he comes back every week and gets money from them until they die. My God, I thought, this is business? I love it!"

His enthusiasm carried over into the next year. At nine, he and in his eight-year-old brother, Jimmy, became business partners. Walking home from school one day, they noticed a blind man was having trouble feeding and caring for his rabbits. Cottrell asked if they could feed the animals and clean their cages for a payment of one rabbit a week.

Within a short while their rabbits did what rabbits love to do, and the boys had a large supply of them. Easter came and their business expanded as they took in employees—their classmates—who were encouraged to sell rabbits to friends and families around the neighborhood for Easter pets. When Easter was over, the supply of rabbits increased again. Eventually, the Cottrell brothers began selling their rabbit pelts to furriers and meat to depression-stricken families eager for fresh protein, but the sales were sporadic.

Comer sought a job with a steadier income. As he said, "Easter only comes once a year and you've got to have a [constant] source of revenue." He took a job as a delivery boy at a drugstore. He had become a salaried employee when his mother made him quit. She had learned that the store manager needed to give the job to a man who was out of work. Though Comer was disappointed and upset, his mother pointed out that by thinking of others before himself, he was doing the right thing. She always told him that he and his brother could do whatever they set their minds to do. "Nobody can do it better," she would say. The most menial tasks were to be performed with pride. If a thing is worth doing, it is worth doing right.

They were lessons he did not forget throughout his business career. They carry over today into his golden retirement.

> "I never took a job for money.
> It was always to learn."
> —Comer Cottrell

Cottrell went on to graduate at seventeen from Heart of Mary High School in Mobile. He joined the United States Air Force at the time when President Harry S. Truman, himself a military man, had ordered the armed services fully integrated. Comer's natural ability, his education, and his entrepreneurial spirit enabled him to rise swiftly in the first integrated squadron.

Promoted to first sergeant and stationed on Okinawa, he managed the PX there. In that job he first noticed that the post-exchange sold no hair products for black men. Though twenty percent of the air-

Comer Cottrell in 1948—a proud member of the newly integrated United States Air Force.

men were black, the young supply sergeant was met with almost the same argument used to answer Oveta Culp Hobby when she asked for beauty shops for her WACs. He was told that special products for blacks were unnecessary and offered other products that just didn't really work. When he insisted, his requests were dismissed.

His superiors' attitudes reflected the resentment that many whites were feeling at this forced integration. They told him if black men thought they needed something special for their hair, they could write home and have their families send it to them.

Comer never forgot their arguments. He also learned that there were very few products suitable to straighten and control very curly hair so it could be arranged in a fashionable style.

He came back home at the end of his tour of duty but left soon after to go to college for a year at the University of Detroit. College wasn't for him. In 1952 he left school to go to work at various places and tried to start several short-lived businesses with little market analysis or capitalization. Not surprisingly, they went bust in a very short time. He married and he and his wife had a daughter, Renee. In 1961 he and a partner started a construction and drywall sales company.

He recalls that time as the toughest in his life. He came home at Christmas to a find his daughter and a friend surrounded by candles. He thought they were really in the holiday mood until his wife told him the lights had been cut off for nonpayment of the bill. About the time he got the lights back on, the water was cut off. He had a friend at the water department who came out and turned it back on without Cottrell's paying the bill. He did the same thing with the gas company's bill.

Cottrell's business limped along, sometimes going well, sometimes going poorly. He finally decided that he had to go back to work at a steady job to support his growing family. Two sons, Comer III and Aaron, had come along in the meantime. In 1964 he took a job at Sears Roebuck where he worked as a sales manager to supplement his income. In 1965 disaster struck his company as it did most of South Central Los Angeles.

The Watts riots erupted. Cottrell's partner went to the bank to withdraw cash to pay their employees. The story that his partner told was that he saw people running out of stores with stolen goods and merchandise in their arms. "He stopped his car and went into a liquor store to steal. His car was broken into and he lost the payroll," Cottrell recalled. "He didn't know what happened, but he lost the money trying to steal liquor."

The partner and the business disappeared as a result of the fearful violence that rocked the country. Fortunately, Cottrell had already gone to work for Sears Roebuck. Otherwise, his family might have suffered greatly.

Comer Cottrell readily admits that he is a poor judge of character. His experiences when he has tried to help people have in most cases been greatly rewarding, but in some cases they have been devastating. In this case, however, the partner's lack of character destroyed the company.

> "Come away; poverty's catching."
> —Aphra Behn

Cottrell continued to work for the country's largest retailer at that time as a sales manager until 1969. While he would never have gotten rich, if he had continued, Sears profit-sharing plan would have given him a comfortable retirement in twenty-five or thirty years, but his entrepreneurial spirit still burned.

In 1968 three colleagues at Sears approached Cottrell with an idea to market cosmetics to blacks. One had read an article in the *Wall Street Journal* about a successful black hair care company in Watts. Cottrell remembered the problems involved in getting supplies in the air force. One company, Johnson Products, dominated the market, but their product line was limited.

Color television and an explosion of entertainment all across America had created a deep desire among ordinary Americans to look beautiful. As more and more people of all colors and heritages realized the American dream, products and services long been thought luxuries became virtual necessities. The beautiful people of Hollywood were no longer unreachable icons in the dark in movie theatres. They were in people's homes only a few feet away. Not just women but men all wanted to look the best they could look, and the surging economy enabled them to accomplish their goals.

Manufacturers of beauty products for women—Revlon, Avon, and Mary Kay—were making millions of dollars daily. It seemed to Cottrell that the whole spectrum of black beauty products had yet to be explored. He had the idea that a marketing niche of enormous value was awaiting those with the products to fill it. With partners to provide capital, he began.

In 1970 the "Afro" hairstyle was coming into popularity. After years of straightening and pomading their hair, African-Americans were letting it grow and "picking" it out into a bush around their heads. It became a symbol of the emerging acceptance of blackness and a source of black pride. While taking advantage of the natural curl, the style required special products to give it a desirable body and shine. Although *avant-garde* young white people were adopting the style too, it was a segment of the market that white hair-care conglomerates mistakenly viewed as insignificant.

Cottrell approached some chemical companies in the Los Angeles area to see if they could create products to enhance the new style. When one agreed to begin experiments, he and his partners took the big leap. With only $600 and a borrowed typewriter, they rented a 700-square-foot warehouse in South Central Los Angeles and began the Pro-Line Corporation. To get a reprieve on paying the rent for six months, Cottrell agreed to make improvements on the warehouse.

The $600 wasn't a sufficient advance payment for a company to manufacture his formula. The situation looked hopeless until he finally convinced two small firms to take a chance on him. The chemical company continued to work and rather quickly developed the formula for the product Cottrell had in mind. The other agreed to package the goods. He entered the cosmetics market with an oil-based hairspray that supplied sheen.

The product had a faint strawberry fragrance that appealed to the young men and women who had embraced the Afro style. The black spray can decorated with a gold hair pick bespoke "cool and hip" to the young purchasers. Pro-Line had made a big breakthrough in an underserved market.

Cottrell himself promoted the product to black barbers and beauticians. It was instantly popular, enabling him to pay off his manufacturer in less than a month.

His next sale came when he approached the U.S. Air Force, where he still had access and connections. Trading on his veteran's status, he received a contract to sell his products at a military exchange in California where many black soldiers purchased their toiletries.

Ambitious and spurred on by his first small successes, he sought to expand. Other products including hair sprays, conditioners, and shampoos swiftly followed. A year later two more businessmen invested $10,000 each in Pro-Line. Cottrell's three business partners, satisfied with their return of investment, sold their shares of the company. Comer's brother James bought one of their interests.

The Cottrells soon realized they had nowhere to go but out of California. Their first efforts in nationwide distribution involved the brothers' driving their own truck. They loaded their products and took off to the city that offered the most opportunities for black success in black businesses—New Orleans.

> "I was raggedy and broke and had to sell a
> case of hair spray to be able to eat and buy gas."
> —Comer Cottrell

Both brothers were aware of a potential problem they faced in leaving California for the southeastern part of the United States. Cottrell was planning to travel through the Deep South where many still harbored deep resentments against black people. Though fifteen years had passed since the Supreme Court had ruled to desegregate the public school system, many places in the South still violently resisted integration.

Other rulings had followed that had garnered unreasonable hatred among southern businessmen. In 1964 in the Heart of Atlanta Motel case, the Supreme Court had driven another thorn into the side of white southerners when it declared that private discrimination in public accommodations (namely a motel on two interstate highways) was unlawful. Businesses renting rooms for the night on public access highways were ordered to rent to whomever drove in first.

Moreover, the brothers were terribly aware that Dr. Martin Luther King Jr. had been assassinated in Memphis less than two years before. Two black men, traveling across the country, doing business in entrepreneurial style, were likely to fan flames among protectionist groups. The physical danger was very real. The chances they took only underscore their determination to succeed. Whether by luck or by the good sense to avoid trouble spots, the Cottrells encountered no problems on their sales trips.

Their perseverance and fearlessness paid off. They had succeeded in taking their product into the heart of its market. By 1973 Pro-Line earned its first million. In 1975 Cottrell opened his first distribution center in Birmingham, Alabama, the state with the second-highest black population in the U.S.A.

Still he was having trouble placing his products because Johnson Products Company dominated the marketplace. Never shy about asking for help and advice, Cottrell contacted Johnson. The person he met with was Isabell Paulding, one of Johnson's managers. The former Miss Black Alabama was taken with the charming, ambitious Cottrell. She saw him as polished, knowledgeable, yet eager to learn. Moreover, his company was on the move upward. Above all, she saw an ambitious man with whom she could further her own dreams. She went into his firm and into his life as his third wife.

Together they worked to create an entire line for the black woman whose skin and hair were enhanced by tints and colors very different from those sought after by white women.

In 1979 the company created the Curly Kit—a do-it-yourself home permanent that tamed very curly hair into glossy ringlets. For young and old black women everywhere, it was a solution that allowed them to manage their hair and arrange it in an attractive, easily maintained style. Men bought it too when Michael Jackson changed his hairstyle from the Afro to shining ringlets and curls. The product became an industrial icon and boosted Pro-Line's sales from $1 million a year to $10 million in six months.

Armed with a fresh cash flow, Cottrell relocated his company to Dallas, a town that had everything he needed to go national and even international. It was a hub for both land and air transportation thereby providing more efficient product distribution. It was relatively cheap in comparison to Los Angeles, which was becoming one of the most expensive cities in America. Most important, Dallas had shed a great many of its southern prejudices. Money was the entry ticket into the entrepreneurial society.

The Cottrells were welcomed everywhere. As a Republican and a conservative, Comer was welcomed into the Dallas business establishment. He quickly became the first black elected to the Dallas Citizens Council.

At the same time his company suffered growing pains. They were the kind of pains known to people like Michael Dell, whose company moved its operations again and again over the first years—always to bigger facilities. For Cottrell the money enabled them to make the move, but the move cost them more than its own expenses. Production lines had to shut down. "Here we were moving our equipment from California to Texas," he remembered. "We couldn't keep up with the orders [for Curly-Kit]."

He caught up quickly however. Working like a demon to increase his market share, Cottrell turned Pro-Line into a business rival with Johnson Products and Soft Sheen. It became the fourth-largest ethnic beauty enterprise in the United States. He became the owner of the largest black-owned firm in the Southwest. Pro-Line was one of the most profitable black companies in North America. Because of the owner's prominence, it was certainly the best-known black-owned business.

Seeking further markets, he took his products international. He set up licensing and royalty arrangements with firms in Nigeria, Kenya, the Caribbean, and Taiwan. Brazil, with an Afro-Brazilian population of 22 million, became a major goal for expansion. He purchased the brand of a hair care company in Brazil to achieve his goal of expanding into their market. As others before him had learned, the time was fast approaching when the way for Pro-Line to grow substantially was to buy smaller competitors or, ironically, to consolidate with larger corporations.

At the same time he was constantly expanding his profit-line, he was expanding his product line. He utilized sophisticated marketing techniques to target salons, individuals, and children. He added Kiddie Kit and Perm Repair to his lines. Later he added the Soft and Beautiful line and Just for Me.

He and his wife and his children were rich beyond anything he could ever have imagined when he and his brother Jimmy started selling rabbits. Rich enough so that none of them would ever have to work again. Rich enough so that he could provide his employees with profit sharing that eventually gave them twenty percent of the company.

He considered selling and living the good life—a sort of early retirement. Isabell convinced him not to do so. He could be a black man with a lot of money. Or he could stay at the head of his company, run it as he had been doing, and let it continue to generate profits that he could do important things with. He could become a beneficent figure in the community. She told him he would be a black man with a legacy.

He would be a truly rich man who could enjoy total economic freedom. He could use his money to do good things for the community.

So at fifty-five, he set himself to work harder than ever for more than money. At about that time he began his annual donations to his alma mater Heart of Mary High School in Mobile, Alabama. Each year $100,000 goes for scholarships for families that can't afford tuition for the private Catholic school. Additionally, in the late 1980s, Cottrell made Pro-Line a sponsor of the newly founded Miss Collegiate African American Pageant.

By 1987 he had turned Pro-Line into the fourth-largest ethnic beauty enterprise in the United States and fortieth on Black Enterprise's list of top 100 black businesses. In 1989 his company had risen to nineteenth with yearly sales of $36 million worldwide.

When the opportunity came for his most important contributions to the general good and to his own legacy, he was ready. In 1988 Dallas's historic Bishop College was forced to close its doors. Established in 1880 in Marshall, Texas, by freed slaves and Baptist missionaries, Bishop had moved to Dallas in 1961. The move was plagued by problems from the beginning. Financial irregularities and bad management clouded its future. Its collegiate status was impugned by scandal.

Cottrell, who held an honorary degree from Bishop, was named a trustee of the college. In 1981 when an audit revealed that the institution was in debt to the federal government for $3.5 million, Cottrell had been appointed acting chairman of the school. He had worked for five years to turn the situation around. He had arranged for significant layoffs and aggressive fund raising, all to no avail. It lost its state accreditation and was forced into bankruptcy.

Undeterred, he was determined to see that minority residents in southern Dallas would have a chance to attend college. In so doing, he became a hero to higher education for blacks. In 1990 he purchased the 131-acre campus with all the buildings for $1.5 million. Bidding took only ten minutes. He had tears in his eyes at the result; he had thought he would have to pay $5 million for the school. In fact, he had waited till the last minute hoping that some other group or individual would come forward. When no one did, he put forth his bid.

As his wife had predicted he was a hero of higher education and became noted as a philanthropist all around the country. Plans were in place for renovations that would have required Cottrell to use his clout to raise money to restore the destitute campus. He estimated $40 million would be necessary to bring it up to "not precisely what it was before. [Instead] It would be a college that is operated as a business."

Few could doubt that he would be able to raise the money. He was determined to have a college that serves the black community. As he told the *Black Collegian* "It was not just a purchase but an investment. I think a company that calls itself black, and asks for black support, is really asking the black community to grant it license to call itself that. And it has an obligation to give back." He felt that the local business community could have no greater return for their money than to invest in higher education. Their investment would be the perfect tie-in. The economic impact would be felt for years. Comer Cottrell had often said that he never took a job for money. "It was always to learn." Now he took his words to live by to the street.

Before the fund raising began, he was able to turn the situation to great advantage for everyone when he persuaded the African Methodist Episcopal Church to relocate Paul Quinn College from Waco, Texas, to the Bishop Campus. For the relatively paltry sum of $3.5 million, the AME purchased the campus and its buildings from Cottrell. He immediately contributed $1.7 million to Paul Quinn for renovations. In return, he insisted that schools of nursing, life sciences, and education be established to train teachers and nurses to work in inner city situations.

In 1989 Cottrell's position in the Dallas community was further acknowledged when he was tapped to be a part of a fourteen-member purchasing group led by George Bush Jr., son of the former U.S. president, to acquire the Texas Rangers. For a million dollars, Cottrell became the first black man to hold such a stake in a major league baseball team. Besides the prestige his new position offered him, he was truly accepted in society everywhere. He had access to some of the real wheeler-dealers in Texas. In a sense he became one of them. He frankly admits to tripling his initial investment as well as listening and learning as he talked and walked among them.

At the same time, he didn't stifle his voice when he became a member of the all-white Texas Rangers. He insisted that black people needed to be part of the baseball club's management team. More than just answering the telephones with a "black voice," in the front office, the team needed a balanced presence to belong in the American League. Through Cottrell's auspices, the team's vice president for Community Development was for a time a black man. Cottrell himself used his new position to induce affirmative action in the realm of professional sports. He was supported in his efforts by his famous friend Hank Aaron.

In 1990 he kicked off the "Say No to Drugs and Yes to Education" back-to-school promotion in company with the Dallas Independent Schools District's ongoing Say No to Drugs initiative. The program encouraged all Pro-Line customers to pledge twenty-five cents each, which would be donated on their behalf to support anti-drug efforts and grant scholarships. He considered the program the responsibility of all black business professionals.

Likewise, taking the time to be with children was a priority with him. One youth recalled that a field trip for Junior Achievement boys and girls in Dallas middle schools was arranged to tour the Pro-Line plant and offices. Part of the trip was a presentation by a speaker who turned out to be Comer Cottrell. The young seventh graders were treated to advice and counsel from the CEO of a major company.

As Cottrell stated in an article for *Ebony*, "I firmly believe that if young persons, beginning even during childhood, spent as much time as possible learning to verbalize their thoughts, reading business publications, practicing the business techniques of successful people, and learning the vocabulary of the business world, they could, by the time they are adults, be 'pros' equipped with all the necessary tools for success."

In 1992 he made another venture into education, the segment of society that would become the focal point of his life and his charitable giving for the next decade. He offered a $25,000 gift to Spelman College in Atlanta, Georgia, when one of its students DeShawnda Gooden, won the Miss Collegiate African-American Pageant. At the time he presented the check to college president Johnnetta Cole, he promised to continue his support and dedication to black colleges and universities.

> "Money is like muck,
> not good except it be spread."
> —Sir Francis Bacon

In 1994 Langston University's National Institute for the Study of Minority Enterprise took a group of black businessmen to the Republic of South Africa. Cottrell and his daughter Renee were among them. Renee Cottrell Brown was then serving as an executive in Pro-Line. The purpose was twofold in a country emerging from the long night of *apartheid*: to make connections with the country's established black entrepreneurs and to help with research and training of new black entrepreneurs.

During that trip Cottrell made the acquaintance of his daughter's secretary, Felisha, who was to become an important part of his life.

At the same time that Pro-Line was selling 12 percent of the nation's ethnic hair-care market for a total of $76 million in sales, the problems of a medium-sized company with a man approaching seventy as its president began to manifest themselves. The company had to grow, but the ways to do so were limited. The only ways open were to either buy a smaller competitor or merge with a larger corporation for which it had constituted a major competition.

Cottrell began to consider seriously selling and getting out. In 1998 he sold his interest in the Texas Rangers. At the same time, his wife of many years, Isabell Paulding Cottrell, sued him for divorce. She had been the one who prevailed upon him to keep the company in the mid-eighties and use it as a means to become not only rich, but also respected. She had encouraged him to make a difference in the Dallas community in the area of education and to use his influence to gain general acceptance of black people.

In March of 1999, three months after his sixty-seventh birthday, he put Pro-Line on the market. In a *Dallas Morning News* article, Cottrell reported that he had tried to buy two different black hair care product companies. In both cases he lost the sales. In one, he was sure he had made the acquisition when Revlon won by offering a bit more money at the last minute and giving the company's owner a high position in their billion-dollar company.

The black hair care products industry, having proved itself profitable, was being taken over by the white giants. Cottrell could feel that they were out to get his highly profitable enterprise. One step was to buy the companies he sought to acquire. Otherwise, he had no way to grow. All too quickly, the worth of his firm would shrink in the face of huge retail organizations such as K-Mart, Wal-Mart, and Target that sell to customers at forty percent less than the suggested retail value. Of course, such discounting takes more money out of the manufacturer's hands even though their products make huge sales.

In competition with Revlon, the French company L'Oreal had acquired Pro-Line's longtime competitor Soft Sheen. The Chicago-based company had been another black family-owned firm absorbed by a worldwide conglomerate.

At that point Cottrell realized there were no companies large enough to raise his company's market share. In effect, Pro-Line had no place to go. One way or another it was doomed. Though he claimed that the *Dallas News* interview did not constitute an official announcement, the business community took the interview as the first of several feelers by Pro-Line's owner to acquire a buyer.

Ownership of the company had already begun to change drastically. Isabell Paulding, having worked hard as an executive in Pro-Line for over twenty years, took fifteen percent of the company in the divorce. She granted her ex-husband the voting rights to her shares, thereby enabling him to retain control of the company. Twenty percent of the company was held by the employee stock ownership plan. To obtain financing for an acquisition that subsequently failed, Cottrell had sold seventeen percent for $10 million to Patricof and Company, a Wall Street investment firm.

Suddenly, he was left with only forty-eight percent of the company he had once owned in its entirety. Without Isabell's shares he wouldn't even have had the controlling interest to sell. Cottrell knew it was time to cut his losses and go.

He took sharp criticism from blacks nationwide when the word got out that he would be selling to a white-owned company with white top executives. "…that doesn't make a damn bit of difference to me," he said. The *News* interviewer noted that Cottrell raised his voice at this point. "If everybody is so concerned about black-owned companies staying that way, I wouldn't be struggling for market share."

In 2000 Pro-Line was acquired by white-owned hair-care giant Alberto-Culver for $75 million dollars. Though Cottrell had hoped to walk away with $100 million dollars, a condition of the sale was that his daughter, Renee Cottrell-Brown, would serve as Pro-Line executive vice-president and her husband, Eric Brown, would be its president. Cottrell himself was signed on as a consultant.

Pro-Line and its sixty-eight-year-old CEO managed to exit the scene in a burst of glory. Cottrell went to Chicago in 1999 for the American Health and Beauty Aids Institute Hall of Fame Industry Awards. The controller of twelve percent of the nation's ethnic hair-care market with $67 million in sales in 1998 earned the Sales Team Innovator of the Century Award.

> "My money is not their money."
> —Comer Cottrell

Since his retirement, many people have come forward to help Comer Cottrell spend his money. He mentioned he was almost overwhelmed by ministers asking for donations. He plans to spend a great deal of time analyzing many possible investments. But first, he gave himself the pleasure of marrying Felisha in an elaborate wedding at the Adolphus Hotel.

They are building a new house in Preston Hollow on Straight Lane where Ross Perot is a neighbor. Cottrell plans the house will be not just a home but also a place where he can entertain important people and continue to exercise influence. He hopes to open doors—both economic and political—not just for Renee and Eric but also for his sons Comer III, Aaron, Bryce, and Lance and his granddaughter. He wants to keep the company's identity in place within the Alberto-Culver conglomerate.

At the same time, he regrets that he has been a bad judge of character as he has worked to develop his new business venture, Cottrell Investments. Some people to whom he has loaned money have not used it wisely, nor do they seem particularly alarmed at the prospect of being unable to pay it back promptly or of losing it altogether.

Still, he retains his hopeful attitude. He says, "I believe in the Golden Rule. Anybody that does that will have success. Treat your customers, your vendors, and your employees as you want to be treated. And pay your damn bills!"

At seventy-one Cottrell is still looking forward to new ventures with the spirit of the true entrepreneur.

Antonio Rodolfo Sanchez Jr.
"El Patrón Criollo"

Standing on a flag-draped platform, looking out over the cheering crowd of men and women all of whom have cast their votes for you must be the ultimate thrill a man can experience. You've won the primary election. The next step could be the governor's mansion. The presidency of the United States, the seat of power for the whole world, is not beyond imagining. As you stand looking at their smiling ecstatic faces, you feel their confidence in you. The very air is electric with their delirious pleasure.

Your success is their success. Every one of them not only has voted for you but also has influenced others, perhaps hundreds and thousands of others, to vote for you. The confidence they have in you and the responsibility they have placed upon you must make you feel incredibly humble and at the same time incredibly proud.

A political party for the faithful and of the faithful celebrating a hard won primary is an explosion of noise, music, and color. Cheers ring out as people mill happily around in front of the stage. They embrace each other for no reason. Men clap each other on the back and shake hands longer than necessary. Some women surreptitiously wipe tears from the corners of their eyes. They are tears of joy and relief. All the hard work has paid off. The campaign trail that began months before has been long. They've dedicated uncounted volunteer hours to many mundane tasks. Some have encountered unpleasant reactions; some have borne downright calumny from the rival candidates' supporters.

What joy to know that all that work, all that effort, and all that time have been rewarded! No one thinks about what would have happened if it had gone the other way. And it could have gone the other way. They are Democrats. Texas is primarily a Republican state.

Red, white, and blue bunting drapes the hall. Signs with Tony Sanchez's name and picture are everywhere. A camera crew is present to record the events for posterity. Print reporters circulate among the upscale supporters getting quotes and opinions for possible inclusion in the story they'll write for tomorrow. A technician tests and adjusts the sound system.

All is in readiness for the great man's entrance. The noise level rises slightly. People crane their necks to see in the direction of the door.

Antonio Rodolfo Sanchez Jr. has spared no amount of money to make this a memorable evening that will inspire his supporters to greater efforts. It is the end of the first phase and the beginning of the second and more important phase of his campaign. The work will be harder than ever in the second phase. The sacrifices will be harder to bear. To be the next governor of Texas—the first one from the Democratic party since Ann Richards lost to George W. Bush in 1996—will require thousands more hours and millions more in campaign dollars.

A door opens. A cheer goes up. Sanchez and his family enter followed by his aides and strategists. Slowly, they make their way through the crowd, shaking hands, smiling, and embracing their well-wishers. Tony smiles broadly; his blue eyes glow. At his side is his wife, Maria Josefina (Tani) née Guajardo. Married thirty years, they are an ideal couple. Their beautiful children, Tony III, Ana Lee, Eduardo, and Patricio, all in their twenties, follow, smiling, caught up in the excitement of the adulation for their dad. Of them all, Ana Lee has the most political poise. She was a former Clinton White House intern.

Tony Sanchez with wife, Tani, enjoys his victory of Primary Election Night. Courtesy Tony Sanchez for Governor.

So picture perfect is the family group that a Hollywood casting director might have assembled it from hosts of headshot photographs. Keeping an eye on all the proceedings is his communications director, Michelle Kucera, who at one time was Tipper Gore's press secretary.

Tony takes the dais. His family gathers around him, perfectly arranged for the photo-ops the press expects to see and the constituency will note later. Texas politics no longer rewards spontaneous behavior. Television newsgathering has changed all that forever. Nowadays, candidates rehearse everything. A bad photo with a candidate looking angry and red-faced or committing some breach of better than good manners can cost many votes. And, of course, no one will ever forget if he misspells "potatoe." Errors of that sort can cost an entire election.

This night all goes well. Cameras capture the moment forever. Cheers ring out. Kucera can relax.

Tony raises his arms in triumph. More cheers. Smiling broadly, he grasps the edge of the lectern prepared to thank them all. It is magic time.

Whether he wins or loses this election, he vows in his heart and soul that he will achieve his goals. Why should he not? He has already achieved more than he ever dreamed. Like his father before him, who drew a fortune from the desert, Sanchez is a living, breathing example of American financial success. Now he is putting that success to use in following a higher calling. In that breathless moment before he begins his prepared speech, Tony knows that all things are possible.

> "Please allow me to introduce myself,
> I'm a man of wealth and taste."
> —Keith Richards

The heritage of Tony Sanchez almost requires that he be elected governor of Texas. Family tradition demands the electorate recognize him. His blood cries out for it. His family has been Texan for seven generations—longer actually than there has been a Texas. His lineage is purer and of longer duration than anyone else who has ever aspired to the office. He has educated himself and prepared himself. When the opportunity for leadership appeared, he was ready. To govern is only the next step.

Antonio Rodolfo Sanchez Jr. is a direct male descendant of Don Tomás Sánchez de la Garza y Barrera, whose own grandfather sailed from Gibraltar for the New World somewhere around 1690. The legend has it that the first Sánchez left Spain to escape the depredations of the Spanish Inquisition.

When he found the Spanish Inquisition even more powerful and more intrusive around Mexico City, he took his family hundreds of miles to the north across the Rio Grande to a land where even Indians had not bothered to settle. It was harsh, dry desert land, but with a wide green river running through it, a man could live free. Horses and cattle could drink from the river and graze on its green banks. There in 1755 Don Tomás founded the town of Laredo, twenty-one years before the United States of America declared its independence.

The blond, blue-eyed Spaniard, who had a reputation of fondness for the ladies, wanted to be a rancher beholden to no man, especially not to the King of Spain. He claimed his land where no man had been before at a crossing where he established Rancho de Laredo. He named himself *capitán de guerra y justicía mayor*—captain of war and major justice. He and his heirs governed for a century.

The success and the aspirations of his twenty-first-century descendant to govern the people of this second largest state in the Union are really a logical step. Today's Tony Sanchez has taken pains to look every bit the part. He has shaved his moustache and straightened his once curly black hair to a wavy gray. With his blue eyes, a gift from Don Tomás himself, Tony is the Spanish don of the royal court, the Mexican *criollo* of intellectual influence, and the Texas *patrón* rolled into one. "He is the best of Texas's past and the best of Texas's future." He is also the man who has benefited most from his family's remade fortunes after a lapse of several generations.

He was born February 3, 1943, in Laredo—the only large town on the direct route between San Antonio, Texas, and Monterrey, Nuevo Leon, in Mexico. More than 175,000 people live in Laredo according to the most recent census. No other towns of any size lie between the two metropolises. Likewise, it is the only large town between El Paso in the far western tip of Texas and the lower Rio Grande Valley—a metroplex of a quarter of a million people living where the big river empties into the Gulf of Mexico.

Sanchez is Laredo's first serious candidate for a statewide office. The town has maintained a splendid, stubborn isolation since Don Tomás founded it. As a result of the Texas Revolution in 1836, the town became part of the new Republic of Texas more by an accident of geography than political leanings. And the children of Don Tomás went with it. Why should they not? According to the legends, they were

Tony Sanchez displays his political image. Courtesy Tony Sanchez for Governor.

escaping religious and political oppression. With a hundred years of living in Texas behind them, they were more entitled to be called Texans than the Anglo-Celts like Houston, Crockett, and Travis who started the fight.

Over the century and a half since Texas became a state, Sanchez fortunes have risen and fallen. When Tony himself was born, his father owned an office supply and typewriter repair shop. The business earned between ten and twelve thousand dollars annually while the elder Sanchez traded oil and gas leases on the side.

Tony Junior described his youth in Laredo when two of his grandparents lived across the river in the sister town of Nuevo Laredo. His childhood was no different from hosts of other children all along the Rio Grande from El Paso to Brownsville. Back in the good old days when children were more carefree, two or three friends would come home from school, take off their shoes and shirts, and go fishing. The boys would amble barefoot down the dusty streets to the river. Perhaps a couple of little sisters would tag along. Of course they would be told to stay well back and stop whining.

If they passed by the house of a family friend or an aunt, they might be called through an open window to come in for some lemonade or some sweets. The object of these expeditions was not to catch fish but to be friends together and perhaps have an adventure. The special relationship of boys and a river, for example Tom Sawyer and Huckleberry Finn, too are part of Americana.

When he grew old enough, Tony worked in the typewriter repair shop after school when he wasn't doing other odd jobs and thinking of other ways to earn money. At this point in time, the periphery of Texas's declining oil and gas business where his father was buying leases barely touched his life.

Perhaps the spirit of Don Tomás burned bright within him. Perhaps simply being an American with the firm belief that hard work and ambition will take a man everywhere was more than sufficient inspiration. Tony made his grades in school. He traded on his Hispanic status and obtained student loans. He took part-time jobs. He worked and went to college at St. Mary's University in San Antonio. He was the first of his family to do so. Perhaps he would have gone to school in Laredo had his hometown had more than a community college. His father had been lobbying for a four-year university for years, but the state had not voted the funding. Laredo, with its huge Hispanic population, was perceived as not needing to provide more than two years of higher education.

In 1965 Tony earned a Bachelor of Business Administration. Four years later he took a Doctorate of Jurisprudence from the same institution, St. Mary's University in San Antonio, where he has since served on the Board of Trustees.

From 1969 on he was torn between politics and the wildcatting life of oil and gas exploration. Four or five days a week, he served as aide to Texas lieutenant governor Ben Barnes. His job was to backslap and *habla español* whenever a Texan with a Mexican surname came in to offer support for

Tony Sanchez at work in the Sanchez-O'Brien Oil and Gas Field in the 1970s. Note the dark curly hair and the moustache. Courtesy Tony Sanchez for Governor.

Barnes's campaign. He found he liked politics. He was good at talking to people. A friend who knew him then characterizes him as "endlessly amiable" without a hint of political philosophy.

Although the Barnes political campaign was eventually derailed by scandal, Tony gained much and lost nothing by the experience. No taint attached itself to him. Today Barnes is one of Tony's strongest supporters.

On weekends Tony drove home to Laredo where he followed his father and geologist Brian O'Brien down to their oil leases at the Lasker O'Keefe Hereford's Nopalosa Ranch southeast of Laredo. Directly across the Rio Grande, the "Christmas-tree" lights from a successful Mexican Pemex well sparkled brightly and tantalizingly in the hot night air. Those lights meant that a crew was working. Oil or gas was pumping, pumping, pumping over there in the darkness.

Unfortunately, oil on one side of a river doesn't mean that oil is on the other side. Indeed, oil coming from one hole in the ground doesn't guarantee that the hole drilled twenty feet away will produce oil. Exxon had drilled two unsuccessful wells in the brush country in the early sixties. No major discoveries had been made in a long, long time. The general consensus of opinion among geologists and their poor cousins, the wildcatters, was that the gas and oil reserves in Texas were all discovered and were eventually and inevitably going to run out. Legendary discoveries at Spindletop, East Texas, Burkburnett, and Midland-Odessa had reaped their huge profits and settled down to regulated, controlled production to sustain them through the next century. But no one really expected anything else.

No. The easily recoverable, that is, the highly profitable oil was gone. Surely, not an inch of Texas remained where the underground strata had not been mapped and plumbed of its wealth.

The true wildcatter doesn't believe any of this, although most of them admit that the strikes now are pretty few and far between. A true wildcatter sees and smells things in the earth and in the air that make his nose twitch and his heart pound with excitement.

In 1973 Tony and his father took a chance that wealth was there. Tony Sanchez Senior may very well have been the first Texas wildcatter in the tradition of Glenn McCarthy and Dad Joiner to be of Spanish descent. Certainly, when he bought the leases initially, he swore he smelled the gas. He told everyone he had the instinct that all the great wildcatters had for finding the precious substances where there was supposed to be none.

Of course so long as the wellhead price of gas was ten cents per thousand cubic feet (mcf), nobody was interested in drilling. Then the Environmental Protection Agency stomped and barged into the fuel business. Coal had already lost its place because of its impurities that heavily polluted air, water, and land. Oil, while better than coal, had problems with the lead added to the gasoline to give it stability. Besides,

America's insatiable gas-guzzling cars made the whole country dependent on foreign oil

And still homes had to be heated. A clean, safe fuel was the answer. The answer was gas. But gas became scarcer as it became more valuable. At the same time more uses were being found for it. The price in Texas rose to $1.68 per mcf. A well cost nearly half a million to drill and $3,000 a day to operate. But for that price the Sanchez men could make a handsome profit—if the gas were there.

Always, always the question with every wildcatter is the big "if." And so many drill until their hearts break over dry holes.

Then in September of 1973, farther north of Laredo near the bend of the river, Consolidated Oil drilled two successful wells. Although Sanchez-O'Brien's hopes were raised, Consolidated Oil's finds guaranteed nothing. They still didn't have enough money for start-up. Then Good Hope Refinery Corporation of Springfield, Massachusetts, contacted Sanchez-O'Brien offering a sweet deal. No one had any start-up money, but Tony and his father sold half of their leases on the Nopalosa in a checkerboard fashion to Good Hope. The corporation hit four winners in four wells on leases all around Sanchez's acreage.

Almost dead certain of success, Sanchez drilled on his ten- and twenty-five-dollar leases—that people had once thought were worthless—and hit gas at 7,200 feet. On Thanksgiving Day the new corporation plugged into a pipeline. Three more wells followed in quick succession. Southern Pipeline, a subsidiary of Good Hope, sold the nearly pure fuel to Lo-Vaca Gathering Company, who in turn sold it to their customers in Corpus Christi, Austin, and San Antonio.

With the money they received, the Sanchez family began buying more leases, 4,000 acres within the city limits of Laredo as well as other acreage in the town of Zapata fifty miles southeast. At the same time Laredo, the town that had been bypassed for so long, was changed forever. A quarter of a millennium of relative peace was gone forever.

Every fortune hunter and con man left from the old glory days of oil exploration descended upon the town. Famous names in Texas oil began to acquire leases in what has been proved to be the biggest gas field in the United States, perhaps in the world. Its size is believed to be twenty to thirty miles wide and seventy miles long.

Brian O'Brien, the geologist who was best friend to Tony Sanchez Senior, reported that one *trillion* cubic feet of gas have already been developed. His considered estimate based on past production and his own experience is that perhaps five to ten trillion cubic feet of gas remain in this area.

At a $1.68 per thousand cubic feet, the amount of return staggers the imagination. The Sanchez-O'Brien Field made its owners multimillionaires overnight. Not only did the three partners become rich, but many people living in Laredo became prosperous as well. To the surprise of many pessimists, not just a few of the old ranching families became richer. Citizens from all strata of society were affected by the influx of people, who needed workers and their support services. An area of relative poverty suddenly had more wealth than it could imagine what to do with.

> "South Texas got left behind.
> In the twenties, thirties, and forties...
> we didn't get the infrastructure, the colleges
> and universities, the expenditures for public schools."
> —Tony Sanchez

What does a man do when he has so much money that he can't count it all? The answer seemed logical to the Sanchez men.

They opened a bank.

In 1966 the International Bancshares Corporation (IBC) was founded. Its stated purpose was to meet the needs of small businessmen and to promote economic development in South Texas, a section of the state with tragically few financial resources. Its growth has been phenomenal. In thirty-five years it has established over 100 banks under its umbrella.

Soon after Sanchez-O'Brien made their strike, they invested in the bank holding company. From an initial investment of less than $1 million, their stake has grown and grown. Suddenly they've risen to the heights of *patrones criollos*. A *patrón* is a man who exercises authority over his people. In return for their allegiance, he protects them. At the same time they understand that he gives the orders. A *criollo* is the Spanish word for Creole, one whose blood is pure, who is a direct descendant of people who came from Old Spain.

While most people of Laredo responded favorably, some muttered under their breaths. After nearly three hundred years in Texas, no one's blood is pure. Just because Tony Junior has blue eyes, they don't mean a thing. They could have come from anywhere or anyone.

Money, be it old or new, makes a noise, especially so much of it. Its soft rustle is quite capable of covering up all the muttering. No one uttered a discouraging word when the family shared with the people of the area the rewards of the gas wells they had drilled.

The Sanchez family now controls the International Bancshares Corporation, which has spread to more than thirty communities throughout South Texas and the Texas Gulf Coast. A *banc* is different from a *bank* in that it may invest in all sorts of things so long as those things involve money and the investment of it. For instance, a banc may invest in insurance companies, in stock operations, and in savings and loans.

"[Tony Sanchez's bank] has prospered by doing things that few other banks are willing or able to do. One is to make loans to the Mexican American community along the border—one of the poorest parts of the United States and a place most other big banks avoid.... The other is to finance trade in the corridor between Monterrey, Mexico, and San Antonio." The last part of their strategy seems likely to garner more success and more money especially in the years to come. As Mexican trucks and Mexican services begin to roll across America, their success cannot help but create jobs and bring prosperity to a long neglected section of the United States.

On the other hand, the business of making loans to a people with few resources to fall back on when times turn tough has proven time and again to be risky. The cycle of poverty is extremely difficult to break. The reason why banks do not make loans to poor people who need them is because they have an obligation to the people who don't need the loans and who trust their banker to keep their money safe.

In this case since Sanchez was his own banker, perhaps he felt he could loan money in more risky situations than more conservative bankers might do. Still, his good heart provided no guarantee to ward off the calamities of others. He is not the first man, nor will he be the last, who has lost some of his own money trying to help people who have nothing but a strong back and only one way to make a living.

Part of the financial structure the Sanchez family chose was to establish Tesoro (Treasure) Savings and Loan. The younger Sanchez became the chairman of the board. He loaned and invested money as he saw fit. At the same time, he set about raising the image of his family in Laredo society.

He sought to establish his Spanish rather than Mexican-American origins. His home on 13,000 acres of ranchland just outside of town reflects the way he thinks of himself. According to Jan Reid, writer for *Texas Monthly*, he has built himself a mansion, not an adobe *hacienda*. When he chose the style, he studied and carefully modeled it after pictures that he acquired from Andalusia in Spain, the homeland of the original Sánchez.

Facing into a center courtyard are rooms looking out on beautifully landscaped fountains and riots of flowers. The Old World appurtenances include a wine cellar and a chapel where circuit priests perform masses for hunters and hands. Like Spanish lords of old, Sanchez's special pleasure is to take his friends and colleagues for hunts. Rather than gallop over the plains on Andalusian stallions, his guests roar across the

Tony and Tani Sanchez at their home near Laredo. Courtesy Tony Sanchez for Governor.

desert in off-road vehicles with raised platforms from which to shoot deer and javelina.

Despite the home, the lineage, and the history of the Sanchez family, Laredo aristocracy viewed them as *nouveaux riches*. The Benavides family, whose son married the daughter of Don Tomás, had assumed their place for over a century. Even today the name of Civil War hero Colonel José de los Santos Benavides commands immediate respect in St. Agustín Plaza, the historic heart of Laredo. People still tell visitors the story of how the colonel and his brothers barricaded the streets with cotton bales and saved the town from the invading Yankee soldiers. Benavides was the real *criollo,* they whisper.

At first, the Sanchezes, father and son, were confounded. Their efforts to join the *hidalgo* society were met with snubs and coldness. Their sworn enemy surfaced as longtime Laredo mayor J. C. (Pepe) Martín. Idealistic young Sanchez and his father fought Martín's regime by supporting local candidates and financing construction and businesses whose less well-to-do owners refused to knuckle under to the political machine.

In 1977 Tony Junior even founded a newspaper, *The Laredo News,* to compete with the historic *Laredo Times,* one of the oldest newspapers along the river. The battle was joined in 1981 when the elder Sanchez came under scrutiny from many sources. He retaliated by filing an unsuccessful $609 million invasion-of-privacy suit against the *Times* for using Small Business Administration records to estimate his private worth.

A full-fledged war erupted when the *Times* led with a story focused on Tesoro Savings and Loan, the company that the younger Sanchez headed. The story accused the family of drug trafficking—always a severe problem along the border. It claimed the S&L had laundered money for dealers and was continuing to do so. Tesoro, which already had a reputation as a freewheeling thrift, was damaged by the allegations.

Bent on protecting their investments at the same time they defended their reputation, the family waged a war of words against the entrenched *patrón*. Martín came forward with more serious allegations. According to his investigations, two of Tesoro's brokers had laundered almost $25 million in drug proceeds through the savings and loan.

Not satisfied with tainting the Sanchez family with money laundering, his investigation dug deeper. More allegations appeared that the laundering was done for the notorious Guadalajara drug lord wanted in the United States for the kidnapping, torture, and murder of U.S. narcotics agent Enrique Camarena Salazar. While the Sanchez reputation lay in ruins, the worst was yet to come.

In 1986 he was forced to sell the newspaper because it was losing so much money. The details of the deal were hazy, but it was executed in haste. No provisions had been made for the people who worked there, some from the very beginning. In an uncharacteristically cruel move, the Sanchezes told their employees to clean out their desks at ten in the morning on Christmas Eve.

For men with so much money, both seemed little able to handle it.

In November 1988, one day before the Internal Revenue Service was scheduled to freeze all Tesoro accounts, an unknown person purchased $1.7 million in money orders from the funds. After the freeze was instituted, Tesoro officers chose to ignore it and allowed the money orders to be cashed in and wired to Panama. The better part of $2 million going south, perhaps into the coffers of some drug lord, remains a blot that will follow Tony Sanchez wherever he goes in his political and professional life.

The Federal Deposit Insurance Corporation immediately sent in a team that included two outside law firms to scrutinize Tony, the chairman of the board, as well as the twelve directors and officers. Their conclusions were that the management structure was unstable. They were subject to questionable enforcement of adequate controls, policies, and procedures.

Closer investigation revealed "risky lending practices, reckless growth, conflicts of interest, questionable expenditures, weak internal controls, and noncompliance with regulatory agreements." Not the least among the discoveries was money skimmed off the top for the usual luxuries. The S&L was paying for two fishing condos for Tesoro officials, a hunting lease, and a plane owned by Sanchez Enterprises.

Tony's law school friend Tony Canales served as Tesoro's lawyer. He advised Sanchez that the savings and loan could not prevent the money's being wired to Panama. Officials were reluctant to accept that story. The investigation continued. Eventually, Tesoro Savings and Loan collapsed from all the bad loans it had made. Depositors lost their savings and vilified the Sanchez family for their losses. Even though a federal district judge ruled that the bank had technically done nothing wrong and ordered that the charges be dropped against the two men who had bought the money orders, the scandal remains.

What did Tony Sanchez know and when did he know it? How much did he know about the daily business of Tesoro? If he was not a good overseer, what does his performance say about how he will lead the rest of his life? Did he allow a drug kingpin's money out of the country when the poor, helpless investors were left with no recourse but to lose their savings? Should he have held the money orders until proper investigations could be made? Did he have a personal reason for letting go of the sum in the face of his own certain losses?

The investigation dragged on for six years. During that time Tony Sanchez Sr., the multimillionaire with the wildcatting spirit, developed leukemia. The tragedy of cancer—and the unfairness of it—rocked the family on its foundations. In 1992 he lost his battle with it. His grieving son buried him and assumed the leadership of the family.

> "If making money is a slow process,
> losing it is quickly done."
> —Ihara Saikaku, *The Millionaire's Gospel*

The Tesoro failure cost the citizens of Texas $160 million according to *Dallas Morning News* reporter Pete Slover. The money was spent to protect insured depositors and dispose of loans with "slow" payments, loans overvalued, or loans otherwise flawed. The S&L was $129 million in the red. Not until 1994 did Sanchez reach an agreement with the FDIC. He personally paid $1 million but never admitted wrongdoing.

Since the two outside law firms that investigated Tesoro for the FDIC recommended that the government file a $10 million lawsuit against him personally, the payment of a mere tenth of that without admitting anything seems less than fair. The citizens of Texas paid so much, much more.

The *Laredo Times* pursued the story to the finish, taking the lead for all the major newspapers across Texas. A feud once begun in a town that is ninety-four percent Hispanic does not cease when one combatant withdraws from the field. Indeed, an insult given or even an imagined slight will sometimes cause unpleasant repercussions for generations.

Tuesday after Labor Day in 2001, Antonio Rodolfo Sanchez announced himself the Democratic candidate for governor of Texas in his hometown Laredo. His wife, Tani, and children arranged themselves behind him in historic San Agustín Plaza where his cousin Santos Benavides fought the Yankees from behind a barricade of cotton bales.

This Sanchez was much different from his valiant cousin. He was nervous as only a man who knows that every word he says will be scrutinized mercilessly can be. He had purposefully pulled himself away from anything that smacked of Mexican. Today he was Texan. His speech bore not a trace of a foreign accent. He looked like exactly what he was—a very rich American oilman and banker.

As he said that day, "I'm not running to be first in anything." Certainly, he was not playing the ethnic card, calling on all the Mexicans living in Texas trying to learn the language and working at entry-level jobs. He was making an appeal to Democrats everywhere, those with Mexican names as well as those with European, Asian, South and Central American, and African names. As such he represents what Texas has become almost in spite of herself. It is home to hundreds of different descendants of immigrants who are exactly what he is—an American and a Texan.

At that moment in San Agustín Plaza he was at the height of his success in life. The more successful he becomes, the more of a threat he becomes to the Republican Party, whose candidates call him traitor because Sanchez had switched his allegiance from Democrat Ann Richards to Republican George Bush in Bush's second run for the gubernatorial mansion.

Many Democrats also label him a traitor because of that move and the $320,000 donation that accompanied it. Richards's margin of defeat was small enough that Sanchez's

loyalty might have made the difference. That and his contra-
dictory statements regarding whether he is pro-life or
pro-choice (almost a litmus test for both parties) represent his
waffling. Some want to know where in the hell he came from.

Where the Sanchez candidacy came from is an interesting
story in itself. Supposedly, he was asked to run by John Sharp,
the former state comptroller who is running for lieutenant
governor. Sharp, a longtime politico and perennial candidate
who lost to Rick Perry in 1998, concluded that he could win
the office he wanted if a rich Hispanic candidate ran on the
ticket for governor and turned out a large Hispanic vote who
could then be expected to vote the straight ticket. He
approached Tony Sanchez with the possibility.

Of course Sanchez denies the story. Why should he not? He
must be thought of as his own man. People must believe that
he had strong political ambitions that evolved over many
years of seeing the problems of neglect and poverty in Laredo
go unaddressed by the government in Austin. He must stick to
his scripted speech topics: education, healthcare, and economic development through job training even in prisons.
Reforms high on his agenda are the Texas Public Utility Commission, referencing the Enron scandal, and insurance
reforms. Opponents can find nothing to quarrel with in that
platform. It is identical with theirs.

What they wait for are his mistakes.

He has already made one that made the big papers statewide. At the end of April 2002, he accused Governor Rick
Perry of never having held a meaningful job. Perry has indeed
been employed for seventeen years in a variety of government
jobs. Few take umbrage at the idea that a man who has
worked seventeen years in government might have been
underemployed, but Perry was a pilot in the United States Air
Force from 1972 to 1977. He left service with the rank of
captain.

The Perry camp immediately arranged for a group of veterans to hold a news conference labeling Sanchez's attitude
toward the military as "insulting" to those serving, those

retired from service, and those who have sacrificed their lives. In a state where military service is an honored profession, particularly among Americans of Mexican descent, the news conference resonated.

Sanchez took college deferments during the Vietnam War. While the Republicans were cranking up that information, Sanchez's own camp had formed a "Veterans for Sanchez" group and quoted their candidate as replying angrily, "How dare he question my patriotism?"

Opponents will take full advantage of his past mistakes, and they are eagerly waiting for him to make more. And he will make mistakes. All candidates do. Whether the past scandals will defeat him or backfire against his opponents will be seen and evaluated later.

If the race gets tight, Rick Perry, the Republican incumbent, will pull out all the stops to gain re-election. Sanchez may try to play the race card—accusing his opponent of racial prejudice—but he may have trouble doing so. His own campaign strategy has been to pull away from the heritage represented by his Mexican name. He looks like what he is—an American. His speeches for his television commercials carry not the faintest hint of an accent. Even though his name is of Spanish origin, even though he can speak the language, his purpose seems to be to garner votes from all segments of the population.

Despite the problems with Tesoro Savings and Loan, the International Bancshares Corporation has been dramatically successful. It now calls itself the "nation's largest minority owned bank." Tony continues to serve as a director. Unfortunately, the *Bankers Digest* reported on May 6, 2002, that it had been fined $7,500 for failing to report its political contributions in 2000. To Sanchez the fine was insignificant. A man whose PAC donated more than $100,000 to recent federal and state political candidates can hardly be bothered with such a small amount.

Indeed, he is a man who now enjoys total economic freedom. In 1993 Laredo State University, which had opened too late for Sanchez to study there, changed its name and expanded its curriculum to become Texas A&M International University. As one of its first directors, Tony was instrumental in raising millions of dollars needed for capital improvements.

In 1998 Iris Sanchez died of ovarian cancer. The Sanchez scion demonstrated his commitment to Laredo and his love for his family. He dealt with the double personal tragedies of father and sister by funding a cutting-edge cancer treatment center in the form of Mercy Hospital. It is the only one of its kind in South Texas.

When the Sanchez children, especially Tony Sanchez III, complained that they had absolutely nothing to do in Laredo, his father set the town intellectuals a-buzzing by endowing a lecture series, not only first-rate, but first along the Rio Grande from south of El Paso to north of Brownsville. In memory of his father, who had lobbied since 1971 for a university for Laredo, Tony named it the A. R. Sanchez Sr. Distinguished Lecture Series.

Twenty-nine years after drilling its first successful well, Sanchez Oil & Gas Corporation continues to explore and develop operations concentrated in Texas. Tony Sanchez Jr. acts as Chairman of the Board and Chief Executive Officer. His political interests as well as his business education have enabled him to step smoothly into many important advisory positions. He sits on several boards as well as the Interstate Oil & Gas Compact Commission. In 1994 he was appointed to the National Petroleum Council, which advises the U.S. Secretary of Energy.

Laredo has prospered as a result of the Sanchez family's wildcatting success. Some estimates run to 75,000 new jobs created by their businesses, holdings, and activities.

Sanchez doesn't play as well as he might with many of the very constituents he seeks to impress—that is the Americans whose grandparents and sometimes parents came from Mexico across the river. When asked about him, some second and third generation Americans curl their lips beneath their moustaches. "He's a Spaniard," they say. And so he seems to be.

Like his ancestors before him, he holds himself a little above his neighbors.

That may be so, but none can doubt that Tony Sanchez has the health and education of the people of Laredo at heart. So far, he has tried to use his total economic freedom well. Whether as man of the people or *el patrón criollo,* the blue-eyed descendant of Don Tomás has done more than his progenitor could ever have imagined.

Michael Saul Dell
"Young Man in a Hurry"

In 1985 Michael Dell's new company "PC's Limited" had been in business something over one year. In the fast-changing world of personal computer sales, it was the maverick, using the direct sales model to customize and sell its machines direct to the consumer rather than through retail stores. Huge companies that sold their models strictly through stores paid it no mind. They considered it a fly-by-night endeavor.

They were wrong.

The first day that "PC's Limited" did a million dollars' worth of sales, someone brought in cupcakes with $1,000,000 written in the icing on each one.

In *Direct from Dell,* his combination autobiography, philosophy, and business strategies manual, Michael devotes one sentence to the occasion. We can assume the employees had some sort of party that day. Who made the momentous announcement is not recorded. Perhaps for a few minutes they slapped each other on the back, hugged each other, grinned and laughed. They might have given a ragged cheer and a fragmented round of applause. Perhaps they all had soft drinks as they munched their celebratory sweets.

Since it was such a special occasion, perhaps Michael produced his key, the only one, and opened the Coke machine. The company was so small that the boss still carried all the keys. If the boss was late, everyone had to stand around and wait at the front door. Fortunately, he was seldom late.

Michael Saul Dell. Archives
www.dell.com.

Party over, it was back to work because he and his employees were riding a crest, "boldly going where no one has gone before." They didn't have time (or wastebaskets) to spend celebrating (or outfitting a workplace). They were building computers. And they loved doing so. The sight of $1,000,000 on those cupcakes exhilarated them, filled them with ambition. Not to eat the cupcakes or have a party with confetti, streamers, and paper hats. They never thought to take the day off. Instead they got right back to work to exceed all expectations.

Of course, going where no man had gone before was exactly what practically everyone in the personal computer industry was doing in those days. It was all so new and so highly competitive. A brave new world was opening to youngsters barely old enough to shave. In the staid office buildings, machine shops, factories, and retail stores all around the country, the old models of doing business were crashing. But only the young people could hear the crash of metal and tinkle of glass.

The typewriter had suddenly become obsolete, but Smith-Corona didn't know it yet. Acres of typists and bookkeepers recording and transferring figures from ledgers were also doomed, but they didn't know it yet. IBM and Apple had built better mousetraps. Everyone's data, not just mainframe government and insurance company figures, were about to be processed in little gray boxes.

Still the capabilities of personal computers were only emerging. The young companies that built them still couldn't conceive of their possibilities. So they were building them all the same. Whether their names were Commodore, Olivetti, Tandon, Tulip, or Atari, the models would perform essentially the same functions.

And yet they were all different. Each had its own disc operating system and configuration. The software for one brand would not transfer to another. Therefore, the data they processed could not be transferred. Moreover, the companies were jealous. They did not encourage independent programmers to write for them. They preferred to have in-house personnel write their own software thereby severely limiting their versatility.

All the same, all different, but still customers were less than thrilled about buying them. In fact, they didn't know what to buy. They all had special tasks they wanted their computers to do; but no matter how long they looked, they had trouble finding the computers that would do those tasks.

The thinking was that everyone was going to conform to the machines. Business people who wanted to use them were expected to build their businesses around the capabilities of their machines rather than purchase the machines with software installed that would conform to and improve their businesses. Linking those machines together into ever stronger, more capacious tools was believed to be so far in the future that no one bothered to consider what might be needed to do so. Everyone did his own thing.

So the manufacturers of Commodore, Tandon, Olivetti, Atari, and Tulip turned out machines that were obsolete by the time they rolled off the production line. Salespeople who sold these computers through retail electronics stores told customers that the products they were buying had fewer features than the ones that were being manufactured at that time. It was built-in obsolescence with a vengeance.

Radio Shack even had their own computer that was different from all the others. The TRS-80 or Trash-80, as it was familiarly called, even used 8" discs for storing data when the established trend was toward 5¼" floppies.

Everyone accepted the computer industry despite its difficulties. Instinctively everyone seemed to know that it was the future. They just didn't know what the future was going to be like. The uncertainty made the whole phenomenon exciting and unsettling.

The captains of industry didn't want to know how to work the machines. That wasn't their function. They just wanted the machines to work. When they found their purchases less than satisfactory, they cussed them and left it to others to use them. Many men and women in their thirties and forties dismissed the new technology as glorified typewriters and calculators. The machines were expensive. Their performances were disappointing. So the managers didn't bother to learn to operate them. They lost out by the scores and in many cases their businesses lost out as well.

Young people with nothing to lose embraced the new materials. Computer stores sprang up in big cities all over the country. An IBM PC sold retail for $3,000. The software and other components that IBM didn't provide sold for between $500 and $1,000, even though they were much less expensive wholesale. The stores were making great money, selling a $2,000 computer with a couple of hundred dollars' worth of software and a board with extra memory to run the software for upwards of $5,000.

The stores offered no support. No guarantees. The sellers from storeowners to janitors knew little or nothing about the machines they were selling.

But every young person wanted a computer even if he didn't know what to do with what he had. Michael Dell was one of the few who actually knew what to do with a computer.

Why?

Because he'd bought an Apple computer for his fifteenth birthday February 23, 1980. His parents had allowed him to spend his own money for it. Because he didn't yet have a driver's license, his father drove him down to UPS to pick it up. When he got it home, he carried it to his room and took it all apart.

His parents were infuriated.

They were sure he'd demolished what was several thousand dollars' worth of equipment.

He tried to calm them down by explaining that he'd put it right back together again. He'd only taken his new machine apart to see how it worked. The next year, 1981, he switched from Apple to IBM, who had just brought out the Personal Computer or PC.

Before IBM came out with its PC, it went to several different companies and asked them to write software to make its new computer run. They wanted a DOS—Disc Operating System. The company that provided the software that they believed would best suit their needs was a very small company—a micro company. It was Microsoft, and its programmer, chairman, *etcetera* was another kid named Bill Gates. The IBM PC worked beautifully with Gates's DOS. DOS was a platform where almost any software could be installed so that it could communicate with the hardware. IBM was a respected name. Now that it had an efficient system, everyone wanted an IBM PC.

Soon all the programmers were writing programs for IBM that had created a very adaptable system, one that anyone's new components could fit into.

But still no one thought to carry the personal computer to its next logical step.

Enter Michael Dell.

A year and a month short of his twentieth birthday, January 2, 1984, he took $1,000 of his own money to register his new company in Austin, Texas. In May of that same year, he finished his freshman year at the University of Texas in Austin and quit school.

His parents forgave him eventually, seeing that he was never cut out to be a doctor of human beings. Somewhat later he was able to forgive his parents for forcing him to go to college for one year and delaying starting his life's work—building computers for the jobs people were developing for them.

As he explained in the foreword to his book *Direct from Dell*, he wasn't after speed alone but *velocity*. Velocity is the compression of time and distance backward into the supply chain and forward to the customer. In the changing world of computers, velocity was what he sought for his business. Because he understood computers so thoroughly and had a good sense of what could be done with them and what they could do, he knew that the speed with which they were placed in the hands of their users was primary.

His life has always been about speed.

> "I almost had to wait."
> —Louis XIV
> (on seeing his coach approach
> at exactly the appointed time)

Michael Dell was always in a hurry. When he was eight years old, he sent away for a high school diploma. In the back of a magazine, he read that all he had to do was pass one simple test. Though he really liked the third grade, he reasoned that if one simple test would do it, he could skip the next nine years and get straight into the business of business.

He sent away for the test.

Soon a woman came to the house and asked for Mr. Michael Dell. His mother asked a few questions and figured out what he had done. She called him out of the bathtub. He came out in a red bathrobe, still quite wet behind the ears and elsewhere. The two women probably chuckled as he trailed back to finish his bath, but he was a little disappointed. They hadn't taken him seriously. He had planned to take that test.

For him getting on to something more interesting was always the way. He simply couldn't enjoy an ordinary childhood. His father was an orthodontist. His mother was a stockbroker who frequently discussed "commercial opportunities" at the dinner table. Michael's idea of fun was making money. And he discovered he was quite good at it. At twelve he made $2,000 selling collectable stamps through a catalog he typed up himself with two fingers.

In 1981, when he was sixteen, he was making $18,000 a year selling subscriptions to the *Houston Post* to newly married couples and people who had applied for new home mortgages. He had observed and targeted the audiences himself.

Since the marriage license had to be mailed somewhere, an address was provided that was a matter of public record. He hired two of his high school friends to canvas the courthouses in the sixteen counties surrounding Houston and collect the names and addresses.

Then he found out that companies compiled lists of people who had applied for mortgages. The lists were ranked by size of the mortgages. He went after the highest paying people first, figuring rightly or wrongly that they would be more likely to need and want a subscription to the *Houston Post*.

But he wasn't through. He composed a personalized letter that offered them a subscription to a newspaper. "Congratulations on your wedding. Now, here's a special offer." Most bought it.

That was when he discovered that going to school could be disruptive to his business. He had worked hard to set this system up. He didn't want to throw it away. He had to work after school and on weekends because the subscriptions were coming in by the *thousands*. When he reported his income to his teacher, she was startled and probably disgruntled to discover he made more money than she did.

That was also the year he bought his first computer and took it apart to see how it worked. He quickly found out that Apple wasn't the computer for him. Though it was clearly the best on the market and had neat games, its system was closed. It wanted its owner to use only its products, just as the other computers on the market did.

IBM changed all that. It came out with an open system that would allow the user to install as much memory as he wanted, as many systems as he wanted, as much software as he wanted from everywhere. So Michael, with a great deal of hard-earned cash at his disposal, bought all the things that he thought would enhance a PC. More memory, more disk drives, a bigger monitor, a modem, and then a faster modem.

If computers had had hard disk drives in those days, he would have installed one. Though his wealth was far from unlimited, it was sufficient to buy everything he thought he needed. That fact alone proved to him that he could make computers to people's specifications for much less than they were being sold when marked up by retail.

He discovered that he could buy all the things that enhance a PC just as a shade-tree mechanic could buy all sorts of interesting nonstandard parts to soup-up a car. He simply had to go to distributors and buy in bulk to reduce costs.

In June 1982 he attended the National Computer Conference at Houston's Astrodome. He had his driver's license, and his parents didn't know where he was going when he left every day for the better part of a week.

He asked so many knowledgeable questions that exhibitors wanted to know if he were an OEM (an Original Equipment Manufacturer). He wasn't. But he quickly got the idea he should be. He saw his first 5-megabyte hard disk drive. Early microcomputers usually had one or two 360K floppy disk drives.

K stands for thousand bytes of memory. Megabyte means million bytes of memory. Today computers with double-digit numbers of gigabytes are routine. Gigabyte stands for billion bytes of memory. The capacity of present-day computers is truly astounding.

But as much as their capacity has grown, so much more have their functions increased.

The National Computer Conference turned Michael around completely. It did exactly what it was supposed to do. It enabled him to research the business. Everyone was there with everything that they had newly developed. Component manufacturers gave him their price lists and talked freely about their upcoming innovations. He saw what he recognized as one of those "commercial opportunities" his mother spoke of—something he had never missed since he was an eight-year-old trying to bypass nine years of schooling. He was convinced he could launch a business that would save users money, provide better support services, and still make a profit.

He was already buying components and adding them to machines and selling his friends and acquaintances the kinds of computers they wanted. His collectable stamp business had succeeded. His newspaper subscription business had succeeded. He was confident his personal computer business would succeed. It was something he loved. He went home imbued with the desire to learn what else he needed to know to outfit and sell computers.

His parents again intervened. He was seventeen years old. He *would* go to college at the University of Texas. He *would* become a doctor.

So reluctantly he drove off to Austin in his white BMW bought with the money he had made selling newspaper subscriptions. They should have known what he was going to do. He had three computers in the backseat.

> ## "I want to compete with IBM."
> ## Michael Dell, 1983

He began his business in his dorm room. Unofficially, of course, he was just upgrading a few computers for friends, but word spread like wildfire. Students who were computer "geeks" weren't the only ones who were interested. Attorneys and doctors whose private practices would be enhanced by computers rebuilt or built to their specifications came by to drop off and pick up their machines.

No job was too big. He didn't think twice about expanding his business. He applied to the state for a vendor's license, for which he paid $1,000. With it he could enter bids with all sorts of companies to install their new computer systems. Without the overhead of a retail store, he won all sorts of bids. He had to work day and night to fulfill them.

By that time he was eighteen and making money hand over fist. Unfortunately, the University of Texas notified his parents that he wasn't attending class.

His mother and father called him from the Austin airport to tell him they were on the way. He barely had time to stash the nine computers he was working on behind his roommate's shower curtain. He opened biology texts on his desk and tried to look innocent when his parents walked in.

They weren't fooled for a minute. They had come to intervene again. His father demanded that he stop all the "computer stuff" and get back to school.

Their intervention lasted three weeks. For twenty-one terrible days Michael was like a junkie deprived of his fix. Then he broke down. He went back to computers fast and furious. As he writes, "I knew in my heart that I was on to a fabulous business opportunity that I could not let pass me by. Here was a device that so profoundly changed the way people worked —and its cost was coming down. I knew that if you took this tool, previously in the hands of a select few, and made it available to every big business, small business, individual, and

Texas Money

student, it could become the most important device of the century."

Selling computers retail was predicated upon the idea that the buyers didn't know what they wanted and the manufacturer didn't know enough to give them what they needed. In a sense that attitude was what doomed many of the retailers. Buyers were becoming knowledgeable much faster than anyone had ever expected.

Michael had lived, breathed, and dreamed computers for three years. He knew more about them than most people. He believed without question that they would come to be relied on by every segment of society in a very few years. And customers would become more and more knowledgeable as they began to recognize the capabilities of the machine.

The way to give them what they wanted was to ask them and then build it for them.

That way seemed perfectly obvious to him. Why had no one ever thought of it?

He had the proof of his idea's viability in his own success. At that time he was making between $50,000 and $80,000 a month selling upgraded PCs to people in the Austin area. On January 2, 1984, he registered his company "PC's Limited" with the state of Texas and ran an ad in the classified section of the Austin newspaper.

He moved from his dorm room into a two-bedroom condominium, a move he didn't inform his parents of until months later.

In early May he incorporated his company as "Dell Computer Corporation." He moved his business into a 1,000-square-foot office space in a small business center in North Austin. He hired people to take phone orders and people to go out and buy parts. He hired three guys with screwdrivers to sit at tables and assemble the machines to buyers' specifications.

> "I decided I'd be a whole lot more credible if I
> had a location instead of operating out of my car.
> Maybe I ought to get a tie.
> Maybe not."
> —Michael Dell

At the end of May, he took his exams and left the University of Texas. He had the option of returning in January if things didn't work out, but he really didn't think he'd ever go back.

To his way of thinking, he had no choice. He had found his calling. He still had the only key to his company. At first they all started work at 9:30 A.M. Then as more and more people came to work and they were more and more interested in what they were doing, he opened up at nine.

He was recruiting directly from local companies and from their competitors, but by far the largest number of new employees came from the University of Texas campus among people who wanted to stay in the Austin area. When the firm had so much business he had to open up at 8:00 A.M., he gave the key to someone else.

He literally had so many people wanting to work for him that he never created a business hierarchy. The company grew too fast. He would sit down on the floor with a stack of résumés and deal them out as if they were a deck of cards. This person would be good for finance. This person would be an excellent manufacturer. This person could develop information and technology.

The business overran its space with alarming regularity. People were sharing cubicles. Salespeople would come in and stuff RAM chips into tubes to ship to customers as they took orders over the phones. The phone systems would get backed up until engineers had to come over and answer them. Dell Computer Corporation was a picture of American business at its dynamic best.

Dell Corporate Campus, Round Rock, Texas. Archives www.dell.com.

> "The Naval Air Warfare Center has
> Dell customer number 14."
> —Michael Dell

In 1985 Dell Computer Corporation introduced an IBM-compatible PC clone called Turbo. It was cheaper than an IBM because it didn't have the name on it. The sales force began selling it by phone and in ads placed in trade magazines. The clientele of businesses and experienced computer users grew.

He introduced chip sets into his computers. They were based on the Intel 286 microprocessor, but instead of requiring 200 chips, they required only five or six Application Specific Integrated Circuit (ASIC) chips. In this way he simplified his PC design and made the computers even cheaper to build and sell. Again they were sold only to order. Dell's inventory costs were still minimal because they could order everything they needed.

By the end of the first fiscal year, sales totaled $6 million. In fiscal year 1986, they totaled $34 million. He employed 100 workers and had expanded into a new 3,000-square-foot manufacturing facility. By the end of calendar year 1986, he had to expand into an 83,000-square-foot building in North Austin.

The world was going PC happy, and Michael Dell was the happiest of all.

Of course he made mistakes. He'd taken no classes in high school or college on how to run a multimillion-dollar business. The faculties and staffs of most high schools and colleges had no idea what a million dollars might be except a faraway figure. Early on he had developed a cash flow problem.

In 1986 Michael hired Lee Walker as president while he continued to operate at CEO. Walker, who had been a company president and venture capitalist, called up the Texas Commerce Bank and got the fast-growing corporation a loan and a line of credit.

Dell himself continued to talk with prospective customers constantly. He also continued to talk with his employees via their brown-bag lunches. He knew exactly what customers wanted through his sales force. They passed the knowledge on to the engineers, and the computers were built accordingly. The sales force itself was geared not to the product but to the customer. Some salespeople were experienced in selling to large corporations; some, to government agencies; some, to educational institutions; and some, to companies and individuals.

The direct sales model worked especially well for them because it didn't require the terrific outlay of capital for parts to build large numbers of computers to stock resellers and retail stores. As the users needs changed, Dell could respond more quickly to their needs because they didn't have a huge inventory to "use up" before they could shift to the next phase of the quickly changing industry.

Michael's requirements for speed and his recognition of its importance in the modern world were illustrated that year. Dell set up a booth at the Comdex show for computer dealers and resellers. They were one of the few direct sales companies there. They were the only one to feature a 12-megahertz 286 PC. (They had actually achieved a 16 MHz machine in the laboratory but didn't believe they could produce it in volume.) Twelve MHz was by far the fastest-performing machine at the show.

Both the attendees and the press lined up at his booth. The press wanted to know why anyone would want a machine that could perform functions that rapidly. The rest of the people wanted to know where they could get one.

PC Magazine put Dell Computer Corporation on the cover shortly thereafter. The machines started winning five stars for quality, support, and service. The key magazines were recommending them as a best value. The business community flocked to their doors.

By the end of 1986 they were doing $60 million in sales.

They had reached a crisis point. People were trying to throw money at them. They could no longer be a small company. They had to target the bigger companies and make the bigger sales. Yet, how could they do so and maintain what had made them great—their reputation for best support in the business?

They had to figure out how to combine those two things. If they did, then they figured they could achieve $1 billion in sales over the next five years.

> "The world is his, who has money to go over it."
> —Ralph W. Emerson in "Wealth"

In June 1987 Dell opened for business in the United Kingdom, which had—as twenty-year-old Michael had observed on his visit to London in 1985—a "high markup/lousy service phenomenon" that was easily the equal of the United States. At the press conference to announce the new venture, twenty-one of twenty-two journalists predicted failure. Of course, as they all found out, the customers—even British customers—knew what they wanted. The business was a success almost from the word go.

Buoyed by success, Dell moved into Europe with very little problem. They were unique. They stepped on no toes, because no one knew how to compete with them. The PC market had the same gaping holes where direct sales and customer support could move in effortlessly. When cultural differences appeared, they hired local management to head off the problems before they arose. Moreover, they were sufficiently capitalized to make their move efficiently.

Michael decided to take the first step toward taking Dell public. He and company president Lee Walker invited investment bankers to meet at their Austin headquarters. They settled on Goldman Sachs because they recommended *not* going public but making a private offering to a small group of investors. It was a slower way to go, but it would give the company a chance to grow a little more. The young man in a hurry (only twenty-two years old) decided to wait.

The private placement memorandum was published in July 1987. By October they were ready to raise $20 million. *And the stock market crashed.* He was sure they were doomed, but their investors were more interested in finding a safe place to invest their money than withdrawing from the market entirely. By the end of the week, they had $21 million. The following June 1988 they went public, raising $30 million. At that time Michael decided he needed to create his first board of directors. The market value of his three-year-old company had grown from its initial investment of $1,000 to a worth of $85 million.

In 1989 Tim Berners-Lee (not Al Gore) created the World Wide Web (WWW). Previously the Internet had been a system that allowed universities and government systems to transport information. It was envisioned as a device for the exchange of ideas between professors and research projects across national boundaries. Students could use it if they were seated at a mainframe computer in their libraries. But Berners-Lee's practical hypertext system opened the world. Users could get on line on their own PCs through their phone lines and talk to each other. At first few people possessed computers with those capabilities, but the ideas spread like wildfire—and so did the sales of replacement computers.

Michael, who loved to get on his computer and explore, saw the possibilities for commerce instantly, as well as the possibilities for support systems. He also saw Internet-commerce as a way to avoid problems altogether. In 1989 Dell had gotten caught with too many memory chips, as the industry went from 256K chips to 1-megabyte chips overnight. The corporation discovered that inventory of almost any kind in the technology industry has "the shelf life of lettuce." Suddenly they were trapped, just as their indirect computer competitors were, with obsolete materials. And they couldn't in good conscience deliver them to their clients.

What they had to do was sell off the inventory, which depressed their earnings to the point where the company earned only a penny per share in one quarter. At least they earned a penny. Many computer companies began to disappear from the scene as doomsayers predicted that the boom was over. Everyone who would ever want a computer had one for at least the present time.

Michael believed that the demand for computers would never be over. New machines with new technology must replace old ones just as the demand for telephones has never ceased. In the last ten years, those instruments and their capabilities have changed almost with the speed of light. No one seems to mind having five, ten, a dozen phones at his disposal. Indeed people consider them a necessity. Phones must be in every room of the house. No car is complete without one. They are as far away as your arm's length on the seats of airplanes. Every woman must have one in her purse; every man must have one in his pocket. Computers would be the same. Why have only one or two in a house? One for every member will be the norm because no one will want to wait for anybody else to get information.

Still mindful of the lessons learned when the company overbought the memory chips, Dell approached their next stage with caution. They had planned a launch of one product that would combine *all* the technologies in one package—a sort of desktop with graphics and disk technology, workstation, and server that would do pretty much everything. While still in the development stage, they took prototypes to the next Comdex.

Almost from the onset the customers backed off. They didn't need that much technology. Like stepping back from the precipice, Dell abandoned the idea. They had grown because they had given people what they wanted. They had almost abandoned their direct marketing concept to give their customers what they believed they should have. They abandoned the idea in a hurry.

It wasn't a total loss however, because some of the new technologies interested the customers. Those were incorporated into the new offerings.

Dell set their sights on relevant technology rather than trying to give everyone everything, when they probably couldn't use it. Rather than "If you build it, they will buy it," they were determined to design products based only on clear customer need and input.

As a result of this expansion of the original direct marketing model, many of their engineers quit rather than listen to their customers' needs. The ones who thrived allowed themselves to be trained in the buying and selling process. They only profited by their experiences. They were bright technicians to begin with. Soon they were able to function as equally bright customer relations persons.

Riding the wave of initial success, the boy wonder and his brilliant company swept out of the eighties and into the nineties, compounding annual sales at a rate of 97 percent. Net income grew even faster at a compounded annual rate of 166 percent. It was phenomenal. It was unbelievable. Growth was all they had ever known.

In 1992 when Dell joined the Fortune 500, at twenty-seven he was the youngest CEO on the list. His corporation had expanded all over western and central Europe and was planning to launch operations in Asia. They were still a small company, however. And the trend was toward consolidation of small companies, as customers didn't want choices. They wanted standard brands.

The situation was much like the automobile industry in the first half of the twentieth century. From dozens of car manufacturers, the United States customers came to choose among only three—Ford, General Motors, and Chrysler.

The choice for Michael and his company was stay small and face the prospect of being absorbed or taken over—or grow BIG. They were at $1 billion in sales, but that didn't really matter. They had to get bigger to survive.

So they violated all three of their own rules. They acquired inventory. They distanced themselves from their customers. And they determined to sell indirect. They started selling PCs through CompUSA, Price Club, and Sam's. They were selling well, but Dell had no real sense as to whether the company was making money on them. They began to convert their entire desktop product line to feature Intel's 486 microprocessor. They adopted an aggressive pricing strategy to drive their growth to $2 billion. They wanted to do none of these things; but if they didn't, they might not be alive at the end of 1992.

At the same time that business grew more precarious, Michael dedicated the Michael S. Dell Computer Lab at the University of Texas at Austin, a rather ironic development

Dell Corporate Campus, Japan. Archives www.dell.com.

since he attended school there only one year. Dell Computer Corporation announced their Critical Care unit, which was dedicated to even more rapid response for customers' service problems. *PC Magazine* named Michael Man of the Year.

With all these wonderful honors and recognition, despite projected revenues of $3 billion, the company almost didn't make it. They had outgrown their phone system, their basic financial system, their support system, and their parts numbering system. The factory system was stretched far beyond their original capacity.

They needed help!

> "What happened? And why?"
> —Michael Dell, 1993

The near calamity that befell Dell Computers was the same one that caused companies to disappear all across the United States. America was enjoying a prosperity that it had never known before. More people were making more money than they had ever made before. The baby boomers of the fifties had reared and educated their children. They were at the top of their earning power and looking around for things to spend their money on. Luxuries of the previous decade became necessities to them. Likewise, ever mindful of retirement looming ever nearer, they were looking for places to invest their money.

Technology seemed to solve both problems. The stock market went up and up, and electronic items bloomed and metamorphosed into ways of life. For the first time sales and purchases of shares on the NYSE were no longer carried on by brokers with their accompanying fees. Ordinary people could invest for themselves via the Internet. And the staid brokerage houses were forced to lay off people by the hundreds.

Computers were more important than ever. As Michael had predicted, every family had to have one. Indeed, some family members had to have at least two.

Dell Computers was riding the crest of that wave in United States and Canada. They had been on the Internet for years. Now www.dell.com became a website so brilliantly designed that people at tradeshows complimented Michael on it. Yet other people were predicting that Dell was in danger of crashing beneath the weight of its own growth.

Michael was savvy enough to know that the company needed a wiser head than his. He hired Tom Meredith away from Sun Microsystems to be the company's chief financial officer. Meredith's predictions were also dire. Michael believed him; the company tried to issue a secondary public stock offering, but with the stock at only $30.08 per share, they decided to cancel it. That quarter they posted their only quarterly loss. At this point they completely revised their business.

Their new goals were "liquidity, profitability, and growth." Instead of letting their business grow harum-scarum, they changed their information systems so that a salesperson could see the level of margin for a product as he was selling it on the telephone. The new systems also showed each salesperson what percentage of his sale was his profit. Rather than push the same old things, people with only eight percent profit margins went after sales that would create twenty-eight percent.

At that time problems with their notebook developed. They couldn't abandon the fastest-growing segment of the industry. Still there were problems. While the company over-hauled the project, they went to their customers via the Internet—their new direct sales model. They told them, "We're bringing out a new line. Here's our phased strategy and our service and support plan. Here's why you shouldn't be nervous about doing business with us."

Their customers were more than pleased. Many undoubtedly became customers for life.

The solution to their notebook problem came in the form of a lithium ion battery developed by Sony of Japan. It became breakthrough technology because it weighed less and provided by conservative estimates four hours of notebook time. (Conventional nickel hydride batteries lasted only two hours.)

In order to launch the new product, Michael loaded fifty industry analysts and reporters into a cross-country flight from JFK Airport to LAX. Five-and-a-half hours later when the plane landed, the new batteries were still going strong. By the fourth quarter of 1995, the notebooks were contributing fourteen percent of revenue.

Michael Dell was named "Turnaround CEO of the Year 1993." He frankly admits that he doesn't ever want that title again.

At that point Michael acknowledged that the job of managing the company was too big for him. They were a multibillion-dollar company. They had offices in fourteen European countries, were the second-largest computer company in the United Kingdom, and had direct operations in eleven countries in the Asia-Pacific/Japan region. They needed a multibillion-dollar management.

Rather than drive himself crazy or burn himself out, he hired people to manage and left himself free to make speeches, to spend time with his employees, to meet with customers, to be the point man, but at the same time have fun. He was only twenty-eight years old. He had a lovely wife and a growing family. And he'd been working since he was thirteen.

The new man, Mort Topfer, came from Motorola. Together he and Michael put together a three-year plan that set as its goal $10 billion in sales by 1997. The plan turned out to be eminently achievable since they hit $12.2 billion. The key to their incredible success besides good management and Michael's lack of ego was data. They were, after all, a computer company. They now apply four thousand different types of analyses to their profit and loss statements. In this way they maintain a tight grip on their business. They also have reduced their inventory to six days. They are aiming for hours.

The next logical step seemed to be servers in PC formats. They had tried those back in 1989 but had abandoned them when customers said they didn't need them. Now they needed them and servers were a great match for Dell. For a company that got its start adding components to standard PCs, the server was the discovery Michael had been waiting for.

Servers are advanced computers with additional technology added to allow them to link all aspects of a person's business, a company's business, or a government's business literally across the world through the use of the Internet.

www.dell.com had been on the web since 1994. In 1996 they prepared their company employees to launch their servers. First came "Message from Michael" emails. Then came posters and brown-bag lunches that had always been one of Michael's favorite ways to communicate with his employees. Because 1996 was an Olympic year, they staged an "Olympic Torch Event" with Michael, who is an avid runner, carrying an Olympic-sized torch into the auditorium in downtown Austin. He was followed closely by Server Man in tights, a cape, and a big red "S" on his chest. Everyone laughed and cheered. The company was psyched to get their servers off the ground.

Again the same techniques that had stood them in good stead opened the markets for them. They prepared their price list and went out into the marketplace to ask their customers to buy a server from Dell or be sure that their current provider could meet Dell's pricing. It was hardball with a vengeance. Those who did not buy Dell forced down the price of the equipment to install servers. Most, of course, bought Dell outright, proving that servers were a logical sell for the direct sales model.

By the end of 1997, Dell had gone from tenth to fourth place worldwide in sales of servers.

At the same time the logical leap forward was to the ultimate in direct sales to customers through online sales and service. They knew if they didn't establish a presence on the Internet, one of their competitors would. The industry observers were predicting a surge in electronic commerce. They believed that by 2002, the dawning of the new century, Internet commerce would reach $300 billion annually. In June 1996 Dell began to sell desktops and notebooks over the Internet via www.dell.com. The response was overwhelming. The company added servers later that year. By December they were doing $1 million a *day*.

Dell added the ultimate in customer satisfaction, "Dell Premier Pages." Each customer has a Premier Page that gives its company employees Internet access to password-protected, customer-specific information about Dell's products and services. It's constantly updated and allows customers to configure, price, and buy systems at the agreed-on price. They can track orders and inventory. Through Dell they can better manage their assets. It's rather like ATM machines for banks. While the Premier Pages aren't a substitute for live sales representative, they can save everyone time.

And time is money.

The Internet was a self-perpetuating generator. All the Fortune 500 companies have websites. They cannot afford not to.

Therefore, Dell is now doing $35 million a day.

> "Now! Now!" cried the Queen. "Faster! Faster!"
> —Lewis Carroll

A new name has entered the picture at Round Rock, Texas. Kevin B. Rollins is being talked about as the heir apparent to Michael Dell as chief executive officer. Michael is twelve years younger than Kevin and shows no interest in resigning his position. Still people within the corporation give Rollins credit for carrying Dell to a position of supremacy through the recession at the end of 2001.

The story of Michael Dell and his company must end here only because this book must go to press. As of January 2002, the *Wall Street Journal* reported that Dell Computer Corporation "pulled away from rivals during a historic slump in the personal-computer market." A later article in April, coinciding with the release of the annual report, announced that the first-quarter profit for 2002 would be sixteen cents per share, down from last year's seventeen cents. However, considering the recession following the tragedy of September 11, Dell has done well for itself.

Kevin Rollins, president of Dell. The newest in a line of men who have been rumored to replace Michael Dell as CEO. Archives www.dell.com.

Riding the wave of cutting-edge technology, excellent support and service, and excellent reputation, Dell's unit sales total has risen while its competitors are in disarray. Gateway has pulled back from international markets. IBM has decided to outsource its PC production. In 2001 Compaq and Hewlett-Packard were both outsold by Dell. As of this writing the two have completed a merger of their firms to allow them to regain their position. The *Wall Street Journal* on May 21 termed it a union that asks a dysfunctional company (Hewlett-Packard) to "undertake the assimilation of Compaq, an even more dysfunctional company."

In the heat of battle they've both neglected their customers while hoping to please their stockholders. So far they've ended up pleasing neither.

As any young man in a hurry knows, when you're going where no man has gone before, you have to keep your eyes on the horizon, the mountaintop, or the next star. Michael Dell's company had a great deal to celebrate at the end of 2001 with worldwide market sales increases of 18.3 percent and national sales increases of 13.5 percent.

At thirty-seven his story is far from over.

The Power of Money

Why is the most valuable institution of society the object of so much calumny? Why does the exchanging of paper promises arouse such wrath? Ministers, moralists, philosophers, and politicians exhort us to eschew the vicious things, for the pursuit of them will surely lead us into a sink of sin and depravity. They complain that what they buy corrupts us and keeps us from being the honest, natural men that we would be if only we didn't want so many things and work so hard to buy them. Yes, most people can quote chapter and verse the horrors of those promises and the vice that they seem to generate.

Ah, yes. If only we didn't feel the need to beautify and perfume our bodies, heat and cool our homes, travel over great distances at faster speeds, and store large amounts of data. If only we were primitive food-gatherers, how happy we would be! Ah, the happy primitive people living a thirty-five-year lifespan in the Amazon Rain Forest. So much happier than our octogenarians tooling around the golf courses and keeping time in the concert halls.

Happily, most Texans don't heed the warnings. The naysayers' exhortations fall on deaf ears or ring hollow even to themselves as they, from time to time, are forced to acknowledge that those very paper promises keep them in business. Frequently, they call for the promises after particularly vigorous denunciations of them. Primitive, natural hunters and food-gatherers have no need of ministers, moralists, and politicians. It is only from society and its institutions that these men arise to do their parts in the regulation of the accumulation of paper promises.

Hail to MONEY! And to all of the wonderful things that it has led us to do. For we see that the RICH with their total economic freedom can do good or ill. Surprisingly, most of them do great good. They leave us legacies of beauty and comfort, for in order to earn paper promises, they must provide most of us with what we need and want.

As Adam Smith said in the beginning, "It is not from ...benevolence...that we expect our dinner, but from... self-interest." All of us in society work in our own self-interest —the poor and the rich alike. The rewards of our self-interest are MONEY.

> "Certainly there are lots of things in life
> that money won't buy,
> but it's very funny—
> Have you ever tried to buy them without money?"
> —Ogden Nash, *The Terrible People*

Bibliography

Ash, Mary Kay. *Mary Kay*. New York: Harper & Row, 1987.

Baldwin, Pat. "Ranking Texas' rich: Got $130 million? Welcome to the club," *The Dallas Morning News*, August 15, 1991, p. 1A, 22A.

Bartlett, Donald L. and James B. Steele. *Empire: The Life, Legend, and Madness of Howard Hughes*. New York: W. W. Norton, 1979.

Buckman, Rebecca and John Wilke. "Microsoft Comes Under Fire from Nader for its Practice of Not Paying Dividends," *The Wall Street Journal*, January 7, 2002, p. A16.

Casad, Dede Weldon. *Texans of Valor: Military Heroes of the 20th Century*. Austin, Texas: Eakin Press, 1998.

Clark, Don. "Dell Soars Above Rivals Amid Slump in Market for PCs," *The Wall Street Journal*, January 8, 2002, B4.

"Comer Cottrell, 1931-" http://www.google.com/search?q= cache:Jed72Q8xaCMC:www.africanpubs.com/Apps/bios /0.1.

Cottrell, Comer. Personal interview, April 22, 2002.

Davis, Wallace. *Corduroy Road: The Story of Glenn H. McCarthy*. Houston: Anson Jones Press, 1951.

Dell, Michael. *Direct from Dell: Strategies that Revolutionized an Industry*. New York: HarperCollins Publishers, 1999.

_____. "Keynote Address," Connecting Technology Conference, Virginia Beach, May 15, 2001. www.dell.com.

Dreazen, Yochi J. "FCC Asks Hughes Electronics, EchoStar for More Data on Deal," *The Wall Street Journal*, February 6, 2002, B18.

"Electronic Data Systems." The Handbook of Texas Online. http://www.tsha.utexas.edu/handbook/online/articles/view/EE/dne2.html.

Follett, Ken. *On Wings of Eagles*. New York: Signet, 1983.

Goldstein, Alan. "Dell gets directly to the point," *The Dallas Morning News*, February 28, 1999, 8H.

"H. Ross Perot," *Famous Texans*. http://www.famous-texans.com/rossperot.htm.

Harris, Joyce Sáenz. "For consultants, Mary Kay Ash exuded the power of pink," *The Dallas Morning News*, November 27, 2001, 2-3C.

Harrison, Crayton. "Mary Kay reps foresee stability," *The Dallas Morning News*, November 24, 2001, 1,3F.

Hensley, Scott. "Twelve Physicians in Research Win Howard Hughes Funding," *The Wall Street Journal*, May 28, 2002, D4.

Herman, Arthur. *How the Scots Invented the Modern World: The True Story of How Western Europe's Poorest Nation Created Our World and Everything in It*. New York: Crown, 2001.

Hobby, William Pettus Jr. "Hobby, Oveta Culp." The Handbook of Texas Online. http://www.tsha.utexas.edu/handbook/online/articles/view/HH/fho86.html.

"Hughes, Howard Robard, Jr." The Handbook of Texas Online. http://www.tsha.utexas.edu/handbook/online/articles/view/HH/fhu60.html.

Hurt, Harry. *Texas Rich: The Hunt Dynasty from the Early Oil Days through the Silver Crash*. New York: W. W. Norton, 1981.

"IBC Bank, Laredo, Fined for Not Reporting Gifts," *Bankers Digest*, May 6, 2002, p. 14.

Jones, Kathryn. "Comer J. Cottrell Jr." http://www.texas-monthly.com/mag/issues/2001-09-01/business5.phpComer J. Cottrell, Jr.

Kirkpatrick, John. "End of Pro-Line," *The Dallas Morning News*, March 3, 1999, 1D, 12D.

Knowles, Ruth Sheldon. *The Greatest Gamblers: The Epic of American Oil Exploration. 2nd Ed.* Norman: University of Oklahoma Press, 1978.

"Laredo: Fuel's Paradise," *Texas Monthly*, April 1975, p. 12,14.

Lessons and Legends of Mary Kay Ash, Volume 1. Dallas: Mary Kay Inc., 1999.

Malone, Michael. "HP-Compaq Mess Isn't All Carly's Doing," *The Wall Street Journal*, May 21, 2002, B2.

"Mary Kay Ash: She led the way for generations of women," *The Dallas Morning News*, November 24, 2001, 30A.

"Mary Kay Cosmetics." *The Handbook of Texas Online*. http://www.tsha.utexas.edu/handbook/online/articles/view/MM/dhm1.html.

"McCarthy, Glenn Herbert." The Handbook of Texas Online. http://www.tsha.utexas.edu/handbook/online/articles/view/MM/fmcaw.html.

McWilliams, Gary. "Dell Computer's Kevin Rollins Becomes a Driving Force," *The Wall Street Journal*, April 4, 2002, B6.

_____. "Dell Revenue to Top Estimates," *The Wall Street Journal*, April 4, 2002, B6.

McWilliams, Gary and Kortney Stringer. "Dell Tries Selling in Kiosks, on TV as PC Sales Drop," *The Wall Street Journal*, December 20, 2001, B2.

Obituary. "Ash, Mary Kay," *The Dallas Morning News*, November 25, 2001, 42A.

Pasztor, Andy and Yochi J. Dreazen. "Hughes, EchoStar Offer to Span the U.S., *The Wall Street Journal*, February 27, 2002, B4.

Peppard, Alan. "A Hunt family affair," *The Dallas Morning News*, Sunday, April 28, 2002, p. 1,5F.

"Perot: Biography." http://www.perot.org/hrpbio.htm.

Porch, Jimmy. "Honoring a Legend," *Eclipse*, November-December 1999, p. 7.

Presley, James. *A Saga of Wealth: An Anecdotal History of the Texas Oilmen*. Austin: Texas Monthly Press, 1983.

Price, Lori. "Comer Cottrell, Reflections of a Legend," *Eclipse*, November-December, 1999, pp. 30-39.

Reid, Jan. "Tony Sanchez's New Deal," *Texas Monthly*, November 2001, pp. 150-51, 153, 180-85.

Robinson, James W., ed. *Ross Perot Speaks Out: Issue by Issue, What He Says about our Nation—Its Problems and Its Promise*. Rocklin, CA: Prima Publishing, 1992.

Salute to the Winners: Seminar '96. Dallas: Mary Kay Inc., 1996.

Sanchez Jr., A. R. (Tony). May 2001. http://www.utsystem.edu/bor/regents/sanchez.htm.

"Sanchez's remarks offend veterans supporting Perry," *The Dallas Morning News*, Friday, April 26, 2002, p. 36A.

Scoper Jr., Vincent. *Come Drill a Well in My Back Yard*. Laurel, Mississippi: N. Pub., 1971.

Sheehy, Sandy. *Texas Big Rich: Exploits, Eccentricities, and Fabulous Fortunes Won and Lost*. New York: William Morrow and Company, 1990.

Shire, Al, ed. *Oveta Culp Hobby*. Houston: Private printing by William P. Hobby and Jessica Hobby Catto, 1997.

Simnacher, Joe. "Cosmetics icon Mary Kay Ash dies," *The Dallas Morning News*, November 25, 2001, 1A, 32-3A.

_____. "Paying tribute to Mary Kay Ash," *The Dallas Morning News*, November 29, 2001, 1A, 33A, 39A.

Slover, Pete. "Tony Sanchez: the Tesoro truth begins to unravel," *The Dallas Morning News*, December 16, 2001.

"Tony Sanchez for Governor, Inc." http://www.tonysan-chez.com. Biography, 2002.

Thinking Like a Woman: The Life and Times of Mary Kay Ash. Dallas: Mary Kay Cosmetics Inc., 1994.

Index

Howard Robard Hughes Jr.

Oveta Culp Hobby

Glenn Herbert McCarthy

Mary Kay Ash

Haroldson Lafayette Hunt

H. Ross Perot

Comer Cottrell

Anthony Rodolfo Sanchez Jr.

Michael Saul Dell

Other titles by Mona D. Sizer

The King Ranch Story:
Truth and Myth
1-55622-680-2 • $16.95

Texas Politicians:
Good 'n' Bad
1-55622-876-7 • $18.95

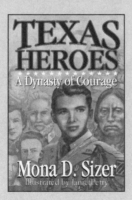

Texas Heroes
A Dynasty of Courage
1-55622-775-2 • $18.95

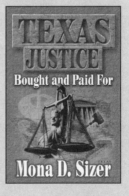

Texas Justice, Bought
and Paid For
1-55622-791-4 • $18.95